Reality, for a Change

Order additional copies from www.Amazon.com.
www.reinventministries.org and www.realityforachange.com

REALITY, FOR A CHANGE

CHANGE

Embracing What is Real,
Discovering What Can Be

A Journey of Transformation

ENNIO SALUCCI

2011

The weakness of a soul is proportionate to the number of truths that must be kept from it.
Eric Hoffer

Dedicated to my wife Dawn:
you bring joy to the journey.

CONTENTS

ACKNOWLEDGEMENTS

A book is created by the imprint of many people and experiences in an author's life. Reality, for a Change, is no different; in fact this book could not be written except for the myriad people I've encountered in the common pursuit for transformation. This book is truly your story. The struggles and breakthroughs I've watched you go through in your desire to transform and make your life different have contributed so much to what I share here. I am forever indebted to you all and appreciate the opportunities I've had to work with you.

I count it a privilege to mention some of the ones who have marked my life and thus this book- I anticipate in advance there are more people who have had influence than will be mentioned here and I apologize to anyone I may inadvertently miss.

First of all, I am grateful to my colleague Hendre Coetzee. It was he who firmly planted the idea that I had something to say and to say it in writing. You have a great gift of stimulating people to greater achievements. Thank you for helping me to see and believe it. You are a good friend- continue to raise leaders.

There are many, many who have been supporting me, some from the beginning, and others along the way; Carole O'Connell, Carol Sheneberger, Brandon Cook, Paul Schulte, Len Netti, Jan Terpstra, Marsha Volkers, Alston & Sheri Hamilton, Eddy & Candy Richey, Kelly Tate. Thanks to all of you for the practical, spiritual and emotional support as I birthed this work.

Dan Leadbetter, your early input into this work helped me to think more clearly about what it was I wanted to say. It was a blast to go over the early editions with you. Thank you for your gift. Ed Stewart, thank you for the patience and refinement in making this flow.

Karen Robison, you have been my biggest cheer leader and a great source for exploration of ideas, concepts, experiences and thought-provoking discussions. You kept me going when I considered giving it up. Thank you.

John and Barbara Sunofsky, you have personally inspired this book to be written and shared practical transformational experiences. Your continual hearts of generosity are refreshing and life-giving. It's great to be in your lives.

Mary & Dennis Trine, your practical and generous contribution and belief in me made it all come to fruition. Your own trek to transformation, individually and as a couple, is encouraging and your stick-to-it-ness inspiring. Grateful thanks are not enough and I'm thrilled I get to walk out my life with you.

Kyle Barber, Russell Grigsby, Joe Featherstone, and Dean Blaine, wow, your belief in this book and your insistence it happen called me up and stimulated me to bring it all together. It probably wouldn't have happened without you. Thank you for your friendship, support, and encouragement.

My former colleagues, Lawrence Edwards, Kris Kile, Amy Maxwell, Linda Costa, Derek Watson and Tammy McCracken- thank you for all you've invested in me.

Ron and Alexa Jensen, your stand with me through my illness was selfless, sacrificial, and generous. Thank you for your care and love.

Jean-Marie Jobs: words are inadequate to express the value of your love, encouragement, challenge ("faithful are the wounds of a friend"), good times and continual friendship. It's a privilege to know you.

Daniel Tocchini, thank you for allowing God to use you to awaken my soul. Many of the concepts, insights, and nuances contained in this book came from and through you. You have a rare gift and are extremely generous in sharing it.

To Doug and Valerie Richardson, thank you for your role in launching Reinvent Ministries. Additionally, I so appreciate your vision and courage in inviting us and this work into your Church community. Again, thank you.

To my mother Cristina and father Cadorna for embarking on a journey of discovering new possibilities by leaving everything they knew behind and coming to a new land and embracing all the new realties they encountered there. Thank you for your sacrifice and vision and love.

To my children Gianennio and Cristiana, you both are a main reason I continue to long for maturing in love and embracing what is needed and wanted to do so. You all make my life rich beyond measure—I'm delighted and blessed to be in your lives.

To my wife Dawn, you are the singular most transformative force in my life. Since we've met you have continued to call out more and more from me which has invited me to continual change. Moreover, your love, patience, grace, and belief towards me has challenged, supported, and sustained me. I love you and anticipate with joy the years ahead.

FORWARD

When Ennio sent me the manuscript of this book I read it and wept and then I read it again. Personally, I have read thousands of books and learned many things through them but very few of them impacted me to the point of moving me to consider changing how I actually live and interact with the reality of my life. *Reality, for a Change* is a book that has produced that longing in me and as a result has helped me to live differently, purposefully, fully.

After I read the manuscript I reflected back on how I came to know Ennio. It was the year 2000. My wife, Valerie, had just returned from a Christian-based training in Northern California. She had only been home a few hours when I observed an amazing change in her manner of interacting with us, her family members. How do I describe that change? In a "nutshell" she embraced the reality that was in front of her rather than resisting it by avoidance. Those realities included engaging unexpected and unwanted turn of events and the difficult conversations that needed to happen as a result. I watched the way she maintained a full presence in the reality at hand and was able to notice the amazing difference it produced for her and the rest of our home. This moment was so powerful and revealed so much possibility to me that I told her right there on the spot that I would go any where in the world to experience and learn whatever had produced this new way of being in her. Within three weeks I was on a plane to Nashville and the rest is history or maybe I should say the "rest is future", because this is what opened up for us. We began living our life being drawn by the possibilities of our future rather than being confined to the repetition of our history. That is the amazing thing that opens up for every person who is willing to engage reality as it is really showing up in our life right now. Rather than trying to resist reality, we began to embrace it and explore what was available to us, even in the most unwanted of circumstances. What possibilities! What change!

The providence of God is a wonderful and mysterious reality. It is just amazing how He orchestrates the details, gifts and surprises of life into a tapestry of beauty beyond human imagination. You may be asking "What's this moment of praise and adoration about?" The answer is that in God's providence He led the person who facilitated "that training" in Northern California to become a member of our congregation in Long Beach; that trainer was Ennio Salucci. Ennio and I quickly became good friends, no, dear friends, no, "heart-friends". That's better. Ennio and his wife Dawn, along with their children Gianennio and Cristiana soon invited us into their lives where Valerie and I have experienced such love, grace, strength and hope. All of this against the backdrop of "life" as it has shown up in their lives as well as our own.

I have been inspired by the realness of how Ennio has chosen to engage his reality and have been equally impacted by the change it has produced in him, his family, my family and our church congregation. Thank you Ennio for showing me that life is not a march with detailed prescribed steps but rather a dance full of wonder if we will but open our eyes and yes, our very lives to what is really in front of us. Now that's *Reality, for a Change*!

Dr. Douglas P. Richardson, MDiv, Doctor of Ministry
Senior Pastor, Long Beach Christian Fellowship

INTRODUCTION

Life is not a problem to be solved, but a reality to be experienced.

Soren Kierkegaard

Face reality as it is, not as it was or as you wish it to be.

Jack Welch

Transformation, real change, is a pursuit that seems built into the fiber of our being. I believe everyone desires to accomplish change in some aspect of his or her life. In our culture the subject of transformation is ever present, as evidenced by the myriad of self-help books in Christian and secular bookstores, as well as countless Bible studies, seminars, and retreats on the subject of transformation.

For some people, personal growth through change is almost an insatiable obsession. For the Christian, transformation is central. Make no mistake: Christians are to be transformed into the image of Christ, and God is unrelenting in that regard, using any and all means to accomplish the work.

Too often, however, change is sought primarily because we desire to have life work out as we think it "should" or as we prefer it to. As creatures dedicated to control and comfort, we have very clear notions about how things "should be." Our life experiences are measured against this standard of how we think it should be and are left wanting. We can be so heavily invested in this standard we may resist seeing the reality of how our life really is. Our preferences extend to self and others in relationship with us. When all these elements are not as they "should be" we get busy setting them straight or, conversely, withdrawing in some fashion until things "get better", i.e. as they should be.

Truth be told, a lot of Christians are primarily motivated to follow what the Bible teaches in order to keep life manageable, using the Bible as a hedge to ward off tragedy and as a lever to keep blessings flowing. The problem is life doesn't usually work out as planned even for the most devout believers. No wonder so many have a subtle and subterranean resentment toward God. He just doesn't seem to live up to their interpretation of specific Scriptures that imply that if they "live rightly" then life can be pretty much tolerable and even pretty good. A friend of mine was distraught as she painfully recounted how she raised her child in "the way he should go"[1] (a good Christian home replete with prayer and regular church attendance). But instead of "not departing from it" the child has vehemently turned his back on his upbringing.

There is a greater reason to pursue change than getting what we want out of life. That reason is to become like Christ. It's pretty clear that life doesn't always turn out the way we think it should. So instead of persisting in a futile effort, why not give it up and go for the brass ring of Christ-likeness.

I've been a Christian since 1974 and have participated in many activities with countless others in the pursuit of transformation during those years. Since 1994 I have been involved in transformational training and coaching in many expressions and through various organizations. I have worked with thousands of people for the express purpose of experiencing change.

One motivating factor in undertaking this book is a pattern observed repeatedly during and after intensive three- and four-day transformational seminars and trainings I conduct through Reinvent Ministries. In each case, personal change is the primary focus. I've noticed, after these events, that many participants experience a profound alteration in their interaction with others and in how they relate to circumstances in their lives. The results are a reawakening of hope, a host of new possibilities opening up, and a deep satisfaction in the experience of life.

Subsequently, they are convinced that transformation has been achieved, that they are *in essence* different. I have found this interpretation of change to be a certain recipe for frustration, disillusionment, and disappointment.

Many of you can relate to the all too fleeting "mountain top" experiences that happen during a retreat or seminar. When you leave for home there is a faint hope that something substantial and permanent has happened this time. Perhaps *this experience* was the elusive key!

And then, in a matter of only hours or days...*slam!* The same old patterns are back! Many people are genuinely shocked to discover that patterns and habits they thought were gone are, in fact, still with them.

This is no different for people who become Christians. They too find that many dynamics of the old life are still with them even after conversion to Christ. The reality of the Scripture which states that whoever is in Christ is a new creation, that old things have passed away,[2] seems somehow just outside their experience.

And so the frantic search to change continues, and we go from book to book, retreat to retreat, seminar to seminar, therapist to therapist in a quest that feels much like the search for the Holy Grail.

In undertaking this book, I quickly was faced with the vastness the subject. There are many elements involved in transformation! In addition, human beings are complicated, dynamic, and they stubbornly refuse to be categorized. This is because there is something utterly mysterious about human beings and about God, in whose image we are created and into whose likeness we are to be changed. Transformation ultimately is something God does in us, and God works in mysterious ways.

In all of my years of coaching people in transformation, I have been privileged to work with people from all walks of life and of all religious persuasions. I have learned more in those interactions than I have taught. I have gained much insight into what change is and isn't, and yet I have so much more to learn. I also write to share with you the biblical principles I am learning, implementing personally, and teaching others through seminars and life-coaching. It is from this perspective and experience that I offer this book. I have, through practice and training, observed what facilitates change and what doesn't. I have also found many avenues by which real change is welcomed, as well as what obstructs it. It is these possibilities that I share with you.

I must also caution that I have not found "The Answer." In other words, there is no magic formula that works every time in every person to effect permanent change. At the same time, I am persuaded by experience that the precepts contained within this book, both from the Bible and from life practice, can contribute to life change.

Paul David Tripp notes that people write books either from expertise or from desperation.[3] If prompted to choose, I would say this one is written from desperation, in the sense that I personally want to "arrive," to be done with the struggles of transformation. It seems I have always been asking, "How many times do I have to repeat the same breakdowns? When will I ever learn?"

Sometimes I just want to *scream*!

I am a firm believer that God works through our weakness and that, as we share with each other from that place, God mysteriously ministers both to us *and* through us. At the same time, I frequently *resist* embracing my weakness, opting instead to portray myself as a man who is strong, self-sufficient, and has it together. The paradox of strength through weakness is often far beyond my egocentric ability to grasp.

The road of transformation is one on which we move from glory to glory. I refer to transformation as a process, and I am writing as a fellow sojourner who is clearly still on the path. I have not mastered any of the dynamics I set forth in this book. And even though I write this book out of desperation instead of expertise, I am an expert according to Heisenberg's definition: Someone who knows the worst mistakes you can make and how to avoid them.[4] It is the insights gained from my mistakes and learning how to avoid them that I wish to share.

There are things we can change in ourselves and our life experiences, things we cannot change, and things only God can change as He continues the work He has begun in us. This work will continue until we see Him face to face—and some believe even beyond that! As daunting as change may seem, we can be "confident of this, that he who began a good work in you will carry it on to completion until the day of Christ Jesus" (Philippians 1:6 NIV).

So come along with me on a journey, an adventure, a road that leads us home; until we lose our false selves, find our true selves in God, and finally find our rest.

PART ONE

THE LONGING FOR, AND RESISTANCE TO, CHANGE

ONE

Longing for Transformation

The mass of men lead lives of quiet desperation

Henry David Thoreau

If our condition were truly happy we should not need to
divert ourselves from thinking about it.

Blaise Pascal, *Pensee's*

J ohn knew he was missing something. Having been a Christian
for 18 years, he still struggled to make his life work the way he
envisioned. His marriage was healthy, his kids were well-behaved,
and he was a well-respected elder in his church. Yet when he thought
about his life and his relationships, he felt oddly disappointed. After
absorbing the content from hundreds of books, numerous retreats and
seminars, and countless church services, Bible studies, and personal
closet times, John was at one of the most frustrating stages in his life: a
plateau where things were not "bad" but where he clearly knew more was
available. Not knowing how to attain what was available only added to
the frustration. What's worse, he had no clue about what else he could do
to reach the pinnacle of "arrival."

His wife, a godly woman committed to stimulate both of them
to continue their growth, was another loving albeit constant reminder
that indeed more was possible—and she was not shy in pointing it out.
The resulting awareness of these realities heightened the disappointment
until it nearly spewed forth into a full-fledged eruption of exasperation.

Although married and having many friends, John felt strangely
alone. At times he sensed emptiness. What bothered him most was his
ineffectiveness to make things different.

Why couldn't he change his life after trying for years? Why did he always revert back to old patterns after experiences in which he thought so much had changed? Where was the life of victory Christ had offered him? Should he just settle for life as it had always been? After all, it wasn't really that bad. He knew plenty of people who seemed to have accepted the way they were, and certainly their lives were no more "together" than his. Did they secretly harbor disappointment or frustration as he did, or was it that he was one of those people who was always looking for the next thing to work on in the sense of always trying to better himself- a person so focused on himself that he could be categorized as a navel gazer. He often asked, "Is that all there is?"

We'll revisit John's story often, but for now let me say John's life experience has changed in profound ways. As a result of applying several of the dynamics explained in this book his life is more hopeful and far richer than ever before. If you struggle as he does to experience transformation into Christ-likeness, your story has bright hope as well- journey on with me to discover truths that transform.

The Hidden Longing

It's all around you. It's lurking just below the surface inside people you encounter everywhere you go: at home, at work, at play, at church, at the supermarket. And when you are very quiet, you can sense it in yourself. It's an underground frustration and despondency that Kierkegaard defines as "despair that doesn't know itself as despair." Since this anxiety is most prone to surface when the soul is at contemplative rest, many people avoid this kind of reflectivity. The busyness of our present culture works well to facilitate this evasion. But in avoiding quiet reflection and evading our despair we end up *resisting* the very thing we long for, namely the transformation we seek.

We are created with the capacity to become glorious reflectors of our Creator, but it's clear that to fill this role we require transformation of many areas of our character. We want the makeover and resist it at the same time. This resistance is born out of the easily substantiated conclusion that transformation can be illusive and that it will compel us to face areas we'd rather not face. Adding to this resistance is the fact that we're not completely convinced the effort is worth the price. We survey our life, conclude it's not all that bad, or that we're pretty much like most other people, and decide to be "content" with what we have. This evasion serves to anesthetize us against the dissatisfaction that lingers as a result of not changing.

Resistance is one of the main roadblocks to transformation. A basic premise of this book is that *resistance to facing reality is the foremost inhibitor to change.* What I mean by "facing reality" is dealing with things as they are, not as I would prefer them to be or the way I think they should be. There is a way things really are.

Imagine an angel observing all our accomplishments and interactions. Surveying our lives with no personal investment in how they are turning out or how they look, he could conclude from the evidence much about us. He would clearly see what we've accomplished and what we haven't. He could ascertain the number of friends we have and the depth of those friendships. He could see how consistent or inconsistent our character and behavior are, both publicly and privately. These would be obvious simply by observing the evidence.

Think of it on a very practical level. Reality is what the scale says when you step on it. Contrast that to the subjective feeling of "I think I've been doing pretty well in my eating and exercising routine." Or, "I've been doing much better lately." A person can go weeks, months, and even years, convinced of their subjective reality.

This evidence is what I sometimes refer to as the "physical universe." By physical universe I don't only mean the material world; I mean the stark reality we can see here and now. This is the real world; the way things really are apart from our biases, hopes, and dreams. There is no lying when it comes to this kind of impartial assessment: there is only what *is so.* Stark reality doesn't lie, because it doesn't care and isn't invested in how things are supposed to be or are going to be; it only reflects the way they are. Intentions are not taken into account, only reality is. In this way facing reality also involves accounting for the disparity between what *is* so as opposed to what I *wish* was so or think is *supposed* to be so.

Reality, for a Change: The Truth shall set you free

The Scripture teaches, "You shall know the truth and the truth shall set you free" (John 8:32 NIV). The Greek word used for truth is *aletheia,* meaning "universally, what is true in any matter under consideration (opposed to what is feigned, fictitious, false); subjectively, truth as a personal excellence; that candor of mind which is free from affectation, pretence, simulation, falsehood, deceit."[5]

In other words, *truth equals reality.* An experience of freedom happens once we encounter reality or truth. It is the freedom of knowing what we're really up against. How alluring it is to "feign" something, or to create a "simulation." How much easier it seems than having to face the harsh reality of life as it really is and subsequently our seeming inability to change it.

I believe there is much bondage in life from resisting what is so, in other words, resisting reality. As long as we do not address what the real issue is, we must of necessity be frustrated trying to change things.

It's like trying to fix a chilly draft in the house by yelling at the kids to keep the door closed, when in reality the breeze is coming through a hole in the roof. Perhaps we ignore the hole because the roof was repaired recently and so it "couldn't be that." Or it's easier to yell at the kids because we don't have money to fix the roof.

Resistance often shows up as refusal to accept what is really happening in favor of something we make up that fits in better with what we hope is so. In our arrogance we may even fool ourselves into believing that what we make up actually *is* so. Then we wonder why we are confused and ineffective in instituting change.

I assert that when we "get real" we can effect "real" change. I believe coming face to face with reality, while it may be difficult and painful, is the only way to make substantive and lasting change. Not facing reality is avoidance.

Marc Gafni, a rabbi and author of the bestselling book *Soul Prints,* cleverly points out that avoidance is "a-void-dance," a restless dance around the emptiness we feel.[6] We are created with a longing for the fruits of the Spirit: love, joy, peace, etc. When we don't have these in our lives, or we experience the opposites instead, we are left unsatisfied. The resulting desperation, restlessness, and emptiness is mainly connected to the loneliness born out of our ineffectiveness to love as Christ does. We are made from love for love. Woven into our design is an inherent yearning to truly connect with others and share ourselves with them: unique individual to unique individual, i.e. to love. This lack of a loving, intimate connection is a primary driver in our desire to change.

Peter Kreeft, Ph.D., professor of philosophy at Boston College and renowned author, writes about the universal experience of loneliness in *Love is Stronger than Death:*

"We are each born with a secret, a secret we try to hide every second of our lives by a million clever devices, both internal and external. The secret is that each of us is terribly alone, each finds that loneliness unendurable, each reaches out desperately to overcome it in those million ways, never fully succeeds, and cannot admit that failure."

This emptiness, desperation, restlessness, and loneliness can be expected in people who are disconnected from God, because true intimacy is rooted in Him. But, strangely, I work with many people who have a relationship with the Lord who have much the same experience. While maybe not to the same devastating depth, Christians are also susceptible to emptiness, ineffectiveness, loneliness, and quiet desperation.

The disinclination to effect real and lasting *fundamental* change in ourselves and therefore alleviate our desperation adds to the frustration. Like John, we know (even if only in a vague sense) there must be more to life, and if only we could change, things would be better. Christ said He came to give us life, abundant life,[7] and we yearn deeply for it. But how do we experience it?

We also recognize that there is something thwarting us from changing into people who live the abundant life Christ demonstrated, that willingness to love passionately and completely. We keep searching for a key to unlock what feel like shackles that keep us stuck and prevent us from bridging the chasm of loneliness with love. If we can just find that key we can become the person we desire to be and have been created to be.

Christ also said He came to set us free.[8] The freedom He offers is definitely freedom from sin, but Christ also demonstrated freedom in how He engaged life. It's a freedom which shows that we need not be the helpless victims of everything life throws at us, as if we had no say in the matter. We want to access the inherent power in this freedom demonstrated and offered by Christ in order to impact and change circumstances and people around us.

There is something intrinsically wrong with the notion that we are *just* the passive recipients of our circumstances or victims of how people choose to treat us. Where is the power and freedom in that? We not only want to make a difference, as in making things a little better; we want to make things *different*—to transform them. While we can't change anybody else we don't have to be maddened by them either. Yet people and circumstances do at times feel exasperating. Often our attempts at change are vain efforts and yield yet more feelings of hopelessness and impotence.

Many intrepid souls, like John and his wife, instead of resisting the sense of emptiness, desperation, ineffectiveness, and loneliness, have allowed it to surface, and some have even stirred it up. These brave people actually use negative feelings to drive them toward change instead of running from it. It's not uncommon for people like John and his wife to go from books to seminars to retreats to studies to therapy to solitary retreats ad infinitum in order to change themselves and thereby alleviate this dissatisfaction.

Yes, an incredible transformation occurs upon conversion to Christ, but that is only the beginning of the journey. For the typical Christian, character transformation lags significantly behind spiritual rebirth. But in the end, being made into the image of Christ—developing and expressing His character—is what it's all about. He truly lived life! That's what we really want, and why we want to change.

We know we are to become "like Christ" in every facet of life, but what does that mean? In order to find out, we must look at how Jesus engaged life. Jesus loved without fear, passionately throwing Himself headlong into whatever life threw at Him. He answered the call of love on His life irrespective of the circumstances. He was equally passionate in times of celebration, in times of ministry, in intimate home settings, before His accusers, among outcasts, standing before rulers, alone in the Garden, embroiled in conflict, pressed by the multitudes, huddled with one or two, teaching in the Synagogue, facing temptation, suffering betrayal and pain, and enduring a criminal's death. The journey of transformation will draw us into His character.

As I consider the process of transformation God works in us, I am struck by the inexplicable blending of God's love, mercy, and grace (which initiate and sustain the possibility of change) with human desire, will, and commitment. God's role and ours are interwoven, and clearly nothing happens without all these elements operating. Yet God's role is superior. Even in the area of our will, we are primarily in a responsive role since He has given us the freedom to choose.

Trying to understand God and how He works in the transformation process brings us ultimately to silent worship and awe, just as it did when God revealed to Job who He is and what He does. In the same manner, as we explore all the aspects involved in transformation we are left with mouths agape, incapable of fully apprehending how it all fits and will unfold. We truly "see in a glass darkly"[9] when it comes to seeing how we'll be perfected.

But that doesn't mean we don't see at all.

When we catch a glimpse of what's possible for us, the reality of the vision God has for us, that *reality* beckons to us. With this vision as a backdrop, facing things that are unpleasant, hard, or frustrating begins to take on new meaning. We can relate to these things as Christ did. I'm sure the cross was unpleasant, hard, and frustrating to say the least! He made the shame of the cross insignificant in contrast to His vision for our redemption.[10] We, too, can de-signify the challenges of transformation when contrasted to the vision.

In that context, if resisting reality hinders what is possible in our lives, and if getting real about what is actually so promotes change, then questions of whether something is pleasant or unpleasant, challenging or easy, become secondary to the vision of transformation. Later in this book we will look at many of the commonly employed human strategies we use in our attempt to have life look the way we think it should (the very same strategies used to avoid reality and render us ineffective in actually changing) and how to disable them. This step in the process may not be pleasant or inspiring, but it is an essential one nonetheless.

In the next chapter I'll look more fully at God's purpose for us in transformation and then jump right into some avoidance strategies we commonly use that keep us from accessing the grace needed to accomplish the transformation.

TWO

A Masterpiece in Progress

"Before I formed you in the womb I knew you,
before you were born I set you apart..."

Jeremiah. 1:5 NIV

Most men die at 27, we just bury them at 72

Mark Twain

The transformation for which we all yearn is the process of becoming what God created us to be. Before we were formed in the womb we were set apart. We were created and set apart for glorious purposes. Talk about being special! You are an amazing creation! The inherent possibilities deposited in all of us by God are beyond what most people achieve and develop. Paul says, "We are God's workmanship, created in Christ Jesus to do good works, which God prepared in advance for us to do" (Ephesians 2:10 NIV).

You and I are God's workmanship. The Greek word for workmanship in this verse is *poiema,* from which we get our English word "poem." It connotes masterpiece or work of art. God has written a love poem to the world in the life He has created in us. Each poem is special and unique. Michael Card's song, *The Poem of Your Life,* says it brilliantly:

> Life is a song we must sing with our days
> A poem with meaning more than words can say
> A painting with colors no rainbow can tell
> A lyric that rhymes either heaven or hell
> We are living letters that doubt desecrates
> We're the notes of the song of the chorus of faith
> God shapes every second of our little lives
> And minds every minute as the universe waits by

The pain and the longing
The joy and the moments of light
Are the rhythm and rhyme
The free verse of the poem of life
So look in the mirror and pray for the grace
To tear off the mask, see the art of your face
Open your earlids to hear the sweet song
Of each moment that passes and pray to prolong
Your time in the ball of the dance of your days
Your canvas of colors of moments ablaze
With all that is holy
With the joy and the strife
With the rhythm and rhyme of the poem of your life[11]

Our lives are songs we sing with our days. These songs are sung in the way we choose to engage in—or disengage from—the daily challenges of our lives. How we act, respond, and interrelate with people and events contributes to the symphony of life. The tune we sing day by day will either coincide with the melodic joy, creativity, and hope of heaven or the cynicism, destruction, and hopelessness of hell. Only doubt can desecrate our song. The many cruel blows of life can disfigure the "art of our face" and we can quickly come to doubt who we are created to be.

Dare we grasp the grace to believe we are the work of art God has created each of us to be, unique individuals who never need to wear the mask of shame? How can we live in such a way that we actually pray the symphony of our lives be prolonged, even when the passage at the moment is more like a requiem than a triumphal march? How can we join in the sacred dance instead of a-void-dance? Dare we believe that our moments of joy and strife are notes in the song we will offer in worship to God for eternity and that will move others to worship Him as well?

Furthermore, the way we sing our song each day influences everyone else's song. The impact I make in life and the stakes involved may be much higher than I think. In reality, we are either adding to the harmony or just making a lot of noise. Many times, because of a lack of love for others—or an exaggerated self-love—we are just banging cymbals (1 Corinthians 13:1). C.S. Lewis puts it this way:

By loving our neighbor we rightly learn to love ourselves...It is a serious thing to live in a society of possible gods and goddesses, to remember that the dullest and most uninteresting person you talk to may one day be a creature which, if you saw it now, you would be strongly tempted to worship, or else a horror and a corruption such as you now meet, if at all, only in a nightmare. All day long we are, in some degree, helping each other to one or the other of these destinations...There are no ordinary people. You have never talked to a mere mortal.[12]

Yes, you are His artwork. But more than that, you are a unique *masterpiece in progress* of the Master Artist. You are a very limited edition...one of a kind. No serigraphs or lithographs here. No printing press production churning out multiple replicable copies. You are an original; a painstaking endeavor of love, signed by the Artist's own hand in crimson ink. He saw the finished product before you were born, and He exclaimed, "It is good!" Now He is committed to fashioning you into the finished masterpiece He saw in the beginning. It's a lifelong process of transformation.

The work of art God is shaping in us is not for display in a gallery. We are vessels that the Artist wants to use for His glory (Romans 9:23; 2 Corinthians 4:7). And His purpose for each of us is as beautiful and unique and His handiwork.

The strange thing about the raw material the Potter uses is that He gives each lump of clay a will of its own. We can opt to partner with Him in the transformation process or attempt to hinder Him. Since He is a committed Artist, resistant clay will need to be kneaded harder. He will allow difficulties and pressures in the process if it achieves the desired result.

Imago Dei

In the original creation, we were fashioned out of clay, but then God breathed upon us and made us in His image (Imago Dei).[13] Consequently every human has the capacity to reflect God's glory. Of course, in his rebellion, mankind, through Adam, became marred and fell short of the glory of God. God earnestly undertakes the actual outworking of that potential in Christians—who've received the incorruptible seed and become born again[14]—in order to fashion them into the image of His Son. The Artist of the universe won't stop retouching His work until it is just perfect.

In the ongoing process of being worked and shaped by the Artist, we may feel like shouting, as C.S. Lewis puts it, "Enough! Can't you just be happy with the way I am?" Lewis goes on to point out that, in such a request, we are really asking Him to love us less than He does by not completing His defining masterpiece.

Yes, there is a plan and a purpose for each of us and, as our Creator conveys to us in 1 Corinthians 2:9, "No eye has seen, no ear has heard, no mind has conceived what God has prepared for those who love Him." But we are a work in progress. We must allow Him to finish His work. What is possible is so much more than what we allow. Why then do so many settle for mere survival? It's as if we live in ruts so deep that they are more like open-ended graves. Wayne Dyer asks, "Have you really lived ten thousand or more days, or have you just lived one day ten thousand or more times?" Our Lord has called us to a banquet and we often settle for the crumbs.

As we move through life and encounter its challenges and pains (seemingly ever present) and joys (which seem to pass too quickly), we can come to a place where it appears *too* challenging or *too* painful to hope for *too* much. We end up trading what we really want (our hopes) for the mediocre life we can easily acquire. But most things worth having in life don't come easily. David, God's chosen King of Israel, embraced a different attitude about something for nothing. He determined he wouldn't give God something that cost him nothing (2 Samuel 24:24). We want to give Him ourselves to transform, but we don't want it to cost us anything.

So often there is a disparity between who we sense we can be—what God is calling us into—and who we know ourselves to be. Peter Kreeft says in *Christianity for Modern Pagans*, "Man is a living oxymoron: wretched greatness, great wretchedness, rational animal, mortal spirit, thinking reed...His nature is double (body and spirit), his consciousness is double (exalted and wretched), and his potentiality is double (Heaven or Hell)."

We do, at times, see both. We see the beauty placed in us by our Creator God, and we see our wretchedness. At times we aspire to fully develop and have God bring forth that beauty and leave the legacy of a life fully developed and lived. We long to contribute our unique beauty to those we love and have our world (whatever size and however many people it includes) be impacted by who are created to be.

Too often, however, this beauty is marred and obscured. It is darkened by many things: sin (committed by and against us), our history (things that have happened to us and that we've done), our self-limiting belief systems (imposed by ourselves or others), comparison of our beauty to that of someone else (and discounting ours), and many other factors.

When I stop to consider who God has made me to be, I have many different internal discussions. There is a mixture of hope, despair, repentance, regret, joy, sorrow, determination, desire to give up, possibility, loss, and on and on and on. Above all else, however, I am suspicious, if not certain, that I am meant for more than I have discovered about myself to this point. This is true even though I have come to a place in my life where I am engaging more of my purpose than ever before.

Over the last several years I have come from a place of being shut down to most of what was possible for me in life to a place where I am consistently (albeit not *always*) sharing my unique gifts with others. I have overcome many limiting self-doubts and come to a place of developing new possibilities both for myself and others around me. I actually like myself and others more. And I am not threatened by others' gifts the way I used to be, but rather I enjoy them, learn from them, and am blessed by them. The transformation occurring in me is certainly not finished. Rather, the more I open up to God's work in me, the more I see of what is possible. The progress has come through difficult and challenging encounters.

Even with the successes, when I think about transformation, many different internal conversations continue to take place as well. There is a mixture of anticipation, trepidation, excitement, dread, willingness, unwillingness, and so on. Above all these there is both suspicion and fear, based on past experience, that change will be difficult and demand more than I want to give. Even though I *know* that my ultimate transformation is in God's hands, I'm also aware that I have sabotaged His creative work in me by refusing to cooperate with Him. Perhaps this rebellion reveals arrogance in me, seeing myself as a hard case that Christ Himself can't reach.

So what will it take from us to partner with God in the ongoing transformation we all desire? What are you willing to give up in order to become the person God has made possible for you to become? Unless and until you can answer these questions with a heartfelt, "Whatever it takes," and give up your demand life be the way you prefer, the Christlikeness God wants to fashion in you will continue to elude you.

Abundant Life?

There are two questions you must ask yourself when considering diving headlong into the transformative process. The first one is, "Why would I want to change?" Since you have picked up this book you apparently have an interest in exploring transformation. Even so, many times change feels too much like a visit to the dentist. Your toothache lets you know you need to make an appointment, but you really don't want to go. Maybe the pain will just go away if you ignore it or wait it out. It's not so bad; you can live with it, you can survive. And maybe you can. But I'm talking about more than surviving. I'm talking about thriving.

And that's what Christ is talking about: "I am come that they might have life, and that they might have it more abundantly" (John 10:10 KJV). Enjoying the abundant life necessitates changing some things that hinder us from it. The reality is that we continue to hold onto what is not working, even though it hinders us from the abundant life Christ offers. It's as if we are unwilling to let go of what's not working because we're afraid we won't have anything left.

The second question is, "What am I willing to pay (give up) to see this needed transformation take place in my life?" There is a theme in Scripture which encourages us to "count the cost."[15] Changing any pattern takes a willingness to let go of anything habitual or comfortable that is keeping us from where we want to be. This is costly to be sure. But consider what it costs you to stubbornly cling to these unfruitful hindrances. You're paying a price either way. You will either suffer the momentary pain of having a bad tooth removed or live with an ongoing toothache. You need to weigh your options. This book will challenge you to do a lot of weighing, but the payoff will be well worth it.

Embracing God's transformative work is similar to receiving grace. Although we can't earn grace—it is unmerited—we cannot receive it if we are holding onto other things with tightly clenched fists. We must open our hands and let go of all we hold onto to receive the free gift.

The paradox of grace is that, although it is free, it costs us everything we think we need. Similarly, transformation doesn't happen until we give up our manmade strategies to have life be the way we think it should.

Purpose: The Greatest is Love

What is the ultimate purpose of our transformation? Is it just to spend the abundant life on ourselves? Is it to show the world that we are "somebody?" Is it to impress others with how powerful or accomplished or mature we are? In asking this question we are really asking the ultimate question: *Why are we here?*

My first Pastor, Len Evans, used to sum up the whole Bible and our purpose in the world with one word: love. God is love, and we are to become like Him. That's what it's all about in the end. That's what transformation is for: that we become passionate, radical lovers like our God, who in the triune Godhead of Father, Son and Holy Spirit has from eternity lived in perfect love.

Being transformed into lovers, we answer the essential question Jesus asked Peter. Perhaps it is the *only* question: "Do you love Me?" (John 21:17). Oswald Chambers comments on this verse in *My Utmost for His Highest,*

> Whoever *confesses* Me before men [that is, confess his love by everything he does, not only by his words], him the Son of Man also will confess before the angels of God (Luke 12:8). Unless we are experiencing the hurt of facing every deception about ourselves, we have hindered the Word of God in our lives. The Word of God inflicts hurt on us more than sin ever could, because sin dulls our senses. But this question of the Lord intensifies our sensitivities to the point that this hurt produced by Jesus is the most exquisite pain conceivable.

There are many things that get in the way of us fulfilling our great purpose to love. As we reach out to love as we are commanded, all the hindrances within us that keep us stuck are challenged. So we pursue transformation in order to move past the hindrances that keep us from experiencing Christ's abundant love life. All our shortcomings in need of change must be faced and contended with. These are the "deception[s] about ourselves [that]...have hindered the Word of God in our lives." But the Word of God "will not return empty, but will accomplish what I desire and achieve the purpose for which I sent it" (Isaiah 55:11 NIV). This is why all men and women, at some level, I believe, *want* the hindrances removed; another reason change is something we are drawn to.

And yet the perceived pain of discovering these deceptions and facing the honest prognoses causes us to resist the examination. We can't seem to conceive the "exquisite pain" Chambers refers to. The reality of change will only happen as we allow the Physician of the universe to examine us, show us how we contracted the ailment, prescribe the cure, perform radical surgery, outline our new lifestyle regimen, alter our diet, and do intensive follow up treatments.

Of course, after surgery we must wake up.

THREE

Wake Up to Reality

Wake up, O sleeper

Ephesians 5:14

I thought I was a new creature, but I feel much the same.

"Walk to the Well," Ashley Cleveland

To Wake Up or Stay Asleep, That Is the Choice

If you have been walking with God for more than a month, you have no doubt identified a few areas you sense He would like to transform. Scripture declares, "If anyone is in Christ, he is a new creation; the old has gone, the new has come!" (2 Corinthians 5:17 NIV). This reality is beyond dispute; let God's Word be true and every man a liar (Romans 3:4). Yet, what does being a new creation mean? For many Christians, the Ashley Cleveland song strikes a deep chord: "I thought I was a new creature, but I feel much the same."

It is unarguable that when someone first makes a commitment to Christ, or converts to Christianity, there are often immediate and striking changes. And it's also true that some things just feel the same. We awaken to new possibilities and yet are haunted by old memories and even nightmares of past failures, numbed but unhealed wounds, questions of adequacy, betrayals and what they mean about us, and repeated shortcomings and sins.

The quiet desperation Thoreau noted can be a disturbing general malaise, a sense that all is not right, or even an intuition that there *must* be more. While some will protest that these ailments are confined to non-Christians, I find this quiet desperation to be true even for Christians.

Perhaps it is even more disturbing for believers, since their eyes have been opened by God's grace: "I once was blind but now I see."[16]

You see, there is no more real "waking up" than being born again. While this experience is often the most exciting and joyful of times, there is also an odd accompaniment to it: pain—a strange portent indeed. Just as physical pain and discomfort precedes physical birth, the pain of remorse and conviction, as well as the pain of recognizing our desperateness and how we've missed it, often precedes this initial spiritual awakening. As focus sets in there is even a "sweet pain" in catching sight of the hope that's set before us.

When we realize how much more is possible there comes a new kind of ache or longing. The Scripture uses painful metaphors to illustrate change: pruning, refining fire, and seeds falling into the ground and dying, just to name a few. As we grow we awaken more and more to these realities.

Waking up hurts.

But waking up is just the beginning. The next step is walking. And the walk reveals many more areas that necessitate further awakening and conviction and (dare we say it?) more pain as God shows us what else needs to change.

When you come face to face with all that life is and demands of us, it hurts. It hurts to live in a fallen world, facing disappointment, betrayal, rejection, and pain. The irony is that God asks us to love as if we've never been hurt. He also asks us to forgive, deny ourselves, repent, and die to self. And even though we catch glimpses of the hope that these commands point to, we also face the despair of noticing our own shortcomings, imperfections, and downright refusal to obey. With all that is required of us and in light of the struggles, life would be close to unbearable without the hope, promise, and joy of Christ.

Living in the Tension

"Ennio, this is all interesting but I want to know what's going on with you, you look like s___t!"

It was Saturday of the Impact training in Michigan and Tracey was speaking. Tracey is a powerful woman; perceptive, gut honest, and direct. I loved this about her immediately.

You see, Tracey was in the medical profession and something about my coloring and swollen neck indicated to her that something was extremely wrong with me.

"Tracey, I'm not here to talk about that, I'm here to talk about what you're up against."

I had just arrived in Michigan late Wednesday night after having had a biopsy of a lump on my neck. I was told the results would take a few days and truth be told I had been anxiously waiting to hear what the test revealed. I kept my phone on silent but would check at the breaks to see if my wife had called-perhaps she had heard from the doctor.

To my dismay, Saturday came and no word yet. I was waiting in uncertainty grappling with all the vivid bad news scenarios I kept conjuring up. I had lived through enough of life to know that random "bad" things happen-even to good people. Not that I consider myself innately good mind you, but that aside I had already had my share of scary and bad things-including a mysterious infection that happened to me two years earlier which left me looking somewhat like Job, complete with boils and scabs that oozed a nasty puss all over my body.

Tracey was unrelenting. "Listen, you say the things that happen to us can be used by God for the benefit of others. Don't you believe that's so for you with this scenario?"

I had brought this point up several times in the training and in fact had shared a lot about my life with the participants; the good, the bad, and the ugly. I guess I just didn't believe this particular event, since there was really no diagnosis, was worth talking about.

In retrospect I see how it could have been a discussion that could has produced some benefit. My concern was that because of the authentic concern my prospective condition might generate it could be used to derail what participants came to accomplish and that was the last thing I wanted the weekend to be about.

I decided to give an honest answer while maintaining a boundary in regards to really delving into it.

"Tracey," I said to her as well as to the other participants in the room, "I had a biopsy on Wednesday morning, I haven't heard the results yet and I appreciate your concern. But as I said, I'm here to stand with you for what you want to have happen in the midst of your circumstances and not get sidetracked by talking about mine."

With that we engaged together throughout the rest of the training with the proverbial Damocles sword hovering over my head. Many of you have lived with similar concerns regarding the uncertainty of the future.

How often, based on past experiences, do we find ourselves anticipating the future with some cynicism? Sure, things are OK now, but isn't there a sense that all can be altered in a moments notice? In the same manner, according to others reading of their personal history some anticipate that when changes do come they will be good. Either mindset reveals our tendency to anticipate the future with an eye on the past.

Regardless of which camp you identify yourself spending more time in I assert that all humans have an innate sense that all is not as it should be. So often there is a sense that life is not running ideally... where do we get the idea that life should be a certain idyllic way anyway? I believe it is because there was a time it was.

In addition to all this, humans have a vague sense that they are dispossessed princes and princesses and have lost something they once had. Man is "lost in the cosmos," as Walker Percy writes, and this adds to the unsettledness. He feels out of place—something is wrong, as though he is in exile. As Blaise Pascal says, "Man does not know the place he should occupy. He has obviously gone astray; he has fallen from his true place and cannot find it again. He searches everywhere, anxiously but in vain, in the midst of impenetrable darkness."[17] We once were in Eden and we have lost that.

We have been promised something even greater than Eden and also have the promise of our full transformation. In between then and now, however, we live in the tension between our current reality and our future reality. It is in how we manage the interim that makes all the difference. In the times of tension things are not "as they should be" or at least how we'd prefer. People unwilling to live in the tension find themselves resisting more and more. It is all these dynamics which add to the void. No wonder people are always searching for the missing ingredient—for something to change how they feel.

This sense would certainly be true about people who have no eternal perspective (perhaps those who don't believe in God or eternity), but in an odd way this quiet desperation is perhaps most noticeable in those who are continually moving closer to God. The closer you get to His pure light, the more imperfections are revealed and the clearer you see just how far there is to go. The distance looks daunting, and turning around often looks like an attractive option. Especially when you get bushwhacked.

You've *Got* To Be Kidding!

"Hey Ennio, what's going on with your neck?" Robb Sheneberger is a good friend and a great doctor specializing in HIV/AIDS and we were in church together the Sunday before I would travel to Michigan and meet Tracey in December of 2003.

I had just noticed a lump on my neck slightly above my collar bone a couple of weeks back and had it looked at by the nurse practitioner at my doctor's office, so I was pretty confident it was no big deal.

"Well," I replied, "the nurse practitioner looked at it and did a blood test which came back with elevated white blood cells and concluded that it could be some kind of infection I'm fighting off which has caused my lymph nodes to swell. She said we'd keep an eye on it but…it has increased in size since she saw it. What do you think?"

As he manipulated the lump he looked at me with his searing blue eyes and said, "Yeah, I'd probably have that re-looked at as soon as you can." His expression, while kind and reassuring also conveyed urgency.

"Oh brother," I thought to myself, "I don't have time for this!" I was leaving for Michigan early Wednesday morning to facilitate a training where I would encourage people to look at and embrace the reality in their lives. I didn't have time to do this myself.

Reluctantly, on Monday I made an appointment with my regular doctor and amazingly got an appointment for Tuesday morning.

I negotiated myself into a frame of mind that said "it's probably nothing…I'll just go and get this taken care of" and yet I intuited something more was up. Maybe it was the way Robb had looked at me…

Then a sobering sense came over me–this was nothing to be cavalier about.

Run Away!

Tuesday, after Dr. Long looked at and felt my neck, and asked a gazillion questions she concluded, "I'm making an appointment for you to have a biopsy on this tomorrow."

"No, Dr. Long," I protested, "I have a 6:45 AM flight out tomorrow and must get to Michigan." I so wanted to avoid what I feared would be a "disruption" in my immediate plans. How ironic! And how telling- here I was being confronted with a sobering reality and I didn't want to be bothered.

"Ennio," she responded, "I'm concerned about this lump. Now you can choose to wait, it may turn out to be nothing, but if it is something I'd rather know as early as possible."

I'd had enough of the vague references. "What do you mean it could be something, what is the possible scope of 'something?'" I asked.

"We'll, it could be an infection, and your lymph nodes are swollen while attempting to fight it off or it could be a sign of a tumor."

"A what? I feel fine."

And it was true...sure I had been a little tired at times but nothing really felt wrong.

"It doesn't really matter how you feel. Sometimes these things give no warning."

I'll say. Isn't that just like life: some things just don't give any warning. You're walking along getting by "just fine thank you" and all of a sudden you're sideswiped.

I've found that the way we *respond* to these unforeseen events, regardless of the upheaval, pain, and uncertainty they bring, have everything to do with the transformative power they do or don't introduce into your life. But it's not usually fun and games.

Oftentimes reality flat out hurts-no wonder blissful ignorance is alluring to so many.

As I survey my own life, I can see that challenge, conviction, and pain coincided with the most transformative times I experienced. While challenge, conviction, and pain may all be a matter of my interpretation, this interpretation is shared by many others I have met. Why this *should* be the prevailing interpretation is academic. It may, in fact, not be the "true" or "real" interpretation; in other words, it may be possible to have real change without these accompanying painful experiences. And yet, the fact that challenge, conviction, and pain is the prevailing interpretation *is* indeed the point.

Real change and growth just doesn't seem to come without these experiences of challenge, conviction, and pain. These experiences are understandably resisted and there-in lies the main dilemma.

Waking Up Hurts

In the film *The Matrix,* Thomas Anderson (the lead character) describes himself as a nobody. Unbeknownst to him, he is stuck in the Matrix, an elaborate illusion that exists for the sole purpose of using the people trapped within it. Without fully knowing why, Thomas is searching for something more; he has a sense that all is not what it appears—something doesn't feel quite right. The engineering within the Matrix deceives its prisoners into thinking they are really living when in actuality they are asleep. It is the epitome of barely surviving. Thomas is living out his days without passion (in quiet desperation) but knows somehow he was meant for more than what he has found and what he has become. Although he doesn't quite know what it is, Thomas Anderson longs for something more. So he searches.

His quest introduces him to others who have also sought the same path. Then he finally meets Morpheus, a character who is much farther down the path. Morpheus says he can show Thomas what reality is, but that opting for reality will make it difficult to turn back. Thomas is presented with a blue pill and a red pill, and he must decide which to take. The red pill will lead him on a continuing journey into reality by waking him up, but the blue pill will enable him to live in the ignorant bliss of the Matrix and stay asleep.

Thomas chooses to face reality, which begins with waking up. The process of waking up is very much like the traumatic birthing process which ends with a painful, interruptive slap on the bottom. And when Thomas is finally awake, reality is more than he bargained for; it is stark, frightening, and overwhelming—especially his sense of being out of control. There is grogginess, and it takes a little while to shake it off. Much of the time reality certainly doesn't look good, feel good, or lend itself easily to being controlled.

The same is true with us upon awakening to God's reality for us. After a long sleep, muscles have atrophied. Limbs tingle and even burn. The grogginess may be thick. As things come into focus, reality may not be as pretty as in our illusions. We may wish to crawl back into the womb (the word "matrix" actually means *womb* or *mother*). Many have embraced sleep, both metaphorical and literal, as the only way to make it through a life that lacks the illusions of comfort and control.

Once Thomas realizes how harsh reality is, another character commiserates with him, "I bet you're wondering right now, 'Why, O why didn't I take the blue pill?'"

Oh yes, waking up hurts.

We, too, have moments when we sense, like Thomas Anderson, that there must be more; that we are meant for more. As a result, many people go about asking themselves hard questions and searching for reality. This quest leads to catching glimpses of what life would be like if only we could change—and change the status quo. As in *The Matrix,* waking from our slumber is painful. The pain is not an evil pain. It is evidence of things coming alive.

For example, I met John, the man I introduced in Chapter One, at a Training I conducted that supports life transformation. After some diligent soul-searching provoked by the Training, he experienced considerable self-revelation. John discovered a disparity between what he *said* he believed and what he was *actually living out*; between what he believed himself to be (illusion) and what was true (reality). He became aware that there were many dynamics in his relationships, based on how he was interacting with people that were causing hurt to the ones he loved. While this realization was painful, John found hope that he would now change.

John was waking up.

These revelations, along with subsequent disciplines practiced for the four days of the training, drove him to make declarations of how he had changed. Upon returning home, John began "the walk." He accounted for his shortcomings, committed to new behavior, and set upon his new way of being. John was dedicated to transformation, and his wife was excited.

It was not long, however, before it became obvious that John's willpower and revelations alone would not bring about the envisioned change. And since he had been a dedicated Christian for many years, it was also evident that prayer, Bible study, and church involvement alone would not bring it about. It was all too easy to fall back into the old familiar patterns. Reverting to familiar patterns happens without thinking, without planning, without warning. Automatic. And, so subtly. Before you know it, you are back into the old ways.

It is the major fall that happens so often after a key spiritual victory. Even though we should know it's coming, we still find ourselves vulnerable; seemingly stuck in repeating the past mode of behavior.

A few months after John's training, his wife had an opportunity to attend one of the same events her husband had attended. John asked if she was going. In a moment that revealed the despair many of us carry regarding our inability to bring about real change, his wife answered, "Why should I go? You haven't changed." Ouch.

Isn't that the rub? It seems that no matter how much we learn, how many "steps to successful living" we master, how much insight we gain, or how much determination we muster, real change remains elusive.

Frustration can set in. It doesn't feel very good and a desire to make it go away can take over. Just like Thomas Anderson, we hit control-alt-delete on the keyboard in an effort to regain ourselves. And yet the *choice* is before us all: Will it be the red pill or the blue one? Take the red pill and the journey continues, and you get to find how "deep the rabbit hole goes." Take the blue one and you can go back into the Matrix and sleep.

Even though people work hard at minimizing the feeling of frustration, most people sense it. And yet they do not want to fully identify it, bring it to the surface, and expose it, thereby opening themselves to the possibility that the greatest of all human fears will befall them: rejection. Unfortunately, it often seems this rejection happens in church—the one place struggling people should experience the most freedom to be honest about themselves.

It is the rejection that often comes in life when a brave soul authentically reveals that he doesn't have it all together, that he has not triumphed over the challenges he has battled for years. This rejection is not vicious or blatant; often it's just a subtle detachment. Friends don't call or come around as much, and when they do they focus on "the problem."

Even worse, it is the self-rejection/dejection felt deeply in a person's core, the discouragement of hitting the same wall over and over again, causing an identity crisis of sorts. It brings into question competence, worth, and essential goodness.

Because these feelings are so unsettling, so agonizing when not numbed by some strategy, people try to handle them in an amazing way: By entering into delusion—a false impression that they've changed or that change is just a circumstance or two away.

Oftentimes our relationships are conspiracies built around our mutual false realities. We go about trolling for people who will reinforce the illusion we desire to maintain about ourselves, or for people who allow us to maintain the strategies that serve to keep us in our comfort zone. Instead of having reality conversations with the people in our life, we remain silent about—or ignore—truth. Arthur Katz and Paul Volk write about this dynamic in *The Spirit of Truth*.

> There is an unspoken covenant between the deceiver and the deceived that allows the pretense to go on. There is no preacher who allows himself to become a performer without a congregation willing to become an audience. There is a self-serving end for both. The flatterer and the flattered, the seducer and the seduced have both ceased to love truth, and for the same, self-gratifying reasons. We have become willing accomplices in each other's illusions. If we do not confront one another in love, we will go on being prisoners of our own illusions. We are afraid to hurt and offend, so *we remain silent and call our silence "love."* What we desperately need, and what true love instills, is a greater sense of horror at the sight of lies eating away the souls of those around us. Love constrains us to speak, not to remain silent.

We remain silent and pretend not to see what's really there. All this despite the promise of Scripture that sin is no longer our master (Romans 6:14), in many ways we still struggle with the same challenges and even sins (albeit on a more subtle level), and still have the same character traits we have been working to change for years.

Many people may find the authenticity that allows us to clearly identify our struggles freeing. And many may come to a place where they are comfortable with the fact that they have struggles. Their spouses and/or friends may not identify these as struggles per se, but rather just a part of the human condition. In a sort of graceful way, loved ones are not bothered by the fact that flaws are present. After all, who is perfect? And who could identify with someone who was? As Christians, we display bumper stickers that proudly proclaim: "Christians aren't perfect, just forgiven." We are all human and have all been marked by life's scars.

While there is some truth in this thinking, I assert that it belies the reality that we all have parts we *really want to change* and have been trying to change for years. And those we love would like to see those areas transformed as well. Just what does it take to make this happen? When will it ever happen?

How Long?

It began as just another typical interaction between my son Gianennio and me. Gianennio is an amazing, intelligent, and gifted young man. His moral character is solid, and he is sensitive, witty, and loving. And at that time he was underachieving in school.

So once again I mustered up the fortitude (with some nudging from my wife, Dawn) to address his lack of urgency with regard to his schoolwork. I say mustering fortitude because I've had this conversation with Gian many times before, and too often the interchange ended in frustration for one or both of us. And so I did not too readily dive back into those areas. I had become somewhat cynical. And sure enough... different day, same result.

I truly approached my son with the initial motivation to have him consider the natural consequences of his actions. I believe I went to him out of love for him and to love him. What I encouraged him toward was born out of years of observing how life works, and I was correct in my assessment. I also knew that if Gian followed my advice it would lead to a greater possibility for him to succeed on his chosen path.

How quickly that changed when my attempts to "help" my son were rejected by him. The rejection was not blatant or cruel or vicious; it was done in a typically teenage way. All he said was, "Alright, Dad" in a tone that communicated, "Yeah, I've heard this before." I couldn't believe how deeply his response hurt me.

As though it was waiting to be triggered, my aggravation sprang up quickly and automatically, as did the sarcasm out of my mouth. I don't even remember the words, but they cut my son deeply. My reaction betrayed the deep frustration I felt about *my* competence as a father, *my* effectiveness as a mentor, *my* image as an important factor in his life. And the frustration set off the automatic reaction of self-protection. As it often is, my weapon of choice that day was sarcasm.

Thinking about it now, I recognize that my frustration that day was interwoven tightly with the all-too-familiar feeling I so vividly recall from receiving similar sarcasm and criticism from my own father. His sharp words had cut deeply, taken root in me, and encouraged me to believe that I was incompetent or somehow didn't measure up to his standards.

Those early messages from my father were consistently reinforced every time I caught even a whiff of rejection from others: not being picked for team sports, having a girlfriend break up with me or being teased by childhood schoolmates and friends (junior high rejection was particularly brutal). It didn't take much to endorse my father's judgment that I wasn't good enough. Sometimes it was simply the failure to receive the reinforcement and validation I wanted so badly. Even when affirmation *was* given, it was often negated if it wasn't given in the way or with the relish I expected from those I considered important.

So here I was standing before my teenage son: forty-six years old, relatively successful in life by all accounts, well-liked by many people, loved by my wife and by my children, engaged with people in a way many say was making a difference. And yet I felt much the same as I did when I was a confused and timid Italian immigrant of six years old: incompetent and insignificant. It's as if I found or *created* another reason to continue to believe what I wanted so desperately to *not* believe.

Even today it seems that all the ground I've taken over the years, all the issues I've worked through, and the spiritual pilgrimage I've been on have not adequately communicated to the deep core of myself that I have indeed changed and overcome lifelong feelings of inadequacy. Not only do the feelings seem the same, but the patterns of responding are also similar. And so the question must be asked: Can we really change?

For instance, over the years Dawn and I have had recurring discussions on the same topics. These discussions revolve around areas of my behavior that I have vowed to her—but mostly to myself—to change. Specifically, the discussions involve how I act, react, fail to act, and at times act out—traits such as procrastinating, being sarcastic, coming off as "needy," criticizing, etc. Whenever she points out that I am relating to her in that "same way," I must fight despair that I am forever stuck in patterns that have been with me for so long.

Even though I still have struggles from my formative years and everything I do today is in some manner tainted by my early "imprints," it doesn't mean I view my life or myself in an all-or-nothing mode. In fact, nothing could be further from the truth. I have taken much ground over the years and, in many ways, the manner in which I relate to others and behave in life would not be recognizable to those who knew me even twenty years ago. Some things have definitely changed!

Ah, but then again, there are those areas I know about (and Dawn knows about) that, frankly, I am sick and tired of, that I want to change. I don't want to be reminded of those moments in my youth when I felt so out of control and subject to my circumstances. How long will it take to fully rise above these things? When, I ask, will I ever be free of them? *When will I really change?*

Later in *The Matrix*, one of the characters who sought reality like Thomas Anderson finds himself discouraged by the continual demand of the very reality he sought. He opts to betray his fellow truth-seekers and be reinserted into the fantasy of the Matrix, even though he knows it isn't real. As long as he doesn't remember the truth, he can live reasonably happy in the illusion and chase after the fantasy comforts and pleasures offered there.

Kierkegaard says that many find "a level of despair they can tolerate and call that happiness."

The desire to change seems to run the gamut from tolerance or settling to apathy to screaming in despairing frustration, interspersed with frantic efforts to change ourselves by many avenues. These frenzied attempts range from following self-help steps (Christian or secular) to exploring our past to uncovering a key that will allow us to change to listening to any of the numerous voices promising us the answer.

Because our labors to date have not produced the permanent change we long for, often it is easier to embrace one or more of the many illusions that serve to defer the painful hope that real change can happen—that we can *in essence* be different. The path to real change certainly doesn't look like an easy, well-paved one. But the less traveled path holds great promise of new discovery. An unknown author penned it well: "There are always two choices, two paths to take. One is easy, and that is its only reward."

The path to transformation, while it can appear difficult, is replete with many joys. In His wisdom, and knowing our frailty, God also gives us tastes of deep satisfaction and hope as we embrace the challenges and fires of life. Yes, at times it feels overwhelming, but there are moments when we are also overwhelmed by the sheer grandeur of it all: the purpose, the hope, the joy, and the love that He sets before us. We come to know in a deep place within us that we are in a noble fight. He gives us these glimpses so that we too can follow in the steps of Jesus, "the author and perfecter of our faith, who for the joy set before Him endured the cross" (Hebrews 12:2 NIV). The joy set before Him was His vision, and that vision essentially was a love relationship with us.

This joyous vision can serve to keep us on the "narrow road" as well. This road, just like the road Christ traveled, leads to our own Calvary where we offer ourselves up, in love and for love, to God the Father. This is not to say that we don't take detours onto "easy street." Easy street is an illusion, though. It is another dead-end street that, unlike Christ's death at Calvary, has no sacrificial benefit (life for others), no transformative power, and no resurrection.

In order to better understand what it will take to truly transform, we will first look at what the detours are. Most of the time these unproductive changes in direction are subtle; in other words, they appear to be the right paths and certainly the ones that make the most sense.

I am aware that the examination of change in and of itself can be frustrating. However, I believe it will serve well to first identify the diversions many people have taken to steer clear of encounters with God and reality. Ironically, it is the avoidance of these encounters that contributes to our sense of quiet desperation. So, before looking at what change is and how to invite it, it is imperative to identify these main inhibitors.

Contrast often gives us a clearer understanding of the true picture. As a point of contrast, we will begin by identifying what I call the illusions of change.

PART TWO

TRANSFORMATION SABOTAGE

FOUR

Underminers of Transformation

Life is a very sad piece of buffoonery, because we have…the need to
fool ourselves continuously by the spontaneous creation of a reality
(one for each and never the same for everyone) which, from time to
time, reveals itself to be vain and illusory.

Luigi Pirandello - 'Autobiographical Sketch in Lettere, Rome'
(10/15/24)

Wake up and smell the coffee

Modern Day Proverb

Illusions of Change

Just as in *The Matrix*, often we are asleep while thinking we are
awake. Unlike the movie, however, this state is not imposed upon us
(except for the "encouragement" from the enemy of our souls). No, this
slumber-like condition is self-imposed because it serves us. Our illusions
are much easier to perpetuate in a state of sleepwalking. But in this state
our dream of transformation will remain only that: a dream. As a card
I read says, "The best way to fulfill a dream is to wake up." Illusions vie
with reality; when we chase illusions we will, by default, evade reality.

Understanding as the Means to Transformation

One of the illusions we embrace is that we will actually be different
when we find out *why* we are the way we are. We assume that when we
finally understand why we relate to people and circumstances as we do,
then everything will be different and we will experience change.

Many people believe that if they can come to understand when
and why they embraced a faulty belief, *that understanding* will enable
them to be free. This desire for illumination, while useful in some

ways, becomes an elusive endeavor when its purpose is transformation. Understanding, illumination, or insight alone doesn't make *the* difference in terms of changing people. Many people I've encountered have a deep understanding of why they struggle in specific ways, and yet they are no closer to the freedom they yearn for. Some have visited psychologists and therapists for years, and while they have uncovered traumatic experiences from their childhood and have talked through them and understand how these events affect their behavior, many experience no true freedom.

While therapy can be a valuable service, I suggest that understanding, in and of itself, does not equal change. People say to me, "I know where all my issues are rooted, but how do I change them?" Perhaps that's one reason the Bible says, "Lean not on your own understanding" (Proverbs 3:5 NIV). Yet it somehow feels right to identify a root cause. Working furiously to understand also serves to lessen the impact of the realization that we haven't changed. "Hey, at least I'm trying to improve myself!" we say.

There are many other strategic deferrals of hope that mitigate the pain of not being able to effect the change we want.

My Life Will be Different When...

One popular recipient of frustration linked to the lack of change is circumstances. We mistakenly believe that when the circumstances dictating our behavior change, *we* will change. In this mindset, we expect that when something addresses—better yet, removes—what we consider to be the factors that make us the way we are, then we will change and be different.

You're convinced that if your financial pressures were relieved, if you had a different job or boss, or if your spouse was more supportive or different then you wouldn't have the problems you do. It's the classic "my life will be different if" or "as soon as" scenario. And it can take many forms, all of which put the onus of change on external circumstances.

It can sound something like this: "If only I can find the right person to settle down with and get married, then I _____." You can fill in the blank: "will have a meaningful life," "won't be so lonely," etc. However, once you discover that your changing circumstances leave you relatively unchanged, you must anticipate the next step on that road, such as owning a house or starting a family, will do the trick.

Here are a few more examples of the "my life will be different if" or "as soon as" approach to transformation:

"When I finally get that dream job I'll be happy and have the freedom to do what I want to do. Then I won't be an irritation to my family."

"When I win the lotto and improve my financial portfolio I will finally get out of debt. I won't be under the stress that causes me to be the way I am."

"I can't wait until I'm old enough to get my driver's license and move out. I'm sure I'll get along better with my parents."

"Once I retire I'll have more time and energy to enjoy life and even help other people."

When you give the keys to your life to external circumstances, you will be irritated, frustrated, bitter, resentful, and unfulfilled when your circumstances don't line up the way you hope. So you must continue to chase after changing the circumstances in order to keep hope alive. Some people tire of the fruitless chase and swing to the other end of the spectrum by anesthetizing themselves from the painful realization that life is not as they thought it would be.

Blaming circumstances for our plight is a victim mindset. Victims place the onus for change on circumstances outside of themselves. Instead of "Christ in me, the hope of glory" (Colossians 1:27), they look to other people and events, for their happiness and to explain the way they are. In this way of thinking, transformation is subject not to God's work in us but to happenstance. There is no power for change in this mindset, and we are bound to face despair as a result. Not only are *we* out of control, but we place God under the control of our circumstances.

Many attempts have been made to compensate for the sense that we really are not in control of our lives. Popular culture offers many tributes to human attempts at making our lives "work" or at least become more manageable. Our music reflects this in lyrics ranging from the positive thinking "Don't Worry, Be Happy" and "Hakuna Matada" to hoping for change in circumstances and ignoring reality, as in "Tomorrow, Tomorrow" to the more cynical and melancholy "Let It Be" to the ultimate power and control song, "My Way."

God Will Do It All

For those who eschew the "I did it my way" mentality, the pendulum often swings all the way to the other side: God does everything. People who "find religion" often take a passive stance to change by "surrendering" to whatever God wants them to do. They are convinced that God is totally responsible for their transformation and that they essentially have no role in the process.

Becoming new creations in Christ and learning that "old things have passed away," we exult, "Great, I won't have those same old struggles anymore!" Of course, as any believer in Christ soon discovers, the reality is that we continue to struggle with many of the same issues, propensities, and predispositions we had before our conversion.

My own conversion happened when I responded to an altar call given by Pastor Len Evans on November 24, 1974, in Pleasant Valley Evangelical Church in Niles, Ohio. Answering that call, I experienced a powerful and life defining personal encounter with Jesus Christ. I remember the excitement of those days near the end of the Jesus movement. The evening services in that little church were so filled with longhaired youth that the only place for all of us to sit was on the floor, which suited our lifestyle just fine.

We also flocked to Christian versions of Woodstock held in the fields of Pennsylvania and other such gatherings. These events, which featured Christian bands, Bible studies, and discussions held on platforms and in large tents continued to feed us, spurring further growth. We would diligently meet at different homes to engage in hours of worship and Bible study. My Christian friends and I spent many a New Year's Eve praying in the coming year as midnight approached.

I vividly remember our hunger for the things of God during that time. The Scriptures were brand new to us and full of wondrous promises. Reading through the New Testament was an adventure. The Bible promised that we were "born again," so we referred to ourselves as "born again Christians." The old former things had passed away; new life had come (2 Corinthians 5:17). The pain and regret of the old live seemed faraway. A fulfilling new life was ours for the appropriating. We were alive with purpose. Even though we didn't know what was ahead, we were certain it wasn't the lame "same old, same old" we experienced prior to making this life choice. We knew we had "changed."

And in many ways, we really were different. The direction of our lives had definitely been altered. Many non-Christian behaviors disappeared almost overnight: smoking marijuana, getting drunk, using foul language, etc. Certainly, the focus of our lives had changed, and today most of us still follow Christ. As a result, the paths we have chosen in life today are dramatically different from the paths we walked as kids, and I'm thankful for that!

Soon after my graduation from high school, I left Ohio to attend a School of Theology in California. My classmates and I worked days, attended class in the evenings, and tried every new spiritual experience that came along. We received the fullness of the Holy Spirit, experienced deliverance from chains of the enemy's bondage from the past, and ventured out on outreach missions of various kinds.

All of these experiences made a profound impact on me and my friends, and they undeniably steered our lives in new directions and effected some change in us. God did begin a transformation, commencing with a move from spiritual death to life through the life-giving salvation provided by Jesus Christ's work on Calvary.

As I got older, however, an unsettling reality crept into my consciousness. I noticed that many of the issues that had held me back from pursuing life with abandon prior to meeting Christ were still with me. Self-doubt sown into my life at an early age continued to grip me so tightly that most of the time I was paralyzed in many arenas of interaction with people, which prevented me from taking the lead in any group setting. I sensed an aversion to being different from what I perceived others wanted or expected me to be.

So what was missing? What would it take for me to actually experience the freedom that Scripture promised me? It was a real conundrum for me because I knew deep within that the promises of Scripture were true. My frustration compelled me to rationalize why my experience was so far from the truth. There was such a glaring disparity between biblical reality and my experience that I looked for and found ways to resolve it. It is these discoveries and the quest of discovery that I will share with you in the chapters to come.

FIVE

Strategies for Resisting Change

...truth eludes us as soon as our concentration begins to flag,
all the while leaving the illusion that we are continuing to pursue
it. This is the source of much discord.
Also, truth seldom is sweet; it is almost invariably bitter.

Nobel Laureate Alexander I. Solzhenitsyn

People only see what they are prepared to see.

Ralph Waldo Emerson

All lies and jest, still, a man hears what he wants to hear and
disregards the rest.

Simon and Garfunkel, The Boxer

"It's Leukemia." The words from my oncologist Dr. David Burtzo seemed surreal. I heard them but it's as if they didn't want to sink in. I had just arrived back from Michigan that morning and as I got into the car with my wife Dawn she told me I had an appointment with an oncologist. We were to go straight from the airport- welcome home! That meant only one thing: cancer. This couldn't be happening. Here I was, heading into my 48th year of life (the same age my wife's father, Donald Anderson, died of cancer) and I was being diagnosed with an incurable form. I still couldn't believe it...perhaps there was some mistake?

This *shouldn't* be happening!

The Blame Game

Numb out and not face painful reality-sounds good in times like this. For many of us, the reality that we have not changed in the deep core of our being is also too unsettling to bear. It's as if we cannot contain the disparity between *who we long to be and who we know we are*. As we defer our hope of change to outside forces, circumstances, or people, the frustration continues to mount as all our efforts fall flat.

To reconcile this discrepancy, we frantically look for someone or something to blame. Someone or something else must be responsible for our plight!

Maybe you or someone you know has experienced that exasperating search for "Mr. or Ms. Right." One thought behind this search is the idea that sharing our life with someone is the answer to us being different. When that "missing piece of the puzzle" is finally in place, life will *finally* be great. But instead, a new relationship makes life even *more* challenging, so Mr. or Ms. Right now becomes the reason our life isn't working. First we assume that this person will complete us. Next we imagine we will be much better without him or her. Then in our disillusionment we complain to anyone who will listen how hard our life is as a result of this failed relationship. Finally, we convince ourselves again that somewhere out there a special someone exists who will understand us and become the impetus for our transformation. It becomes a bitter, vicious cycle of blame.

Our bitterness can even dredge up people from our past to blame for our present circumstance. Perhaps we focus on parents who didn't train us right or who failed to provide a proper education. Lack of opportunity due to financial status or lack of education could be anchored, in our minds, in our ethnicity. This mindset blames race for opportunities that have been opened or closed to us.

Maybe we blame a marriage or an unwanted pregnancy for where we are because it derailed our career plans. If we pinned our hope for change on our job or career, we may carry resentment toward a boss who keeps passing us over, or a mixture of resentment and envy toward co-workers who are more successful.

All of these can serve as outlets for relieving some of the pressures from the supposedly bad hand we have been dealt in life. "Now look at what lousy odds I have to overcome!" we complain. We see ourselves as victims of everything that has happened to us.

Blaming God

As we compare our situation with that of other people, we may conclude, "God just doesn't love me as much and He is really at blame for my awful life. After all, look at all the bad things that have happened to me." We may feel like asking God, "Why couldn't I have been born into a family with money or at least into a functional family? I certainly wouldn't have these problems if I had been brought up in the right circumstances." With this rationale we see ourselves as victims of God.

Even our recognition that God uses difficult circumstances to refine us can be fodder for us to feel victimized. This is beautifully and comically captured in the movie *Fiddler on the Roof.* Topol's character (Tevye) asks God in the famous song, *If I Were a Rich Man*, "Would it have spoiled some vast eternal plan if I were a rich man?" He also laments, "God, I know the Jews are Your chosen people. I'm just wondering, could you choose someone else sometimes?" We seem to say to God as Tevye would, "Do you have any idea how hard it is to be me?"

This certainly resonates for me: "God, I come here as an immigrant from Italy when I'm five years old and end up in the rust belt of Northeast Ohio being raised by a wildly unpredictable and angry father. We don't have a lot of money, I begin working at twelve years old... it seems like my whole life I've been battling odds, and now I have *cancer*? Can't it be different? Can't you do what you need to do with me without all the *drama*?"

The other extreme in blaming God is to completely turn away from Him and religion. We can carry a subterranean resentment toward God for not setting us up in life more in line with how we see ourselves or what we deserve. After all, we think, we're not so bad. To prove this assertion to ourselves, we compare ourselves with others who are clearly less spiritual. Of course, comparison and envy are just another way of blaming circumstances and prolonging despair.

We mask our resentment by contending that we are entitled to God making our life easier because we are His. I have spun out into this mode of thinking often and come up feeling short-changed. My "haves" are measured against my "deserves," which are determined by contrasting myself to those who don't measure up to my conceited view of myself.

Here's how that might sound: "Sure, I'm not perfect, but I'm certainly not any worse than Tim. He seems to catch so many good breaks, never seems to worry about money, and seems to have a devil-may-care attitude toward life. As for me, Lord, I just humbly follow You and try to do what's right. But look at how difficult it's been for me and what I've had to endure by being raised in the family I was and encountering one challenge after another. I'm tired, I deserve a break, I've paid my dues, and I'm entitled to some rest."

You can identify people who live in this mindset because they often develop a transactional way of relating to God. A transactional mindset says: "If I do this, then God will/should do that." For example, if I pray more or study the Bible more or volunteer more, then God will bless me and my life will be different." These dynamics are very subtle because there is an element of truth in them. Following the wisdom laid out in the Scriptures is, while not a guarantee or a formula, our best bet to have life turn out well.

Guilt-Self Condemnation (Blaming Self)

In my work I am constantly amazed at the depth of self-loathing and shame that people choose to carry. It's masked very well and, on the surface, it is difficult to believe that they are struggling with shame and/ or self-loathing. Most people who carry these albatrosses appear well-adjusted, competent, and "together."

Self-blame is popular because it seems to us that taking blame is a way to own the problem. Often, when our lives are not working out the way we hope or when the changes continue to elude us, we resort to guilt and/or self condemnation. There is a gnawing frustration that continues to build as years go by, and still the struggles remain and this frustration is often turned inward.

Assuming blame is not the same as taking responsibility. In fact, blame serves to separate us from the problem at a level where we can actually effect change. Taking responsibility for our predicament is our only hope for growing out of it.

When we fall into blaming ourselves, the possibility for change is stifled. Responsibility looks at what happened with an eye to identify the cause of the breakdown so we can interrupt the pattern and enjoy a better outcome in the future. Blame looks at what happened negatively in order to beat ourselves up for it, thus hampering future growth and reinforcing long held beliefs that that we're no good and we always do something like this.

Both blame and responsibility bring pain. Instead of looking to what happened and/or how we contributed to the chaos (which is the pain of ownership leading to change), we revert to blame and self-condemnation (which is the pain of regret). Then enters the feeling of guilt, and our sense of helplessness grows so big that we are paralyzed.

Along with the sense of helplessness and impotence we wonder, "When will I stop doing the same things over and over? When will I finally accept that I'm enough and that I matter? When will I stop trying to make myself more by making others less?"

This same dynamic is true if we tend to blame the other person in the breakdown. I *get to* be right about what I don't have and then in turn I *get to* be angry and resentful.

Either way, the result is that things stay the same. I exchange what I desire for simply surviving. The pretense that surviving is the same as thriving is to ignore our own longings, deaden our desires, and/or fill our life with diversions that allow us to avoid seeing what is really there.

Conceit

Another way to avoid confronting reality is conceit. Conceit is a favorable or self-flattering opinion of one's self or accomplishments.[18] It is a self-love that denies its own faults. Loving ourselves is natural. But the self-love which deludes us into thinking we are "the cat's meow" is dangerous, and to insist on this lofty view of ourselves means averting our eyes to the truth. Consider what Blaise Pascal writes in his *Pensee's*:

> The nature of self-love and of this human self is to love only self and consider only self. But what is it to do? It cannot prevent the object of its love [the self] from being full of faults and wretchedness: it wants to be great and sees that it is small; it wants to be happy and sees that it is wretched; it wants to be perfect and sees that it is full of imperfections; it wants to be the object of men's love and esteem and sees that it's faults deserve only their dislike and

contempt. The predicament it thus finds itself arouses in it the most unjust and criminal passion that can be imagined, for it conceives a deadly hatred of the truth which rebukes it and convinces it of its own faults. It would like to do away with the truth, and not being able to do away with it as such, destroys it as best it can, in the consciences of itself and others; that is it takes care to hide it's faults both from itself and others, and cannot bear to have them pointed out or noticed.[19]

This hiding of faults comes in the form of denial; and conceit is another type of denial that serves to keep us from facing reality. When we don't face reality we actually resist the truth, and therefore remain bound. Until we know the truth, the reality of what really is, we remain ineffectual in affecting change.

This exalted view of ourselves runs deep and spawns many other attempts to manage our life on our terms. The following strategies are extremely pernicious and, in my view, comprise some of the key dynamics that keep us from changing. They may seem innocuous at first glance, but they severely undermine the transformative process God is looking to work in us.

It's Not the Circumstances; It's Choice

Most of the time, what we have or don't have in our lives, in our relationships, in our bank account, etc. is the result of what we choose and prefer. In other words, where we are in life is not primarily the product of our *circumstances* but the product of our *choices*. Our life has the flavor it does because it's the flavor we want. We have the number of friends we do because it's the number we want. We have the depth of relationship with our friends because it's the depth we want. We have what we have—and don't have what we don't have—because, at some level, it is the desired outcome we have achieved for ourselves.

This may seem foreign to people who look at their lives and say, "This is not the way I want it." But I assert that the way we live and relate to others is mainly our own design. We have the uncanny ability to get what we want out of life and other people. When faced with the seeming inability to change, it is important to realize that nothing we do or choose is by accident. Our choices, actions, and what we see as possibilities are in keeping with what we are really after.

We have been practicing this art our entire life. Watch how crafty a child is in eliciting the reaction she wants from her parents. She may begin by asking, and if she doesn't get what she wants she resorts to crying, screaming, or throwing herself to the ground in absolute fury, kicking and flailing in order to achieve the desired outcome. If this tact doesn't work, perhaps she bats her pretty little eyes and pouts. Whatever it takes.

This concept of owning that everything I have in my life is of my choosing is at times difficult for me to grasp. It doesn't jibe with how I like to think about myself. I ask myself, "Why would I choose anything in my life that leaves me unfulfilled?" It feels better to blame what isn't working in my life on forces and factors outside of my control. Maybe you have similar feelings.

Perhaps one reason we struggle with this concept is that we want to maintain a semblance of "comfort and control" even though this semblance isn't reality. Better the impression of something manageable than the reality that we don't have life figured out or under control. It's painful to own the reality and take responsibility for how life is.

This kind of pain is often experienced by the graduates of our Impact Training. Grads come to realize how much they are responsible for the way their lives are. The following is an email I received from a recent graduate of our program:

> I must share one thing with you. I sometimes wonder if The Training was the best or worst decision I have ever made...[since] that day I stood and cried for so long. At one point, there is hope beyond measure, and the other complete despair. I have chosen to "raise the bar" and do it in love, and finding myself to be more alone in all I believe. I sometimes wish I could crawl like a child back into the womb where everything is safe and controlled. My life seems to be out of control today...

Ouch. Maybe I'll crawl back into the Matrix.

The other explanation for this experience of despair which many of the grads of our work run into is that the way they were holding life, and how it worked, and their place in it has suddenly crashed down. Even though it may not have been idyllic it was mine, I knew what to expect, I knew who I was in it, and how to navigate through it. Egypt was more compelling to many Jews than the unknown and scary Promised Land with its giants and all. It's not unlike the grief and depression people experience over the death of something they had held closely for so long. While this "death" also opens up new possibilities and therefore new hope let's not lose the reality that there has been a death.

As creative beings, we have the main say in what kind of fruit we reap in our lives. These desired outcomes can be as simple as, "More than anything else, I just want to stay comfortable and in control." If this is our most desired outcome then we will implement unconscious mechanisms to produce this result. Some possible strategies of this are that a person may not "believe" that more is possible in their relationships. Or they may settle for what they have by comparing.

The list can go on and on.

Matthew 12:33 says, "Either make the tree good and it's fruit good, or else make the tree bad and it's fruit bad; for a tree is known by it's fruit." This Scripture implies quite a lot of authority on us to produce the fruit we want, and it places responsibility on our shoulders to account for the fruit we have. In this way we can say we have reaped the fruit we have sown and cultivated. If this is true, then as we survey the fruit in our lives we must conclude that, *at some level*, what we have is what we want. We have the results we want because we somehow have determined them as "valuable."

Hidden Payoffs

I call the results we are after "payoffs."

When I speak of payoff I am referring to something I get or receive from acting a certain way. This payoff is something that I consider important. We are receiving some sort of payoff in *all* our ways of relating to life and people, *even the ways we say we don't like*. For example, you may despise yourself whenever you lash out in anger at your spouse or child. But you lash out anyway because of the payoff, which may be the sense of control your outburst gives you.

I assert that if there was no payoff we would not employ some of the tactics we do. In other words, why heap such guilt on yourself through outbursts of anger when it makes you so miserable—unless you are getting something else you want. On the surface, choosing to carry guilt would seem contrary to a payoff.

What we fail to realize is that there are many payoffs for feeling guilty. One of the payoffs is found in self-pity. For example, a possible payoff for persons living in self-pity is that they can gain sympathy from others because of how bad they feel. The fact they feel so bad can draw others into comforting them. In a strange way people can also find a place of comfortableness in the mire of guilt—if that comfort is only that they don't have to do anything about it (which may, after all, be uncomfortable). Also, if someone is beating him or herself up with guilt, it's a way for them to control the amount of punishment they receive. Guilt can also give you an excuse to be lazy, as well as allow you to avoid mourning and feeling the loss associated with the violation that gave rise to the guilt in the first place.

A subtle payoff of guilt is that it gives guilty persons license to lash out in anger again (after all, they're so bad it's expected). And ultimately it allows the guilt-prone person to be *right* about his self-judgment, which is a huge payoff. In addition, feeling guilty proves you are really a good person deep down because, after all, you feel so bad about your behavior. With all these payoffs you don't really ever have to change. You can settle for what little you get instead of risking to give yourself for real love, which can appear very scary and a lot of work.

At first glance, some of the following payoffs may appear instead to be costs. In other words, they appear to be something that costs me as opposed to something of value I receive. I will now review some of the common *hidden* payoffs that motivate people to be the way they are. As you consider them, please be aware that I am not calling into question a person's intention or essential identity. These dynamics are not a sinister plan being generated by an evil person. These ways of interacting in life are simply choices people make because, in their mind, they represent the best way to make it through a cold and hard world.

Looking Good

When people hear this term they usually think of the physical sense of "looking good," and many point out that this is not a big payoff for them. But looking good is a much more subtle dynamic. When someone is driven to look good in the sense I am referring to, it can permeate even the strategies that, on the surface, would seem to be of no use to us.

Take blame, for instance. Initially blame doesn't really appear to serve a person—and certainly not to make them look good! In this way people usually look at blame as a "price" they pay for their behavior. In an odd way, blame is a payoff. It allows them to feel right about what they don't have and "look good" while doing it.

They send the message that it is not for lack of trying that they haven't changed. They blame themselves in the process and say things such as, "I always seem to get myself in this position." But they also make it clear that they so badly *want to* change the dynamic. They spin their tales in such a way that it leaves people nodding in understanding about how hard it is for them to make changes and how much they dislike the fact that they haven't yet made them. After all, if they continue to beat themselves up enough it proves that they don't want to have this problem, doesn't it? Then they garner all kinds of sympathy and understanding from those who hear their tales of woe. See the payoff? They exchange the possibility of real change for the image of a person who is trying *so* hard and has *so* much to overcome.

Therein lies the paradox of looking good by looking bad.

The person who appears to have life figured out represents another aspect of looking good. At first glance, this person has it all together; they are cordial, friendly, outgoing, well-liked, and loads of fun to be around. They don't brood about challenges in their life or obsess on personal character; rather they seem to glide through life virtually unruffled. They don't spend a lot of time navel gazing or preoccupied with whether or not they are growing. They seem to have "insider knowledge" regarding life that allows them to live at ease. They have a great job, model family, nice house and car, and vacations in Cabo San Lucas. If they do get down, it's not for long. They quickly grab life by the collar, shake it, and snap out of the temporary funk.

I have found that many of these people have primarily surface level relationships. While they are well-liked, they are hard to identify with because most people can't relate deeply with those who seem so well adjusted. Outwardly accomplished people are not usually approached by others whose lives seem to be unraveling. People who want to look good can ill afford to grapple with the difficult questions of life they have no answer for. So they convey to their friends and family that such topics are best not discussed.

It is of utmost importance to people in this category that the people they are in relationship with operate the same way. In order for this strategy to work, all parties must continue the façade that everything in life is fine. Dan Tocchini, a colleague of mine says, "Oftentimes we don't have friends, we have co-conspirators."

Feeling Good and Staying Comfortable

Feeling good is another powerful driver. People in this category include those who constantly flagellate themselves with blame. These people punish themselves in front of others and in doing so feel better about not being able to change these areas of struggle. In fact, even though they are miserable in this state, they feel good in the sense that they have made themselves pay. Since they "can't change it," they create a strange comfort zone designed to keep them comfortable in their suffering, much like the masochist who feels "love" in receiving pain. Paradoxical as it sounds, they are comfortable, or in a sense feel good, in this state of stuck-ness.

People committed to feeling good and staying comfortable also may develop different addictions. Alcohol and/or drug abuse can serve to make them feel good or take the edge off their inner pain and can quickly come to be relied on. These people may develop a shyness in relating to others or an aversion to taking any risks that may lead them into unfamiliar or uncomfortable ground. This is dangerous ground because the strong desire to feel good or comfortable takes precedence over anything else and becomes this person's highest good. Consider how often being in relationship isn't comfortable or doesn't feel good. It doesn't take a rocket scientist to see who and what can be sacrificed to this avaricious need to feel good and stay comfortable.

Being Right

Being right is one of the biggest motivators in life for many people. It is so important to some that threads of it run through both of the drivers we've just mentioned. It too unsettling for some people to acknowledge that what they have held so near and dear for so long is wrong. People who have stayed stuck in abusive relationships have actually argued with me that there was no other option! It's as if the prospect of choosing well conflicts with their identity. For these people, conceding that they were wrong, and allowing that the choice was made on purpose, somehow creates an identity earthquake.

For this and other reasons, some people have a strong desire or need to be right. Often they only see what fits in with this preconception. In their book, *Getting to Yes,* Fisher and Ury state it this way: "People tend to see what they want to see. Out of a mass of detailed information, they tend to pick out and focus on those facts that confirm their prior perceptions and to disregard or misinterpret those that call their perceptions into question."[20]

Being right provides many benefits for people, and here are two of them: It gives people an out—or back door—and it leaves them still looking good. For instance, let's say a person is resentful or angry about being betrayed by someone. Such anger seems reasonable; who wouldn't be angry at some level? But what if the anger served a different purpose? What if the anger or resentment allowed the offended person to continue being right about his decision that people are dangerous? Another possible driver for this reaction is a deep-seated belief that people can't be trusted. One may even undermine a relationship on purpose (albeit perhaps subconsciously) to carry on this belief. He may be so committed to being right in his belief that people simply become avenues to perpetuate it. He gets to look good, however, because he has a right to be angry or resentful; after all, he was wronged.

Or if someone is confused about plans that were in place, and he is convinced that he is in the right, he can justify and feel right about not fulfilling a commitment. This is a classic back door that allows a person to live in an "I do what I want" mindset and still shift blame for their behavior to someone else—in this case, "They weren't clear with me." I'm right again. Insistence on being right also blinds you to feedback that can open the door to change into your life. As Ralph Marston says, "Let go of your attachment to being right, and suddenly your mind is more open. You're able to benefit from the unique viewpoints of others, without being crippled by your own judgment."

I have known people who use religiosity as the basis for maintaining the attitude of being right. When someone adopts a religious basis for their stand it is difficult to break through to them. It's as if you are arguing against God Himself. People become convinced they are correct and stand with fervor against others who differ with them. I personally believe this is why God has given us "fruit" to help us ferret out and show us the true impact of our actions and even the true intentions of our hearts. For example, disconnection with a loved one can be viewed as rotten fruit. This fruit testifies to how I have been with them in reality and interrupts my subjective sense that I am connected and loving.

Being right is another attempt to play god and, in a peculiar way, stay in control. It's strange that even though we say we don't want the problems we have, often we would rather be *right* about why we have them than to do the necessary work, and allow God to do what He needs to in us and through us, to effect change.

Being in Control

Many adults convince themselves that they've changed by taking control. Personally, I have at times maintained control by staying away from situations that appear too challenging for me. Sometimes it takes a near crisis before I venture into areas I've failed in before and would rather forget. I already mentioned my reluctance to foray into some interactions with my son. I don't want to remember these unpleasant experiences or face them again because they bring up strong feelings of inadequacy and failure. Instead, I run any number of avoidance schemes in an effort to stay in control and not allow these feelings to run rampant.

The ways to maintain control are as myriad as there are people, and most of us will run a number of strategies at the same time. People detest being out of control, and so they structure their lives in such a way as to never allow themselves to be put into such a situation.

Think about the person who is perpetually angry. Her world is arranged so that most people in her life will not dare challenge her in an area that needs to change. This anger strategy is so effective that even if someone did confront her, the very challenge would fuel an angry outburst and entrench her deeper in the strategy.

Consider the person at the other end of the spectrum: the fragile one. This person comes off as so frail and easily broken that the people in his life handle him with kid gloves in an effort to shield him from potential hurts that could cause him to crumble. Of course, pointing out his shortcoming must be done very delicately if at all. Either way, this person often precludes or efficiently avoids such difficult conversations.

Control is still maintained!

Overt control mechanisms such as violence, abuse, belittling, and sarcasm can also be very effective. I can make myself unapproachable using any one of them. Covert strategies such as shyness, fragility, isolating, sickness, and victim behavior can work just as well. Whatever gets the job done for the control person is just fine thank you!

At its base, the desire to control is, I believe, a refusal to trust God enough to enter into the mystery of life and relationship. It is a refusal to trust that, even when I inevitably miss the mark, God will redeem.

Henri Nouwen puts it this way: "It seems easier to be God than to love God; easier to control people than to love people; easier to own life than to love life…we have been tempted to replace love with power."[21]

For instance, one of the common evidences of this phenomenon that can clearly be seen in men is in the drive to find formulas to do things right. For many men, the desire to control reveals a question of adequacy. This question may sound like: Am I enough to handle this _____ (person, situation, etc)?

Personally, I get so excited when I find a formula that my wife Dawn responds to. If I want a time of connection and intimacy with my wife, I may find that a candlelight dinner or watching a "chick flick" with her may work. If it does work, in my male mind I develop a formula: *candlelight* + *movie* = *connection*! Yes! I'm going to bottle that one!

My newfound formula may even work multiple times. Then one day I break out my tried and true "intimacy formula" and without warning it crashes and burns or even backfires. It's as if Dawn suddenly developed a sixth sense and sniffed out my modus operandi a mile away. And, much to my chagrin, she shuts down my formula, which is exactly what she should do if my formula has reduced her to a human vending machine. Now I have to find another way to reach her next time—and it's such work! And what if I can't? What if there is no other formula? What will I do?

Like I said before, I do so want to arrive.

In the movie *Ground Hog Day*, Bill Murray plays a reporter who gets caught in a time glitch and repeats the same day over and over. Once he figures out what is happening, he uses his increasingly familiar circumstances to unfair advantage by exerting control over his life. He despicably uses each day to uncover the vulnerabilities and longings of the female he is trying to seduce and take control of various situations. While this is contemptible behavior, it's an accurate portrayal of an insecure man attempting to control the mystery that is life.

If only there was a way not to fail and always get what I want—ah, the control of it all.

For some people, control goes as far as telling others what they should think. Controlling people actually get upset when other people don't see things their way. When someone says something that doesn't jibe with what the controller thinks, she sounds off, "No, no, you're wrong about that. That's not what I meant. You always hear me wrong. Fall into line and don't challenge me."

For others, the desire to maintain control will lead them to actually alter reality. My friend and colleague, Lawrence Edwards, loves to watch *Star Trek,* and he especially appreciates the concept of the "holodeck." Lawrence points out that in the holodeck people can create and interact with any "reality" they want. This feature offers them both escape and control. But in the real world, controllers maintain such a narrow view of life and people that they tend to interact with what they make up rather than deal with what is.

For people who want control, predictability is exchanged for the uncertainty of dealing with reality. After all, we all know how unpredictable people and life are! While these mechanisms are somewhat effective for maintaining a manageable little world, the sense that things are not all we make them out to be cannot totally be avoided.

At some level we still want to change. This duality, wanting change and avoiding reality, sparks even more tactics to enable us to deal with the discrepancy.

SIX

Strategies for Coping

I want to run, I want to hide, I want to tear down the walls that
hold me inside.

U2, "Where the Streets Have No Name"

Doing what you've always done will get you what you've always
gotten.

Modern Proverb

Reconciling the Disparity

There are numerous strategies we employ to cope with the disparity
between wanting to change and realizing that, in many ways, we haven't
changed. Like the line in the U2 song, we become ambivalent, wanting
many different outcomes at once. We resort to coping because the
realization that we still struggle with the same issues is unsettling. As
humans, we have a deep need to achieve a certain equilibrium in life, to
arrive at a stage where we feel we are in control and can predict outcomes
in our life.

This tendency to maintain predictability is actually necessary for
some functions of our physiology. Science has identified this dynamic
as *homeostasis.* Peter L. Petrakis says, "Homeostasis is the maintenance
of equilibrium, or constant conditions, in a biological system by means
of automatic mechanisms that counteract influences tending toward
disequilibrium." Bodily functions such as maintaining constant body
temperatures are essential to our physical survival. God has beautifully
wired into us this predisposition so we don't have to think about doing it.

The problem comes when our resistance to change flows over into
our relationships and, even worse, our psychology. Since we are looking

for growth and yet want predictability, we have a double-mindedness about wanting change. We even have sayings which reflect this idea, such as, "Better to sleep with the devil you know then the one you don't." The desire for predictability is a dynamic that chains people in the most abusive and symbiotic of relationships. We have all heard of battered women who continue to stay with a battering husband instead of opting for uncertainty by taking a stand against the abusive cycle.

This predisposition for predictability often undermines the very changes we want. In a Impact Training event, participants experience for four days what it means to live authentically and taste deep passion and possibility in their lives. Early on in the event, most people experience more profound relationships with people and God than they have in a long time or ever before. As with all good things in life, this brief taste creates a hunger for more, and participants leave the training determined to change their relationships.

Sadly, this awakened desire for positive relationships is often stringently resisted by the very loved ones these participants want to draw near! Many of these loved ones feel betrayed because the previous, predictable way of relating, whether it was good or not, is threatened.

The allure and familiarity of the life people know is often stronger than a promising but uncertain hope for what life can be if they could give up the old way of relating. For many the prospect of change triggers fear of disappointment instead of hope for fulfillment. And so most people, as Kierkegaard says, "find a level of despair they can tolerate and call that happiness."

Desiring to Arrive

Our desire to achieve and maintain a state of predictability in life shows up in the way we talk about relationships. We say, "I have a good relationship with my spouse," as though we have arrived at a place where we can switch on autopilot. Such a posture belies the reality that neglecting the disciplines of nurturing a relationship for even a day takes a toll on the relationship.

Our pop-psychological culture also instills in us the sense that we should be able to resolve our relationship issues with finality. It shows up in the language we use: "I've dealt with the pain of being abandoned by my father"; "I was abused as a child, but I have come to terms with it"; "My spouse's affair hurt me deeply, but I've worked through it"; "I've dealt with the death of my loved one"; "I was feeling pretty low there for a few days (weeks, months, years) but now things are going well."

Statements like these indicate the strong underlying belief that life and its events and relationships should be a certain way. And when they aren't as we expect, we frantically set about trying to fix them. At a very fundamental level this thinking reveals a view of life and God that I believe is contrary to what Scripture teaches.

The unmistakable message in this concept of "dealing" with life or tragedy is that we can arrive at a place where life starts looking the way we think it should. This includes exerting control over not feeling the pain we've suffered. While it's true that time offers a perspective that lessens the pain of the wound, it is also true that I have the ability to allow myself to experience that hurt again whenever I choose. In fact, I believe that part of true freedom is the ability to authentically access whatever experience or pain I need to that assists me in connecting. This accessing includes fully feeling the pain. In this way I believe that we never fully arrive at the point where our hurts are completely dealt with and resolved, nor is this the most resourceful goal. Our deep wounds are a permanent part of us (much like a scar) and, instead of being hindrances, they can be an opening for us to connect with others.

Forgetting

Forgetting is just another attempt to take control of things we have no power to change. In fact, many Christians use Scriptures such as Philippians 3:13 to justify forgetting: "One thing I do, forgetting those things which are behind and reaching forward to those things which are before." However, most commentators make it clear that Paul was referring to his past accomplishments, not his past failures and hurts. I believe this view also applies to past wrongs done against us. In reference to this verse, Matthew Henry says, "There is a sinful forgetting of past sins and past mercies, which ought to be remembered for the exercise of constant repentance and thankfulness to God. But Paul forgot the things that were behind so as not to be content with present measures of grace: he was still for having more and more."[22]

It is my belief that past hurts can become points of strength for us without cutting us off from events we would rather leave behind. Later in the book we will look at how to accept the realities of past hurts and failures without becoming stuck in the past.

C.S. Lewis says, "Being alive has the privilege of always moving, but never leaving anything behind. Whatever we have been, in some sort, we are still." If we think we have "left it all behind us" we are of necessity denying the impact, the pain, and the ramifications that resulted. We are also disallowing the possibility that God is sovereign and able to use *all* we have walked through to fashion us into the image of His Son and to use us as, in Henri Nouwen's words, "wounded healers." Wounded healers are people who are effective at reaching and connecting with others *because of*, not in spite of, their wounds.

It's no wonder many people don't hear and encounter God. They are too busy avoiding pain because they believe God doesn't want us to suffer pain! And even if He did allow pain, they believe when they get to a place of fully trusting Him, the pain will go away. Consequently, many who equate the presence of God with the absence of pain become inauthentic with their experience of life. When we insist that we have not been deeply wounded or that somehow the wound has no impact on us, we then work very hard to mask the deep anguish that resides.

Avoidance

There are many ways to avoid pain and difficulties we would rather not face or remember. Since we are highly creative beings, there is no limit to resourceful and imaginative methods of avoidance we can come up with. Anything that can be used for good can also be employed to help us avoid. And, of course, there are things that by their very nature serve to help us evade responsibility, such as plain old sinful behavior.

W. H. Auden's poem captures this drive to numb out what we don't want to face:

> Faces along the bar
> Cling to their average day;
> The lights must never go out,
> The music must always play
> Lest we know where we are,
> Lost in a haunted wood,
> Children who are afraid of the dark
> Who have never been happy or good.[23]

The lights must never go out. In other words, keep busy to avoid the pain of the real world. It's little wonder that life today is so frantic. We fill our lives with distractions to help us avoid what we don't want to face. And the distractions are myriad: busyness, volunteerism, religiosity, pouring ourselves into work, children, hobbies, entertainment, brooding anger, bitterness, resentment, silence, gossip, isolation, always looking for the next gathering, sports, working out, eating, sleeping, sex, pornography, romance novels, studies, ad infinitum. The more we have to busy our minds and bodies, the less time and energy we have for our struggles.

Overcompensating

Overcompensating is another popular route to avoidance. We excel in areas of proficiency to overcompensate for areas in which we feel deficient. Like a T-shirt I saw proudly proclaims, "I'm not very smart, but I can lift heavy things." Whenever we are asked to face areas of weakness, we frantically redirect attention to areas of competence.

Fred is accomplished in his professional life, a deacon in his church, and very devout. After working with him, I realized that his home life was a wreck. His wife felt abandoned and alone when dealing with difficulties the children were facing. When she brought up the fact he was ignoring his share of this responsibility, Fred got angry. *Doesn't she see how hard I work to earn a living?* he reasoned. *And doesn't she realize I am doing it for her and the kids?*

Fred knew that he had neglected some areas of his fatherly and husbandly role. He was also aware that he had not achieved a level of leadership that would positively impact his family, even though he deeply desired that change. But instead of acknowledging the reality of his shortcomings and standing in the pain this might bring, Fred avoided it by overcompensating in his career, all in an effort to make up for an area where he knew he was missing it. He worked feverishly for more and more accolades in his work. Achieving a significant degree of financial success and respectability at work, as well as getting his ego stroked by his colleagues, served to lessen the impact of his shortcoming as a father and husband.

The idea is that over compensating in one sphere will somehow mitigate the failure in others. Of course, this only works as long as a denial of truth in the particular sphere is perpetuated. Being a caring man, Fred did make attempts at change. Small but insufficient movement in the right direction gave rise to hope and, at the same time, a higher level of despair. For Fred and his wife, the sense that the needed change was just out of his reach added to the frustration. Little tastes of change prompted hunger for more.

Settling

After months or years stuck in the same painful place, frustration leads people to settle for what they have. They compare their situation to others who are worse off and conclude that they really have it pretty good.

This is often mistaken for the biblical notion of being content in all things. Paul wrote, "For I have learned to be content whatever the circumstances. I know what it is to be in need, and I know what it is to have plenty. I have learned the secret of being content in any and every situation" (Philippians 4:11-12 NIV). Once again, this belief misses the context of Paul's message. The apostle never "settled." The difference is subtle and yet vital to how our experience of life and the possibilities we strive for are either opened up or closed down.

Many people, out of sheer willpower, continue to settle for a life of despair for years and some even for a lifetime.

Denial

If the frustration builds to the point of seeming unbearable, it often appears easier to deny our reality. Denial can be spawned by our desperate fear that coming face to face with our seeming helplessness at effecting the changes we desire is too painful. Rather than let the full weight of the way things are rest on us, we alter the reality by denying it.

Denial is much more than the blatant refusal to acknowledge a reality. No, denial can be much more subtle. Denial can show up in many clever strategic attempts to control what we don't like.

One way is to minimize the problem. Instead of seeing it for what it is, we make it much smaller and therefore more manageable. "It's not so bad," we say. Or we attempt to make it smaller by comparing our problems to others we know. "I know it's a problem, but mine's not as bad as what Matt and Linda have." Denial can also show up as "I can't believe this is happening!" or "I can't believe they would do this!" In fact, many of the same strategies we use to avoid can serve our desire to deny, since avoidance is, at its core, denial.

The next strategy I would like to more fully explore is one that numerous people employ every day of their life.

Procrastination

Procrastination is an effective way to delay facing something as mundane as answering a letter or email or to something as critical as a life threatening illness. It is one of the most effective tactics because it says, "I'll get to it soon." It's not really avoidance, because we have every intention of following through—at least that's what we say. I have procrastinated to evade many uncomfortable situations, such as difficult tax issues, cleaning out my garage, and having a difficult conversation. It's like sticking my head in the sand, all the while hoping that the dreaded task will somehow become bearable or disappear.

Procrastination is like saying, "I'll try" in response to someone's request. Nothing really happens, but you feel good about yourself because you didn't avoid anything.

Daniel Tocchini suggests that procrastination reveals either illegitimate obligations, "hauntings," or ambitions. An illegitimate obligation is created when you say you're going to do something, perhaps because you think you should, but then withhold what it takes to make it happen. In that way you become duty bound but your heart is not really in it. So instead of being truly committed, you just feel obligated—a feeling you want to put off.

Procrastinators may feel haunted by the memory of past events which were similar to a present obstacle. These events turned out badly, which prompts the individual to put off getting involved. For example, a woman procrastinates telling her husband about getting a speeding ticket because he got very angry with her the last time it happened.

Illegitimate ambitions also cause procrastination. These are ambitions we are not really invested in, but they looked good or sounded good at some point so we committed to them. It can move into the area of performing. For example, a church member promises the pastor that he will spend half a Saturday doing yard work at the church. He succeeded in impressing the pastor with his commitment, but he keeps making excuses because he really doesn't want to do it. And he feels off the hook because he is only a volunteer. An illegitimate ambition can also arise from committing to something you cannot humanly do, like promising, "I'll always protect you."

Inauthentic religious faith can also serve to allow us to procrastinate. The religious saying, "Let go and let God," may be used to avoid things I don't want to face. I can come off like a trusting full-of-faith child of God who doesn't worry about tomorrow (more like Hukuna Matada). We have all had the experience with churchgoers who's pat response to the question of "How are you?" is flashing a fake smile and saying, "God is good, praise the Lord!" Then we come to find out later things were falling apart. Perhaps we've done the same on more occasions then we care to admit. In my experience this is done when I'd rather not deal with what's happening.

Again, I am not saying that there isn't a time to do exactly that, if it is true. We are instructed not to worry about tomorrow.[24] There is a huge difference between faith and fantasy. One leads me to God, the other to some type of self-sufficiency. One self-sufficient way to handle things is to procrastinate. It all depends on where I'm coming from and why I do what I'm doing. I believe anxiety and worry are always outside the parameters of a child of God, for those are the times to go to Him in prayer, trusting He will work in those areas.

So many times in my life I come face to face with the reality that things I had thought were behind me are with me still. They just take a different, more subtle form. How often are we surprised by that reality? "Wow, I thought I had handled those feelings already." Or, "Lord, how long will I have deal with these same issues?" This is another way to resist, and perpetuates what's not working.

What You Resist Persists

You may have heard the modern proverb, "Doing what you've always done will get you what you've always gotten." The certainty of this statement is self-evident. Patterns are identifiable, repetitious events or behaviors. We've seen this happen before, we recognize it, and we can count on it playing out the way it always has—provided we don't change the equation. There is a certain comfort in patterns. Some patterns and habits are helpful. Many people have achieved financial success and physical health by faithfully implementing consistent patterns of discipline over time.

However, if something doesn't work at the beginning, doing more of it probably won't change the results. The only change occurring in unattended problems is the change from bad to worse. A tooth that's infected will not get better if ignored. Masking or numbing the pain does not heal the infection. Patterns that make things worse instead of better are not solutions.

I call this resistance. Resistance, as I'm defining it, is not recognizing the reality of something. When what is real appears too difficult to face and I concoct an easier reality, I am resisting instead of surrendering to that reality. I'm not referring to the type of resistance that is necessary to actually change a situation. Our forefathers and mothers resisted the tyranny of oppressors and yet did not delude themselves as to what was really happening and what it would cost to bring reformation.

Resisting Keeps You Stuck

"This shouldn't be happening; this couldn't be happening; this isn't happening!" As mentioned before, all of these flooded my mind as the diagnosis from my oncologist began to sink in. These statements are forms of resistance. As I resisted reality (I *have cancer*) my choices for moving ahead were highly ineffective. In fact, I wasn't moving ahead at all.

Resistance shows up in the many strategies for coping we have discussed and more: masking, avoiding, denying, minimizing, ignoring, procrastinating, getting angry, giving in, hyper-religiosity, abandoning faith, guilt, blaming, self-condemnation, overcompensation, withdrawing, isolating, becoming the life of the party, developing addictions, etc.

Consider the metaphor of a swimmer who gets caught in a riptide and resists the current. Many a lifeguard can attest to the fact that the harder the swimmer fights against the much stronger current the more he gets exhausted until finally, in utter fatigue, he gets swept away to his death. Much progress has been stifled and much stuck-ness has resulted from resisting reality, not to mention the death of hope that can result from being overwhelmed by the enormity of trying to fight against metaphorical "riptides" seated deep within us.

There comes a point when the swimmer must realize what he's up against, stop resisting the reality of the overpowering current, and surrender to it. Once he does he will get to the place where he can once again head to the shore. He now must swim purposely back to shore even though he is probably tired. It is at the point of surrender to reality, instead of resistance against it, that the desired outcome is possible to achieve.

Resistance is an interesting phenomenon in that it means both having to make a shift and in another way perpetuating the very thing it attempts to eradicate.

Imagine a wife who does not want strife in her relationship with her husband, and so she resists entering into conflict. In her mind conflict is the enemy. Her husband has probably figured out long ago that she will acquiesce when the threat of conflict looms. In turn, her backing down serves to allow him to stay complacent. They both gain something in this dynamic. Over time there develops a deep-seated dissatisfaction with the relationship because they both know she's selling out. Resistance to entering into conflict eventually creates the very strife that she wanted to avoid.

I have a friend whose parents went through this dynamic with one of their children. The parents' two greatest fears were that their children would not succeed (i.e. support themselves) and they would not be close as a family. My friend, their first child, did not cause them many problems. She was a typical first born—high achiever and responsible.

However, her younger brother was not. Though very intelligent, he was not inclined to do his schoolwork. In fact, he was not inclined to do much of anything. In their minds, conflict with their child was something to avoid all costs. The reason they wished to avoid it is irrelevant. It may have been because there "shouldn't" be conflict in the home or because they felt inadequate to handle it or because they excused it by focusing on his positive qualities and realizing he could be worse.

Instead of engaging the inevitable conflict with their son and going through it, the parents dealt with it by giving him what he wanted. They hoped he would realize how much he was loved and would then show them his undying gratitude by doing what they desired. Instead, he asked for more and more and got angry if something was asked in return. Eventually, the parents ended up with a bill for his education in excess of $100,000.

After graduating from college, this young man never got a job, never left home, and refused to take any responsibility for his life. Today he is extremely resentful toward his parents and is always angry with them. He is now in his late thirties and still living at home. He always eats alone and has not attended a family function in over five years. The saddest part is that he has only one friend (from junior high) and no apparent purpose in life. He seems to be paralyzed by fear and unable to venture out into the real world.

His parents' greatest fears have come true: they have a child who does not support himself and who isn't close with his family. In their quest to have no conflict, they have instead reaped a perpetual conflict, one that will require an incredible battle to overcome. As I write this, my friend says her parents feel they will just wait until they die and let others deal with his situation.

What we resist will persist until it comes about. It is like a self-fulfilling prophecy.

The successful avoidance of reality by any of these or other tactics will render real change ineffective. Anything that keeps us from facing the truth will serve the goals of staying comfortable and being in control. Encountering reality and experiencing God is foreign to people who seek to maintain control by any of the aforementioned means. Let's face it: People often settle for what's predictable and familiar, even at the cost of sacrificing their dreams. If staying in familiar territory keeps things the same, then forging into strange and alien regions of our experience may open up new possibilities.

In order for that to happen we must first challenge the way we see many things as either/or instead of both/and. When dealing with both/and truths we must quickly come face to face with paradox. Let's look at this phenomenon called paradox and how it affects our journey into transformation.

PART THREE

DYNAMICS OF TRANSFORMATION

SEVEN

Embracing Paradox

*Christ shows us both our greatness (thus destroying our despair)
and our wretchedness (thus destroying our pride) together.*

Peter Kreeft

There are many aspects of life God uses to transform us that are incongruent with how we prefer it to be. As a result, our attitude and response to God's "mysterious ways" can either facilitate or hinder the transformation.

Some of the elements of God's transforming process contain paradoxes that confuse us, and we consequently find ourselves resisting them. Well meaning Christians, for instance, rightly resist being self reliant. Can this be one of those both/and dynamics? After all, what is self-reliance and what is God-reliance? What faculties do we use when we are being self reliant and are we using different faculties when we are being God reliant? I assert the faculties are the same and that self-reliance is when we use our God-given abilities to attempt to live without following His commands. God-reliance is when we use those same abilities in order to fulfill His command to love, a command that leads us to discard our masks, be honest about what's so for us, and risk vulnerability in order to connect. In this case, *we* are the ones using our faculties but are using them to rely on God.

Another example of a God-given ability is the capacity to interpret our circumstances and ourselves. We spent the first portion of the book looking at how we use our ability to interpret to escape reality—it's that well attuned. However, as with our entire repertoire of God-given talents and capacities, there are legitimate uses for them too.

What must be considered when answering the above question is what are we using the facility for? For God's glory, or ours?

The Freeing Aspect of Paradox

Many of the ideas presented in this book are paradoxical. I mention this here because unless we allow for paradox we will be ineffective in utilizing all the facets of transformation God has made available to us.

Paradoxes are two seemingly contrary ideas that are both true. Paradox is defined in Webster's as, "A tenet or proposition contrary to received opinion, or seemingly absurd, yet true in fact." It is from the Greek words *para* meaning "beyond" and *doxew* meaning "to think or suppose."[25]

Paradox doesn't seem to be inconsistent with God, and we're not very comfortable with seeming incongruities we cannot neatly package. True to our propensity to fully understand and be in control we often resist paradox because it is beyond us. In fact, there are many aspects of what God says and does that seem to conflict and leave us perplexed and dependant. It's as if we aren't big enough to contain these seemingly contradictory truths.

This shows up readily with most little children when we consider the truth that there is just as much joy, if not more, in giving gifts as in receiving them. As a child, when Christmas came around I did not grasp that I would experience as much joy in giving gifts as I did in receiving them. As it stands today, the elation I experience at Christmas is more about the gifts I give. A child does not grasp this paradox until some maturity sets in.

I'm personally coming to embrace the reality that "God's ways are above my ways,"[26] and that I really don't understand how life works. The way life is laid out by the revelation of God in the Bible is full of paradox. I've found the acceptance of paradox to be one of the most fleeting and at the same time freeing concepts presented throughout Scripture.

Paradox is part of our present experience as Christians. As Peter Kreeft says, we are "Both already redeemed and in the process of being redeemed, both eternally secure and battling in 'fear and trembling,' both 'working out your own salvation' and knowing that 'it is God that is at work in you, both to will and to work'" (Philippians 2:12).

Indeed, many of the tenets put forth in Scripture are seemingly absurd. How often in fact have we heard people say just that in response to some biblical truth they are confronted with? "Why would I want to enter mourning and revisit that whole thing again? It won't change anything." "How can I give my tithe when I don't have enough to pay the bills this month?" "I'd be crazy to forgive him after what he did to me." "Love my enemy—are you nuts!?"

Think about all of the paradoxes presented in the Bible. Here are a few:

> Last shall be first (Matthew 20:16);
> Better to give than receive (Acts 20:35);
> Die to live (Matthew 16:25-26);
> Worth everything (Romans 5:8)/ Worth nothing (James 4:14);
> Those who mourn shall laugh (Matthew 5:4);
> Strength in weakness (2 Corinthians 12:9);
> I can do everything (Mark 10:27)/ I can do nothing (John 15:5);
> There is nothing good in me (Romans 7:18)/ I am a child of
> God (John 1:12)

Dealing with paradox requires a very mature mindset and an increased capacity for accepting life's apparent incongruities and contradictions. Peter Koestenbaum says it this way: "The difference between a mature and an immature person lies precisely here: the ability to cope with the paradoxes, ambiguities, uncertainties, conflicts, contradictions, and polarities that are intrinsically inherent in life itself. And what's more, we are by nature equipped to deal with them, and the more we do the higher quality people we are...Polarity training is therefore central to the development of character."[27]

The ability to contain paradox interrupts the "all or nothing" or "either/or" conversations that keep so many people stuck. It helps us allow for being a work in progress instead of expecting that we are now or will always be a certain way. The all or nothing mindset insists that everything in my life must always be positive or that I'm a complete mess and will never arrive.

Embracing paradox makes it possible to realize that, even though we cycle through similar challenges, we are still taking new ground. It gives us freedom in the sense that we don't have to get crazy when we notice that there is still work to do. However, just because we are works in progress doesn't mean we can say our lapses into fleshly behavior don't matter. Paul addresses that attitude in Romans 6:1 where he talks about grace abounding where sin increases: "What shall we say then? Shall we go on sinning so that grace may increase? By no means!" (NIV)

A realization and acknowledgement of both the presence of sin and the working of grace doesn't give us license to slip into a *laissez faire* attitude. Our attitudes and posture of heart are some of God's primary concerns, because these emanate from our character. We will address attitude more fully later on.

Paradox also helps deal with other apparent inconsistencies such as the reality that I by Christ's stripes I am healed- yet I have cancer. How do I reconcile those two things? Here are some of the actual thoughts I had shortly after I was diagnosed with cancer:

> "As people found out, and the calls of concern began coming in, I found myself being both grateful and–the strangest feeling– cynical. As people told me they were praying, I drank it in and noticed how desperately I wanted that, I got their love and concern for me. And at the same time I felt uncomforted. As I explored this aspect what came to mind were all the 'unanswered' prayers I prayed myself and watched other people pray. I categorize them as 'unanswered' because the turnout was not what was preferred.

> As I consider this it brings up the most unsettling aspect of what my family faces. As I have long advocated, God is not that interested in our temporary comfort. While He is a God that heals, He often does not. The 'why's' we don't get to know."

Some may see this as an escape but it works for me: I have chosen to contain the paradox that God is a healer and yet doesn't always heal. It is something that fits in perfectly with the idea of paradox–something beyond what I think or suppose, in the natural mindset–is consistent. Yes, His ways are beyond me. Many times people are not healed... and yet He is the Great Physician by whose stripes we have been healed.

In a practical way, as I've allowed for these seeming in-congruencies, I have found not only peace but also found that I can channel my energy towards making the most of what I have rather than spend it on resisting what is. If His ways are truly beyond me it doesn't always have to make the kind of sense *I prefer*. If some see that as a cop-out, so be it. Dropping the either/or aspect of this dilemma, as well as others, brings tremendous freedom.

Next, I would like to give an overview of what I consider the different aspects of transformation and how they affect each other.

EIGHT

Elements of Transformation

Even as water carves monuments of stone, so do our thoughts shape
our character.

Hugh B. Brown

In the confrontation between the stream and the rock, the stream
always wins—not through strength but by perseverance.

H. Jackson Brown

If you don't change the direction you're headed you'll probably get
there.

Ancient Chinese Proverb

The last chapter briefly touched on the idea of paradox and how our willingness to stay in the tension of two seemingly contradictory truths is one of the elements required to affect transformation. There are many other elements that God uses in transforming us. The following paragraphs offer a brief overview of some of these elements.

Scripture says, "As a man thinks in his heart, so is he." Does this mean that if we *change the way we think* we then change? I say yes, this is where transformation begins. And many self-help gurus have seized upon this biblical concept and run with it. Thinking your way to success is used in spheres as diverse as sales training, wealth-building, athletic achievement, and influencing people, all with undeniably positive results.

Bringing our thinking into alignment with God's revealed truth in the Bible does initiate change. So we must continually ask, "Does the way I am thinking or believing align with what God has revealed? Are my expectations in line with what is real? How much do my attitudes and assumptions affect change?"

In large measure, our thinking is shaped by our history, culture, circumstances, education, and experiences. These influences in turn can affect how we behave or respond to events and relationships in our lives. Other aspects of change grow out of what we believe and how we think, spilling over into how we behave, respond, react, and relate to people and circumstances.

Repeated patterns of behavior can further cement how we are. Over the years, behavioral psychologists have had some success helping people implement changes in behavior which in turn helped change what they think or believe.

For example, we know that changing the way we relate to God, to others, to ourselves, and to our circumstances produces different "fruit" in our lives. Is this fruit evidence that we have changed? In other words, how does *changing the way we relate to people and circumstances* in turn change *us*? If I change the way I relate or respond to different situations and people, will I then change? Which comes first: changing my thinking/believing or changing my actions?

If these questions come to your mind, as they did to mine, then the linear way we often think about progress toward transformation is revealed. I wonder how often we limit dynamic change by investing in the idea that growth must happen in steps or sequentially. It is my belief that transformation is more of a dynamic, and once it is activated change affects many faculties at the same time, not first one and then another followed serially by another. We are not talking about dominoes here.

Linear thinking can be seen in the examples in Chapter Four where I pointed out how people can put the onus of change onto the next thing that needs to happen: when I get married, when I have kids, when I buy a house, when I get that new job, etc. The progression is on a line with one thing following another, all leading to an elusive arriving point where my life—and myself—will be the way I hope. How often do you find yourself thinking not only linearly about yourself, as in "I'm getting better," but also as though each "step" in and of itself is a temporary place of arrival? This thinking is ingrained in our cultural mindset.

This is understandable since our experience seems to show us that, although we can change how we think about things and change how we respond or relate to life around us, deep, foundational, or core change seems elusive. We can go along for a while believing we have changed only to find that it wasn't the real change we were hoping for. What really happened was either a successful removal of the triggers that throw us back into old patterns or that the old patterns have simply taken on more subtle forms.

So how does core change occur? In other words, how can we *change who we are in essence?* True and complete transformation will only happen at our core. Of course, dealing with our core essence brings us full circle because at this level we encounter what we really believe and think, which consequently affects how we behave and relate.

A common understanding of core transformation is that happens once and for all time. In other words, once we change at this level we are changed *for good.* Any mention of core change connotes permanency or finality. This can lead us to believe we are fixed in some aspect of our constitution. What I mean by fixed is concrete, static, done. This even shows up in statements such as "I'm peeling back the layers" or "I'm getting to the next level." These kinds of statements point to a belief that at each stratum we are, at least temporarily, fixed (in the sense of being static). Then, as we continue to move forward, someday, somehow, when we get to the *final* layer or level we will arrive. I question whether this will ever be so in this life and wonder about the next.

So the questions that beg to be asked are: What is our core essence? How do we access it? How is it altered? How do we really change? We will more fully explore these questions later in the book, but for now let me say I don't believe we are fixed, static, or concrete in our way of *being.* We are dynamic creatures and have been given the gift of freewill; therefore a possibility to choose otherwise will remain.

Fundamental and core change is a work of God through the Spirit as He conforms us into Christ's image. Any ability to engage life differently is ultimately a God-given grace, as apart from Christ and as creatures who derive their very being from God, we can do nothing (Acts 17:28).

Even though I have in some way divided these spheres of change into thinking, relating, and core/essence change, all of these aspects influence the others. Each area contains elements of the others within it. We don't have three *separate* parts of ourselves; these facets are not isolated from each other nor do they stand on their own. Furthermore, the division I have done here regarding thinking, relating and core is simply in order to make it easier to talk about the dynamics I refer to and not as though they are "things" at all. As mentioned above, I don't believe we are fixed, concrete, or static. These aspects of our makeup are themselves dynamics and interwoven instead of linear and sequential. It will also become evident that all three spheres sway each other. We will explore these dynamics in the coming chapters.

Once surrender takes place we can start acknowledging the reality in our lives in ways that will invite transformation instead of using all the avoidance mechanisms we been noticing. The path to this will always involve telling ourselves the truth about the way things really are instead of how we think they should be, wish they would be, etc. While we must face reality we must also interrogate the "reality" we make up—our truths rather than an absolute truth. It would serve us well to keep in mind that we "still look through a glass, darkly" (1 Corinthians 13:12) and that in our finiteness we do not possess all truth but are instead seekers of truth. Our culture is prone to come up with answers and resists living in questions, we resist wondering about what we *don't know* in areas we think we *already know everything there is to know*. As Christians we give mental assent to the Scripture that "we see through a glass darkly" (1 Corinthians 13:12) but we live as if we see with absolute clarity. With that in mind, there are multiple areas that need to be faced and many that need interrogated:

- What/how have I been avoiding?
- How does my believing/thinking line up with reality?
- How does even the way I "view" myself (as a fixed/static being) or transformation (as a "thing" to get to) actually impede transformation?
- How does the way I interact contribute to or hinder what I say I'm committed to having in my life and relationships?
- How do I ally with God to have the circumstances of life be elements of transformation instead of further cementing what's not working?

- What attitudes in me need realignment?
- What comfort zone am I unwilling to interrupt or what loss of image am I unwilling to undergo in order to transform?
- What prices to my pride am I willing to pay?
- How can I engage the people and issues that I'm currently blaming for my plight in ways that invite deeper transformation in me?
- Might I be the way I am because in some way I'm getting what I want?
- How are my judgments keeping me stuck?
- How does my need to be right keep me reproducing the past?
- Who haven't I fully released through forgiveness? What haven't I fully released through mourning?

These are but just some of the topics we will investigate as we go forward in our journey. Transformation involves many aspects of our makeup. It involves changing how we think, talk, act, interact, believe, and relate to people and circumstances. Transformation alters our attitudes about people and experiences, our expectations, and on and on. Each of these aspects are pieces to the puzzle of the dynamic of change. The remainder of this book will look at all of these dynamics. Each component contains facets over which we have a great amount of control and others to which we must simply surrender.

Once we surrender to reality, we then must paradoxically stand with all our might to actually change something. Change is something that does not just happen on its own. We are participants and indeed nothing will change without our insistence that it do so.

As you can see from previous chapters, the obstacles to change are many. We both want and resist change. But there is hope beyond measure. We are not alone! The promise of Scripture is that He who began a good work in us, will complete it (Philippians 1:6).

He will also complete us...make us whole...make us perfect.

NINE

Transformation is Dynamic

The most important difference between Christianity and all other
religions: that in Christianity God is not a static thing—not even
a person—but a dynamic, pulsating activity, a life, almost a kind
of drama. Almost, if you will not think me irreverent, a kind of
dance.

C.S. Lewis, *Mere Christianity*

I keep referring to our *being* as dynamic versus static or fixed. This
is not surprising if we are made in God's image and He Himself
is dynamic—meaning flexible and fluid. And paradoxically, He is
unchanging.[28] I believe that God is a perfect Being, and His eternal
attributes are "immutable"- so this is not what I'm referring to when I say
God is dynamic. What I am talking about is how fluid and flexible He
shows up in order to love us. And in my view to love fully is the ultimate
purpose of transformation. Often times we don't tap into these same
possibilities but rather argue for limitations in how we can *be*.

When we talk about ourselves and our ability to love we argue for
how we *are*: as in we "are a certain way", and imply we are static using
it as an excuse stay the same. Or, we indicate we can change but insist
it needs to happen through slow and ponderous personal growth. How
often have you used phrases such as "I'm getting better, aren't I?" Or,
"Hey I'm trying to change!" as ways to actually justify the way we say we
actually *are*: this solid, static, defined creature who is trying so hard to
change but is almost helpless to do so? Instead I assert we are created in
the image of this dynamic God and I assert that as dynamic beings our
transformation, while ongoing, can also be far-reaching.

To understand better how this concept of being dynamic plays into transformation it may be helpful to look at the way it's viewed in the scientific realm. Dynamics is defined as "that branch of mechanical philosophy which is concerned with the force of moving bodies; the science of moving powers, and the effect of moving bodies acting on each other and producing motion."[29] Also, a dynamic is "an interactive system or process, especially one involving competing or conflicting forces."[30] When we actually engage in the type of thinking that is in line with what Christ outlines, a force or power is exerted which produces motion towards transformation. The antithesis is also true: When non-resourceful conversations and interpretations are tapped, these can keep us stuck or unchanged.

If the *force* comes from the conversation or interpretation that is currently engaged, it would follow that when that conversation or interpretation reverts, changes, or is dropped the power exercised toward the transformation would be affected.

For example, let's say that you make a commitment to live honestly and share vulnerably with a person in your life. Up until now, perhaps you had the interpretation that it was better to play it safe, stay comfortable, and be in control. The conversation that generated this interpretation may be one that says people aren't safe, they can hurt you, and so it's better to not be honest and vulnerable. In keeping with the commitment to live honestly, however, you risk being hurt, give up the control, and engage vulnerably.

As you begin to walk this out, you notice the dynamic between you and the other person impacted in the sense there is greater connection, intimacy, understanding, and love. These results are present because of the way of relating you are engaging. Once you've achieved this connection, let's say you once again revert to playing it safe, being in control, and staying comfortable. At some point disconnection will happen again. The results will cease to be if the way of relating that produced the results ceases. That's the dynamic.

Is All Change Permanent?

One of the greatest frustrations reported by many graduates of our programs is a stated inability to maintain the mountaintop "high" experienced at the training event. During Reinvent Ministries' trainings, seminars, and workshops, we struggle as we learn to practice the disciplines of living in the light, confession, honesty, authenticity, repentance, forgiveness, striving to love God and others more than ourselves, etc. Because of the diligence in employing the above disciplines, participants come out of the training feeling hopeful. They are convinced they have changed.

But feeling hopeful and different doesn't necessarily mean real permanent change has occurred. The change was valid while the disciplines were employed; when these are dropped and the old ways of living were drifted into, the "change" disappears too. I assert that our concept of change is flawed. Just because we embrace change, initiate change, or feel changed doesn't mean we have completely changed. This idea is naïve, unreal, and actually works to keep us stuck.

Change is an active and dynamic principle. Through growth we may have come to realize that our experiences did not need to hold us back the way we thought they did in a less mature mindset. Even as we grow, we can have recurring thoughts and memories based on past negative experiences. If we fail to persist in relating to these in the new interpretation that produced freedom, these thoughts can enslave us to previous modes of thinking and behaving.

Changing our thinking is an area in which we have a very active role. As we read the Scriptures regarding the mind, it is apparent that we are the ones who must initiate this kind of change. We are commanded to bring our thoughts into captivity. There are disciplines to help us with this task, but we must not trivialize the importance of this aspect of change and our responsibility to make sure it happens.

Shifting

One of Webster's primary definitions of change is: "To put one thing in place of another; to shift." To shift, in turn, means: "To change; to give place to other things" or "A change; a turning from one thing to another; hence, an expedient tried in difficulty; one thing tried when another one fails."[31]

Putting one thing in place of another? Giving place to other things? Turning from one thing to another? This may not sound like change. It may sound more like choosing one way of thinking or being over and above another. It sounds more like a cognitive decision to try something else when what we've tried hasn't worked. This doesn't sound very spiritual and certainly doesn't sound very permanent.

So how close is this to the biblical concept of change?

In all actuality, this fits perfectly with the teachings of Scripture. The Bible makes it clear that we "were taught, with regard to [our] former way of life, to put off [our] old self, which is being corrupted by its deceitful desires; to be made new in the attitude of [our] minds; and to put on the new self, created to be like God in true righteousness and holiness" (Ephesians 4:22-24 NIV).

"To be made new in the attitude of our minds" in the New American Standard Bible reads "that you be renewed in the spirit of your mind." It is interesting to note that one of the primary illustrations of the word "shift" is to change clothes (Webster's). In Ephesians we are urged to "put on the new self," as if we are taking off one outfit of clothes and putting on another. Isaiah 61:3 talks about the same dynamic, "a garment of praise instead of a spirit of despair." Both suggest putting off, laying down one way of being and putting on another. In Ephesians 6:11, we are also encouraged to put on the full armor of God as a way to equip us to go forth into battle (life). I offer that another way of saying "to put off and put on" is to shift.

Shifting does not mean a "fake it 'til you make it" type of positive thinking. It is a conscious decision born out of a deep persuasion to believe what God says. A decision to shift the way we think is an act of the mind and the will made possible by the work of the Holy Spirit within.

During the Impact Training, participants practice certain disciplines that most people aspire to live by. We sometimes compare our training to working out in a gym. Personal coaches work with individuals to develop routines and encourage reps to build strength. The rigor of maintaining these disciplines is very high. The accountability in this atmosphere is not unlike being in a gym with a personal trainer coaching you, pushing you, and developing your discipline. Living by these disciplines produces a change. The transformation that takes place during the training can best be defined as a shift.

For example, in the Impact Training we establish that we will be completely honest with each other. We openly share our internal conversations about ourselves and each other. Such authenticity is freeing when done in love. This is not normally practiced by most in daily life. Whereas we may normally practice the self-service of loving ourselves, in the training we practice the self-sacrifice of loving others. In other words, people put off a way of being that has them stuck in a certain mode of living and put on a way that is advocated in Scripture.

This is a good explanation for what occurs in most participants during an Reinvent Ministry event. Engaging in God-given, scriptural disciplines produces a quality of life that is undeniable. Because of the rigor with which we practice these disciplines in our time together, the possibilities that open up for life after the event are enormous, invigorating, and exciting. People think about things in a new way and therefore experience a type of change in themselves. They practice being fluid and flexible in ways of engaging for the purpose of impacting another person in love. Most succeed in this commitment and it feels good. And as we are prone to do, we immediately think "I get it!" and hope that we are done with the old life and have finally and for good been transformed.

People who naively think they have arrived inevitably abandon the disciplines and new thought patterns they practiced in training leaning instead onto how they understand now. Many hope they can mainly coast the rest of the way, expecting to maintain the new ground without persisting in the rigor that opened up the opportunity in the first place. It's the same as thinking that one good workout session at the gym is enough to keep us fit for life. Such an attitude exhibits an arrogance and entitlement that God very quickly undermines. And thank God He does!

A very helpful definition of transformation is found in the great book, *Killing the Victim before the Victim Kills You,* by Watson and Tocchini. They define transformation as "the process of shifting the relationship taken to a person or event; such shifting occurs moment to moment and *is not permanent.*"[32]

In its simplest form, shifting is a decision to release attitudes, actions, and ways of thinking that have not worked to bring about the desired outcome, then going about finding ones that do. Shifting involves a willingness to be fluid or flexible instead of insisting that what we have been doing should work. If it's not working, face up to it and shift!

Imagine driving a car up a steep hill in overdrive because it usually runs smoothest in overdrive. The car begins to lose power and speed, but instead of down-shifting you keep flooring the accelerator.

Sounds ridiculous, yes? And yet many of us engage life this way. I know I have. And when I begin to "lose power and speed" in life, instead of trying something different I get angry with circumstances that don't change or people in my life who don't respond.

Children are very good at shifting and are often the most flexible in the sense of going about getting what they want. I can't tell you how many times my daughter Cristiana has probed and prodded for possibilities for overcoming a "no" from me. She's a master at working all the angles to find a way around something we have forbidden her to do.

Dawn and I have often smiled at Cristiana's persistence. But as her parents we do make the final decision on most issues, and many times we've had to curb her creativity and persistence with firm discipline. We have always tried not to step over the line between sound discipline and breaking Cristiana's spirit. But sometimes parents, including us, are too overbearing and squash a child's creativity for shifting, causing them to reluctantly and resentfully conform.

While this practice can arguably fall into the category of manipulation it accurately captures the idea of finding a way to impact another person. When applied to reaching another in love this "shifting" approaches a characteristic of God. As an aside have you ever wondered what it means to "provoke one another to love and good works"? Is it not finding a way to persuade another human being to choose something they may be resisting? Does that sound like manipulation?

Shifting how we relate and respond to others until we find a way to reach them is essential to changing relationships for the better. The same is true of changing our circumstances in life. If one way of engaging isn't working, try another.

What frustrates many people is that the *shift isn't permanent*. It's like people who diligently exercise, eat healthy, and get in shape. Then they stop the disciplines, become couch potatoes, and eat whatever they want. They become frustrated because they have reverted back to their previously unwanted physical appearance. This frustration and disappointment in itself is very revealing. It indicates an expectation, an entitlement, and a way of thinking many people hold—even Christians— that life should be a certain way: the way they prefer.

This insistence is one obstacle to effecting change. Life works the way it does. We are not the creators of it. It's useless and counterproductive to deny the existence of certain truths. Imagine resenting gravity and pretending it didn't exist. It doesn't matter how resentful we are about gravity; it exists and there's nothing we can do about it. You can pretend— even deeply believe—it doesn't exist, but if you jump off a 30-story building you will still go *splat* on the concrete. But if you acknowledge that gravity exists, you allow for the discovery of aerodynamic lift needed for airplanes to fly.

The way we think life should be also strongly influences how effectively we accept the tragedies of life and allow God to use them to work for our eternal good (Romans 8:28). When we align our thinking with what God says we should expect in life, we somehow gain altitude on the worst things life throws at us. While it doesn't fully remove the sting of difficulties, the frustration is not the same.

Let's investigate how we can shift and thus influence change in these spheres. It all starts with the thoughts. Samuel Smiles, the poet, writes:

> Sow a thought, reap an act.
> Sow an act, reap a habit.
> Sow a habit, reap a character.
> Sow a character, reap a destiny.

Changing our thoughts is a great place to begin engaging in the great effort of demolishing the strongholds that keep us from transformation.

TEN

A New Way of Thinking

The soul is dyed the color of its thoughts... The content of your
character is your choice. Day by day, what you choose, what you
think, and what you do is who you become.

Heraclitus, Greek Poet, Philosopher

...whatever is true, whatever is noble, whatever is right, whatever is
pure, whatever is lovely, whatever is admirable...think about such
things.

Phil 4:8-9 NIV

Changing the Way We Think

How does the way we think influence how we change? Many books
and motivational seminars have tapped into this powerful mechanism for
change. Gurus in secular and religious spheres advocate thinking your
way to change and/or success. Let's look at the impact of changing our
thinking on transformation.

Proverbs 23:7 states: "For as he thinks in his heart, so is he" (NKJV).
It would seem to follow that if belief in the heart changes, so does the
person. The universality of the connection made between *what* we think
and *how* we are is a testament to the truth of this proverb.

So exactly what role do our thoughts have in effecting change? How
much of this process is accomplished under our own power? In other
words, can we change ourselves by changing how we think? What power
is there in positive thinking anyway? To put it another way, what power
is there in changing the way we think into ways that would simply work
better?

The Scriptures have much to say about our thoughts and the impact they have on our life. The Bible exhorts us to examine our thoughts, determine which are contrary to what Christ teaches, and bring all thoughts into alignment with His teaching and all of Scripture. Second Corinthians 10:5-6 states: "We demolish arguments and every pretension that sets itself up against the knowledge of God, and we take captive every thought to make it obedient to Christ" (NIV). The tone of the language implies tremendous responsibility on us to actually do this work.

This passage indicates that the way we are predisposed to think is contrary to how God would have us think. At the very least, once we've examined our thoughts and ferreted out the ones contrary to His, we are to show them no mercy. In fact, terms like "demolish," "take captive," and "make it obedient" are very combative. In short, this is war. If our thoughts are out of alignment, we are to forcefully and ruthlessly subjugate them to Christ. In other words, we are to make our thoughts obey Him.

Barnes comments on 2 Corinthians 10:5: "All the pride of the human heart and of the understanding…is opposed to the knowledge of God, and all exalts itself into a vain self-confidence. People entertain vain and unfounded opinions respecting their own excellence, and they feel that they do not need the provisions of the gospel and are unwilling to submit to God."[33] According to Barnes, it is vain confidence that says we can handle life without God. Self-sufficiency makes us mistakenly feel that we don't need the provisions offered by God. This is a function of pride, and we are commanded to demolish this thinking because it keeps us separated from the transforming work of God.

These self-sufficient thoughts need to be interrupted. In some ways, most of us take control of our thoughts every day. For instance, when we are tempted, we have learned to master lustful thoughts by pushing them away. Or when provoked to anger, we restrain thoughts of lashing out. Inappropriate remarks that spring into our minds are blocked from coming out our mouths. Sometimes we even push away thoughts of good.

In other words, we do *know* how to take our thoughts captive and make them obey.

There is a very real and close correlation between *how we think* and *how we are.* "As a man thinks in his heart, so is he." Of course, "thinks in his heart" is the operative phrase here. It implies more than mental assent; it speaks of a persuasion, a deep-seated belief. Bringing our thinking into alignment with what the Creator of life says is true will certainly yield results in our efforts to change. Romans 12:2 says: "Be transformed by the renewing of the mind."

In this context, let us consider some of what Scripture teaches regarding knowing our thoughts and their effects on our experience of life. I propose that our desire to change is grounded in yearning to be free of what we feel stuck in.

Just How Are We a New Creation?

When we commit to becoming Christians and we read the Scriptures, we are eager to accept the truths that promise transformation, and rightfully so. The questions we need to ask as we read are: How does our thinking and what we believe about these truths play out in reality? Is there a disparity between the two and, if so, is it only a matter of time until the two come into alignment?

For instance, the Bible does say that we are new creatures (2 Corinthians 5:16-21). The old is gone, all things are made new. This promise seems out of place when applied to the areas in our lives where we experience a longstanding, ongoing struggle with the old life or sin.

Matthew Henry comments about 2 Corinthians 5:16-21:

> A thorough change of the heart: For if any man be in Christ, if any man be a Christian indeed, and will approve himself such, he is, or he must be, a new creature, v. 17. Some read it, *Let him be a new creature.* This ought to be the care of all who profess the Christian faith, that they be new creatures; not only that they have a new name, and wear a new livery, but that they have a new heart and new nature. And so great is the change the grace of God makes in the soul, that, as it follows, old things are passed away-*old thoughts, old principles, and old practices,* are passed away; and all these things must become new. Note, regenerating grace creates a new world in the soul; all things are new. The renewed man acts from *new principles,* by *new rules,* with *new ends,* and in *new company.*[34] (Emphasis mine)

The Scriptures are the standard God has given us for measuring our experience of reality. However, it is easy to settle for a watered down version of what they mean. Most people do not go through the rigorous self-examination of their experience in the way that Paul spoke about in Romans 7. There he identifies the reality of his situation ("I don't do the things I want to do, instead I do the things I don't want to do"), embraces the truth, and seeks to allow God to reconcile the discrepancy.

Upon conversion we are in fact new creatures, and we are commanded to engage in the disciplines that verify this fact. "Let him be a new creature" suggests a practice, a daily discipline, a battle to be engaged in.

In his popular book, *The Pursuit of Holiness,* Jerry Bridges writes, "Through our union with Christ in His death we are delivered from the dominion of sin. But we still find sin struggling to gain mastery over us (Romans 7:21). We may not like the fact that we have this lifelong struggle with sin, but the more we realize and accept it, the less we feel its effects."

Bridges then likens this struggle to two warring nations. One of the combatants has the conflict settled in its favor by the intervention of an outside army, with the effect that the faction that won the war assumes control of the government. Yet instead of stopping its fight, the opposition simply changes its tactics to one of guerilla warfare.[35]

In the same way, while we have been granted victory through Christ's work and indeed have been made into new creations, we still have our struggles waging a guerilla war within us. We have been granted this victory by grace; we did nothing to earn it. And yet our thinking has been permeated by the effects of the war sin has waged in us. So many survival strategies have been embraced and integrated in an attempt to keep us from what seemed to be sure death, albeit the threat was really to self-sufficiency and pride. Sin, with its reality of spiritual death, is what has ushered in this condition.

And the repercussions continue.

Our reality is that sin's hold is broken by the work of Christ on the cross. And while a new man is birthed, the old man continues to try to resurrect himself. It's like a zombie in a horror film that refuses to stay dead; it keeps getting back up every time it is apparently killed. In this way we have not changed, or more properly, we can still be plagued by many of the same sin-motivated struggles and propensities we've had for many years. At times it feels like there are two different people (or more) living inside in me. I'm sure there are two natures.

Since my junior high days I have enjoyed the *Lord of the Rings* trilogy by J.R.R. Tolkien, and I have been delighted by Peter Jackson's film adaptations of that trilogy. In the second installment, *The Two Towers,* there is a pitiful creature called Gollum. Gollum was once a rather normal and likable creature called Sméagol.

Sméagol has been corrupted by his long obsession with "the Ring of power" (control) resulting in his transformation into a murdering, isolating, hateful, and self-loathing creature called Gollum. He's forgotten his old good self because of all the bad he has done in his lust for power and control.

Yet deep down there is a small remnant of goodness in him. Frodo (the Hobbit hero in the story) opens the possibility that Sméagol can once again emerge. Frodo does this by reminding him of his former name and by holding out hope for him. Frodo's belief in him encourages Gollum to believe that he can live again. As a result, a shift happens in Gollum. He begins to think differently and act differently, and Sméagol reemerges to a point. He rediscovers a degree of happiness and faithfully carries out the promise he makes to Frodo.

But later, when haunting memories of betrayal and trust are triggered and Sméagol believes he has been betrayed, he begins to revert back to the personality of Gollum. There is a moving scene where the two personalities are fighting for dominance. Gollum tries everything to keep Sméagol in check. In the scene Gollum says to Sméagol, "Where would you be if it wasn't for me? I saved us, it's because of me we survived!" When that doesn't work he reminds Sméagol of all his failures, throwing all the wrong he's done in Sméagol's face. The battle continues.

In my experience, this conflict is so true. Our sinful nature is given free reign when we rely on ourselves rather than God in order to survive and pride-fully refuse to die to self. It is the "I saved us" mentality Gollum talked about. In that frantic effort we do so many things we are later ashamed of. And yet we do the best we see to do at the time.

We just want to survive...to live.

I'm not making an argument for the validity or reality of dual personality disorder. I also doubt Tolkien was writing about it when he penned the Rings trilogy. What I am arguing for is the reality of Scripture. The double-mindedness of Gollum is a perfect example of James 1:8. There is also the reality that what we give ourselves to begins to transform our identity, vying for our hearts and loyalty.

So What Does It Mean To Be a New Creation?

Second Corinthians 5:2 states that "we groan to become clothed with our heavenly dwelling." Romans 8:23 talks about us groaning as we await our redemption. The groaning to become the men and women God intends us to be begins in earnest when we make a decision to follow Christ at our conversion. Our old way of thinking is confronted and an intense battle to bring our minds into alignment with truth begins. Until that time what we called "our thinking" was simply processing thoughts along the cultural lines prescribed to us by the "world." Clear thinking is when we think God's thoughts.

Romans 12:2 says: "And do not be conformed to this world, but be transformed by the renewing of your mind" (NASB). Barnes commentary on this verse states that the renewing of the mind consists of "the making new; the changing into new views and feelings."[36]

God has given us the authoritative ability to change our minds into new views leading to new feelings. In a powerful exercise during the Impact Training, participants have an opportunity to look at circumstances of their life through different filters; not changing the circumstances, but rather changing their perspectives or interpretations of the circumstances.

Amazingly, people find their feelings or emotions changing as their view of the events change. Of all God's creatures, we are the only ones possessing the power to change our perspective, rising above our circumstances and thereby changing the impact of those circumstances. I don't believe we have fully grasped the power God has given us to rise above the circumstances of our life and actually use them to change us in the way we hope.

Another way to state this is that the conversations we engage in about the events of our lives, and the subsequent meaning about ourselves we assign out of these ongoing conversations, come to determine how we see ourselves. You see, things happen but they don't happen in a vacuum. As they happen, we assign an interpretation to them. This interpretation, more than the event, is what works the mischief in our lives and keeps us stuck. We could, conversely, interpret the events in a way that would allow us to access resources to bring about transformation. This begins by really believing God will use whatever happens in our lives.

At the same time, I believe it is counterproductive, if not destructive, to simply reframe all that happens to us with the trite "God will make it all right" patch in an effort to avoid the full impact or hurt of an incident. Instead, we must exhibit a willingness to fully face life and its experiences without utilizing the convenient modes of avoidance we enumerated earlier.

Since God is loving and omniscient, we can be confident in deriving eternal benefit from whatever He allows into our life. If we, in an effort to control what we don't like, attempt to bypass the path He gave us to walk, we will still suffer. Additionally, we also add the unnecessary suffering of not receiving the refining He intended for us. And, since He is sovereign, He even uses the paths we obstinately choose instead of His to continue His work!

What Are You "Listening For?"

This concept may sound a little strange at first. But when you think about it everything we experience intersects with internal conversations we are already having. We then interpret what we experience by matching what's happening with what we are expecting. Our expectation is set by conversations we are always having. These conversations have to do with how we have come to believe we are and should be, how others are and should be, and how life is and should be. These belief systems have been formed out of our past experiences, upbringing, and preferences. We perpetuate, or keep these intact, by the internal conversations we have, conversations that basically assess and validate or invalidate what we experience.

Think about it. Whatever we experience clashes with these conversations. Events that happen to us, things we experience in relationship, our successes and our failures, all these are filtered through the internal conversations we have about how things should or shouldn't be. I call this dynamic what we're "listening for." We are listening for the evidence that matches up to the beliefs we have.

One discipline encouraged during the Impact Training is for participants to bring their internal dialogue into the light. If you paused right now for just a moment and tuned in to yourself, you would discover an internal commentary running through your head. These conversations are taking place all the time. Some people refer to this inner dialogue as the "tapes" playing in our head. Often this internal dialogue goes unnoticed. It is like the oxygen that's always around us, so encompassing that we scarcely think about it. Our internal dialogue is the white noise we always live with. It can cause trouble if we are not aware that it's going on and therefore assume what we're thinking is the *only* way it really is.

Internal dialogue is normal for everybody and it need not be a problem. The mischief comes when this internal conversation undermines what we desire most. Here are some examples of internal dialogues that can conflict with and therefore sabotage our dreams.

I'm not good enough.

That was stupid (self judgment).

I always attract losers (judgment of self and others).

I hate dealing with this.

I'm not good at this.

This will never work out; I can't deal with this (judgment of self and ability to handle circumstances).

He/she will never get it.

They always do this (judgment of others).

This shouldn't be happening (judgment of reality).

As you can see, these internal tapes are judgments either of yourself, of someone else, or of life. When it comes to judging others the Scripture teaches us that we shall be judged by whatever measure we use to judge. This internal judgment of self and others is another way we block change in our lives. When it comes to judging how life should or shouldn't be, change is sabotaged because some things just *are* and it's a totally ineffective transformation conversation to bemoan what *is*.

Imagine one of these tapes constantly playing in someone's head as they interact with others. Often the inner dialogue is so loud that it's all they hear. The person can't hear what's actually being said. For example, someone may tell you how nice you look today, but if your inner tape is saying, "I'm ugly, nobody likes the way I look," you may not hear or accept the compliment. Or, if you do, you'll reject what's being said by assigning a meaning to the person complimenting such as "They are just trying to be nice or they probably want something."

I've heard communication is comprised of 7-20 percent language while the remaining 80-93 percent consists of the tone of voice, mood, attitude, and body language of the communicator. We are constantly sending messages without words, and much of this content reflects what we hear in our heads. Often our internal conversation is communicated more clearly than our spoken conversation.

Furthermore, we will not allow incomplete communication from others to remain in limbo. We finish what others start, filling in the missing pieces. For example, someone who has a conflict with you may not tell you what went wrong, but you will form a conclusion based on what's in your head. What's in our head is not necessarily the most resourceful fountain to draw upon since it could be a view developed by an un-resourceful child. Cycles of communication, or incomplete understanding of something, must be completed in some fashion. We tend to "close the loop" on incomplete conversations and unresolved situations in this way.

Here is an example from my own life. Recently I discovered that three of my colleagues had launched into a venture without telling me about it. When I finally heard about it, I jumped to some conclusions based on the tapes rolling in my head: "I guess I'm not good enough to be included in this venture"; "If only I had more presence in front of a group!"; "I'll just get better and then they'll notice me"; "Why wouldn't they want to include me? Don't they know how much I've sacrificed?" From there I just grew more offended and judgmental.

I resisted approaching my colleagues with what I determined was going to be a difficult conversation. I was reluctant to get into it for fear that my suspicions would be confirmed. In some ways, it appeared easier to hold onto my interpretation that I wasn't good enough than to get into a difficult "reality conversation." When I finally spoke with my friends, I discovered that my perception was entirely wrong. I had been in their plans all along, and it had simply been more efficient for them to plan together because of the logistics, since they live very near each other and I live eight hours away. The missing information filled in by me reflected the internal struggle I've had for so long.

Ironically, avoiding reality conversations perpetuates the very things we don't want. Instead of seeking the truth, we make up interpretations that are in keeping with what we have come to believe. We can find out what is really happening, as I finally did, but we need to be aware of our propensity to fill in the blanks from heads.

Often when a breakdown happens in relationship, a person will be left with uncompleted conversations which he fills in with snippets of information based on what he was predisposed to believe. This person decided that his need to be right took precedence over what was real.

For instance, I've worked with people who have been divorced and never performed what Dr. Phil McGraw terms "an autopsy on the dead relationship." Unaware of all that went wrong leading to dissolution, spouses have concluded, "She just had too many problems" or "I guess he didn't love me anymore." As morbid as the "autopsy" reference sounds, I believe our judgments against people and our failure to take responsibility for our contributions to bad situations is even more ghastly.

Of course, the internal completions we come up with usually cast more favorable light on us than on the other person or make us appear right about what we have decided. As a result, we give ourselves license to act the way we want; we become critical, we isolate ourselves, and we hurt others before they hurt us, etc.

Another way to understand the *listening for* dynamic can be readily seen whenever you have been considering buying a new car and settle on the make and model. All of a sudden it seems the car is everywhere you look. It just presents itself in a ubiquitous manner as if they were multiplied. Of course, in reality there were probably always that many around; it's just that now you are looking for them. Consider how this is true whenever you are in this decision making process.

The implications of this phenomenon that we find what we're looking or listening for, are staggering. We may actually miss information that can contradict what we're listening for, or interpret it in such a way that effectively makes it fit in with what we've decided. I have worked with many people who are *certain* about what they see because of all the evidence they can point to that supports their position. Many disagreements, misunderstandings, and full on separations have resulted from this dynamic.

If we can't make the words they are using fit into our construct, we can seize upon a tone or inflection or look in the eye to bolster our position. Like I said before, we're often committed to being right.

I would now like to look at one of the most powerful forms of intentional internal conversations and what makes it even more powerful.

Declarations

A powerful contributor to causing our lives to change is what we declare through our speech. What we say carries a mysterious power. If this wasn't true, why do we need to "confess with our mouth" to be converted? (Romans 10:9; Philippians 2:11). Clearly, speaking words does more than just create sound waves. Spoken words emanate from our internal beliefs. "Out of the abundance of the heart, the mouth speaks" (Luke 6:45).

Our spoken words are declarations that generate a response, an expectation, a reaction, or an influence in ourselves and others. A spoken declaration sets things into motion. God created the universe by speaking it into existence- is it an accident the words "uni" and "verse" or "one phrase" refers to all creation? And the words we speak, in relationships and to ourselves, can be powerful as well.

If I make the statement, "I'll be there at two o'clock," an expectation is raised in the listener: that I will arrive at the time stated. This is logical, but recognize: it's the declaration which created the expectation. That is quite a powerful principle! What if that kind of power was unleashed each time we made declarations? How much self-confidence is eroded because we don't follow through with our declarations? How much trust is lost because we don't follow through on even the smallest promises we make? One of the reasons we struggle at transforming our lives is the self-sabotage of not following through on our declarations.

The Scripture also says that our words contain the power of life and death. Consider how hope can be created when we speak with conviction to someone. A simple spoken word can give someone something to lean on and carry them through tough times. And a word can also knock the props out from under someone. Think about the times when someone said something that sustained you or tripped you up or even changed your life, either positively or negatively.

In the movie *Last of the Mohicans*, Nathaniel, the hero, finds himself at a dead end, trapped in a cave behind a waterfall. He has just rescued two sisters from certain death at the hands of Magua, who is committed to murder these daughters of his enemy, a British general. The dampness of the cave has moistened the gunpowder and rendered Nathaniel's rifle useless. Magua and his warriors have found the cave and are closing in. Death is certain if Nathaniel stays to fight, but in order to rescue the sisters, he must first escape Magua by diving through the waterfall to the river below.

Cora, one of the sisters, is terrified to see her "knight in shining armor" leave her. Seeing this, Nathaniel grabs hold of her arms, looks her in the eyes, and says to her; "I *will* find you. Just stay alive, I will find you!" The conviction and passion in these words convey a commitment that says, "No matter what it takes, I will come back for you or die trying, but I'm not giving up!" He then turns and dramatically jumps through the waterfall.

These words of declaration serve to carry Cora through and maintain her hope. Her sister, however, loses all hope and subsequently takes her own life by jumping off a cliff.

How often do we miss the opportunity to make declarations that bring hope to others? In doing so, we often shirk the possibility to change things around us.

God awaits our declaration in order to transform us. In loving, wooing, pursuing, and forgiving us, God has initiated the transformative work of forming Christ in us. He awaits our response, just as He did with Mary. Our declaration of "be it done to me" is the invitation He awaits to accomplish His work in us. He is the initiator; we must respond. Peter Kreeft notes that all souls are feminine to God. Like the Lover that He is, He awaits our declarations of love in response to His great love for us.

The other benefit of making declarations is that as soon as they are made *everything* that is out of alignment with the declaration becomes evident to everyone who hears them. Once received by another, a declaration of "I am a man of authenticity and intimacy, and I promise to share myself with you" will expose when I am instead shallow and fake and holding myself back.

Is It *The* Truth or *My* truth?

I must here distinguish between what is physical reality and what is interpretive reality. Philosophy has long argued whether we can, as subjective human beings, really know truth at all. We can certainly know Jesus, who is "the Truth." But aside from the revelation of the Holy Spirit, we know Jesus subjectively as well. It is not in the scope of this book to tackle questions better handled by Kierkegaard, Heidegger, and other great thinkers.

We certainly see the world through filters and live in particular paradigms. A paradigm is defined by Willis Harmon as "the basic way of perceiving, thinking, valuing, and doing associated with a particular vision of reality."[37] So, in a very real sense, what I perceive, think, value, and do is determined by how I see *reality*. This is just how it is and need not be a problem, unless we're not really seeing reality. It's also a big problem if we don't recognize the reality we do see and perceive subjectively, thinking instead we see absolutely! Remember 1 Corinthians 13:12, "we see through a glass darkly... we know in part..."

Also, if something doesn't fit our paradigm we'll probably miss it completely. Thomas S. Kuhn writes in *Scientific Revolutions,* "Data that exists in the real world that does not fit your paradigm will have a difficult time getting through your filters." Just consider the implications of this statement. Reality may be shouting to me and I can completely miss it because of my filters and interact with something I make up instead!

The bottom line is that I probably won't be able to precisely and objectively ferret out what is true and what I've interpreted as true. It is because of our subjectivity that I believe Jesus consistently pointed us to "fruit" in order to judge what is real or not. There are physical realities an impartial assessment can determine. For example, you can objectively answer the following questions through observation: Are my wife and I married or separated? Are we conversing or ignoring each other? Do many people hang out with me or am I basically isolated? Do people seem to be friendly or hostile to me?

But when it comes to ferreting out the reality of our true motivations, intentions, and heart attitudes, the only objective judge is God. However, I believe we can confidently assert that the interpretation which decides whether a relationship or a task is good or bad or easy or hard definitely falls under the category of "my truth." When I speak of good and bad I am referring to quality, not morality. Good and bad certainly exist in a moral sense as well, and Scripture clearly spells those out.

The other aspect of our internal conversations that is hardly ever challenged is the fundamental reality of them. We often speak of ourselves as if we are locked into the way we are. We say with finality, "I'm shy in front of groups" or "I have a hard time asking for what I want." It's as if an autopsy on us would find concrete evidence of a shy component or something else physically present that would it make *absolutely so* that things like that are hard for us. In other words, we talk about ourselves like we have no choice; it's the way we are—period.

What if we're wrong? What if we've bought into a lie? What if we've been deceived? What if it just serves another hidden motivation such as playing it safe, or maintaining control, or being right? Even if we have evidence from the past for our assertions does that mean it must always be so?

Statements such as "I can't do that" or "I'm not good at this" come out as incontestable realities. In reality, they are programmed declarations we have practiced over and over for years. Of course, we have evidence of this "truth," but the reality that we've not had success *up until now* does not necessitate that it will always be that way *from now on*. Claiming, "That's just the way I am" may simply be our way of staying comfortable, in control, or safe.

"Up until now" is one of the most freeing statements you can use. It allows for the truth that certain things have been so to this point: "I'm not good at following through... up until now"; "I never complete things I start...up until now"; "I shy away from necessary difficult conversations...up until now." This statement places a demarcation line delineating between what has been so from what will be "from now on." "From now on I will follow through with excellence." "From now on I promise to complete what I start." "From now on I'll engage in difficult conversations necessary to move the relationship forward."

Of course, simply because we say something does not make it so. Actions congruent with the declaration are necessary to actually have it turn out. But eliminating the self-limiting declarations is a critical first step. The mindset of going again and again whenever we miss the mark is also crucial.

The way things appear to us, and the truth we hold about anything, lives in the domain of language. In other words, how we internally talk, or converse, about the events or "truths" in our lives determines what we come to believe about these events. In fact, I assert that we often don't remember the events clearly but rather form our memories based on the impact we carry with us from the events. What I mean is that, in and of themselves, the events that happen to us are, in a strict manner of speaking, neutral. It is we who assign the meaning of good, bad, devastating, providential, etc. to them. This is not to say there are not moral rights and wrongs; I'm talking about the interpretation and assignment of meaning to the events.

What we come to believe about events is a matter of interpretation and the consequent internal conversations we have about them. Like the two classic views of a glass half full of water—"half empty" or "half full"—a person will see a reality according to their interpretation. Consider the example of Joseph in the Old Testament. On their own merit, the events which happened to Joseph at the hands of his mean brothers—being sold into slavery and lying to their father about him dying by an animal—can only be termed as "bad." Yet Joseph interpreted what happened to him in a way that enabled him to rise to prominence instead of sink into bitterness. I believe that Joseph, who was cheated, betrayed, and victimized repeatedly, didn't "deal" with his bad fortune by having internal conversations such as, "This isn't fair," "This shouldn't be happening to me," etc. If he had, how could he later say to his brothers, "What you meant for evil, God meant for good?"[38]

Our memories of our events and experiences are another faculty that is subject to our interpretations. Our unpleasant memories tend to grow like a cancer in proportion to the injustice we feel was perpetrated against us and the ramifications of the injury we suffered. Childhood memories are especially subject to this dynamic. Benjamin and Rosamund Zander make this astute observation: "How often do we stand convinced of the truth of our early childhood memories forgetting that they are but assessments made by a child? We can replace the narratives that hold us back by inventing wiser stories, free from childish fears, and, in doing so, disperse long-held psychological stumbling blocks."[39]

We are in constant internal dialogue with ourselves about ourselves, others, our circumstances, and our memories. If we allow negative conversations to run uninterrupted or unchanged, the negative results they produce will go unchanged.

Assumption

Another important component of how we think is our assumptions. Assumption is closely related to expectation; it can cause us to see things that are not really there or alter what *is* there. Our expectations and assumptions are woven into our thinking, and it takes deliberate effort to untangle them from reality. Too often our expectations and assumptions are given unchallenged power in framing how we see and don't see life. We come to believe certain things are true and take on the attitude that the facts just confuse our view.

If I assume the worst about you, how much evidence do you think I need to prove my assumption true? I think a little arching of an eyebrow could be more than enough! This kind of assumption is bred by suspicion and is anchored in self-protection.

I have talked with numerous training participants whose description of their experiences was based solely on what their assumptions led them to believe was true. Nothing I could say made any difference. It's like the old line, "My mind is made up; don't confuse me with the facts." This makes communication very difficult indeed because they heard something completely different than what I was saying. These kinds of assumptions are flagrant violations of the law of love (1 Corinthians 13:7).

Changing the way we think includes identifying these expectations, assumptions, and internal tapes, interrupting them, and replacing them with ones that are consistent with how God teaches us to think and with what we say we desire to have with people.

Assumptions and expectations are not always bad, of course. When they are positive and based on truth, we can actually accomplish some good, take new ground, and feel pretty good about where we are.

But when we do succeed in some area, does it mean that we have arrived? I have often rested on my laurels, allowing myself to coast for long periods of time on a success I experienced, using a past victory as a reason to not be diligent for a while. Such complacency is ill-founded. We can never let down our guard against unreal expectations and assumptions.

One of these unreal expectations is the idea that we should be able to get to a place where we can just coast. We wish we'd change in the sense we don't have to struggle anymore. In my experience, this does not line up with reality. I would now like to look how this misconception actually dissipates available resources resulting in disappointment and resignation rather than continued movement in transformation.

ELEVEN

A New Way of Relating

It is commonsense to take a method and try it.
If it fails, admit it frankly and try another.
But above all, try something.

Franklin D. Roosevelt

Whatever you have learned or received or heard from me, or seen in me-
put it into practice.

Phil 4:8-9 NIV

Insanity: Doing things the same way and expecting different
results.

J. Keith Miller

Shifting in the way we think and speak regarding all of these following dynamics is an important first step in the process of transformation. Believing differently is the first evidence that change is taking place. Changing the way we think will spill over into how we interact with people. This mental renovation then begins to impact how we relate to people and circumstances in our life. We can then begin to sow differently, ultimately leading to reaping different fruit. How does changing the way we respond, act, and *relate* bring about change in our lives?

Changing How We Relate to People and Circumstances

To start with, let's look at the word *relate*. It comes from the combination of two Latin roots: "re" meaning *again*, and "fero" meaning *produce*. Together the word means to "produce again." It's the reproduction of the same responses or reactions in our lives that leave us feeling that things have not changed.

Here's an example that helps explain. Someone betrays me, and it hurts! To mitigate the pain, I instigate certain reactions designed to help me make it through the hurt. At some point I may decide not to expose myself to that kind of pain and betrayal again. I might say to myself, "That's the last time I'll allow that to happen to me!" In keeping with that vow, I develop strategies to ensure that it won't. These strategies can become deeply entrenched and so integrated into my relational style that the tactics become automatic reactions, like the autopilot function of an aircraft.

When someone comes along who reminds me of the past betrayal of another person (remember the haunting?), it pushes my button and I go into autopilot mode, reproducing the same reaction as before. I end up relating to this new person based on a prescribed way—a way that worked (got me through it) before.

So it seems I'm always facing the same kind of relationship, and nothing changes!

The problem is self-induced and obvious: I have already judged this person based on my predisposition toward an incident or person from my past. Rather than view this as a new relationship full of possibilities, I have tried, judged, and sentenced the person without giving him or her a chance to testify to my trumped-up charges.

This protective dynamic holds true when we encounter any circumstances or events similar to ones we've had in the past. It can become automatic to relate to the new events in the same way that enabled us to get through or survive earlier circumstances. In both cases we find ourselves stuck in a way of relating that has been operating in us for so long that it feels like normal behavior. Phrases like "That's just the way I am" and "That's how I've always handled it" become our mantra. Thus, our relating style is stuck in a stalemate. And when our lives don't experience change, we are still genuinely surprised. The vicious cycle continues.

Double Mindedness/Conflicting Intentions

Because this self-protecting relational style is so imbedded we often find ourselves, at an unconscious level, internally conflicted. We may cognitively say we desire intimacy, and yet subconsciously remember the pain caused by past betrayal, abuse, or disappointment by someone we had been intimate with. As you can see, there can be a deep association between intimacy and pain.

But we insist we *intend* to have intimacy!

Let's say our conscious (what we are aware of at any time) and unconscious (what we are unaware of) intentions together make up the full 100 percent of our intention. What if our conscious part was 10 percent and our unconscious was 90 percent? The 10 percent we are aware of says, "I want intimacy!" The 90 percent we are unaware of screams out "Intimacy hurts too much, you'll be betrayed, run away!" Which do you think will ultimately win? The reality is that our internal intentions make up a majority part of our full intentions. And if left unchecked, the 90 percent will sway us to self-protection. We sabotage our own conscious intentions and ultimately find ourselves frustrated.

We fail to see that this is the way we really want our lives! In the conscious mind we say we want something different, but the hidden majority continues to act in the that's-just-the-way-I-am mode, and so we feel discouraged. When we see and own that we are actually producing this behavior for self-protection, we have the option to sow differently. We can sow to risk instead of sowing to protect, trusting in God instead of our own defenses.

I have found this "reality conversation" freeing. It doesn't make it easier to choose differently, but at the very least it opens up the possibility that I *can* choose differently. Facing reality makes my life both more exciting and in some ways more difficult because the responsibility is on me to actually risk going back "into the fire." I can no longer say, "That's just the way I am." The honest conversation would be, "I choose a safe, comfortable little world rather than risk and open myself up for possible further hurt and betrayal." Once you really know what you're saying you are poised to say something different—to sow differently.

Sowing and Reaping

I've mentioned how relating differently to people and circumstances brings about different fruit. The way we handled situations in the past came about from how we thought we could make it through those situations without pain. When we establish deep, imbedded patterns and continue handling things the same way, we don't change.

Again, the word "relate" means to produce again. You keep sowing the same seed and you will reap the same fruit. But sowing a different seed produces a different crop. Sowing different seeds in our circumstances and relationships also produces different fruit. The seed we sow is how we respond or relate in situations. The concept of sowing and reaping is universally recognized. Many religions have their own versions of this spiritual law (Karma, for example). Even in the secular community the law of reciprocity, or what goes around comes around, is embraced as true.

Sowing and reaping is *not* the same as cause and effect. A farmer may diligently take all the right steps in preparing the ground, fertilizing, tilling, planting, watering, and tending without reaping a bountiful harvest. One bad frost or hailstorm can wipe out an entire crop. We tend to forget the verse that says, "And let us not grow weary while doing good, for in due season we shall reap if we do not lose heart" (Galatians 6: 9 NKJV). It's not us but God who decides when the harvest will come.

It is incumbent on us to remain faithful in doing our part, choosing to sow actions that will bring forth the fruit we desire.

Jesus also showed us that we can willfully respond in love, thereby producing different fruit from the seed that may have been sown in us by others. He said, "Do good to those who abuse you," "Pray for those who mean you harm," "Love your enemy." We *can* relate differently than we are related to. Isn't that what Jesus was saying when He taught us to turn the other cheek?

While it takes two to perpetuate a hurtful symbiotic cycle, it only takes one to interrupt it by sowing different seed and eventually producing different fruit. Christ commands us to exhibit the incredible power to influence and impact our world. The Scriptures are full of references directing us to rise above how we are treated and pressured by circumstances to conform. We are not subject to responding in like manner and producing again the same fruit. We can be instrumental in breaking generational curses.[40] We can even change legacies.

This principle has very practical and profound implications for our lives. When we are confronted with situations or behavior by others that call for a reaction in kind, we can instead interrupt the cycle and produce a different outcome. We can shift the way we respond and in doing so transform the dynamic cycle.

Given our penchant for staying comfortable, we oftentimes need to identify reasons to get uncomfortable, which can be a byproduct of shifting. I have noticed other elements that are resourceful for us when deciding whether to shift.

Vision Causes Shift

In *The Two Towers*, one of the story's heroes, Aragorn, is destined for leadership—to be king. But Aragorn is a reluctant leader; he is afraid of his weakness. His history reveals a pattern of failure in his family when a hard test came. He fears the same fate in himself because he knows he has the same blood coursing through his veins. In an effort to avoid failing himself, Aragorn tried to run from his calling. He isolated himself for a long time, abandoning the people he was born to lead.

In this effort to avoid his calling, Aragorn succumbs to cynicism at times. He cycles between wanting to make a difference and not wanting to believe he's the one to do it. What consistently gets him out of the whirlpool of not caring is when he focuses on others. The cycle of unbelief shows up again when he finds himself at Helms Deep, a fortress under siege by a vast enemy. Faced with overwhelming odds and not believing fully in his calling, Aragorn becomes morose and downcast. Then he focuses on a young boy who has been pressed into service because everyone able to fight must do their part. In that moment Aragorn shifts from reluctance to encouragement, from potential failure (self-focus) to making a difference for others.

His vision for encouraging others took prominence over his perceived weakness.

How often I have equated not trying with succeeding! In this mindset I foolishly choose to stay out of a difficult situation in an effort to diminish the possibility of failure. I have come to realize that when I choose this path I am focused solely on myself and consequently don't bother shifting. My vision is inward, looking out primarily for my own comfort. I'm focusing so intently on myself that I'm cross-eyed!

When we focus on others and their good, this vision can be the impetus for us to shift out of reluctance to face fear and propel us through what we fear. *Perfect love casts out fear,* even if that fear is a fear of not living up to what God has called us to do. Shifting brings us into confrontation with what we'd rather not face and then moves us further into change. In this way vision serves us in our goal to transform.

Another necessary shift is regarding how we have come to believe life is supposed to be or turn out. When we stubbornly hold onto what we have decided about how life should be and don't shift the way we think, we once again vie with reality and actually add unnecessary frustration to life's tragedies.

Unmet Expectations

In the same way a person who resents the reality of gravity would be frustrated, the way I have thought about life and how it is structured has left me feeling disgruntled, stuck, and has actually worked against what I most desire. I suggest that having false expectations of what life should be adds a great deal to the dissatisfaction of our experience of life. Life, in many of our minds, is *supposed* to be pleasant, wonderful, and fulfilling; we should be able to enjoy heaven on earth here and now!

This expectation borders on entitlement. Never mind the fall, which introduced sin and toil and death into the world. Never mind that we are exactly like our first father and mother in wanting to be our own gods. We want and sometimes demand Christ to restore us to Eden without having to live in the consequences of our rebellion. This insurgence has impacted not only who we are but what we must persevere in this life.

In December of 1999, my beloved thirty-six-year-old brother Carlo was tragically killed in an automobile accident. As of this writing, I can't see any good, in the traditional sense, which has come from this heartbreak. It has been a very difficult and often emotionally brutal experience. This is not the way it was supposed to be. Many in my family, in an attempt to cope with the loss, have accused God of betraying us. Carlo's death is nonsensical, but we still try to make some sense of it through our feeble rationalizations.

I often face the void of his presence and the void of not having a sufficient answer as to why this happened. As I observe the challenges of his son and daughter, my mother, my sister, his nephew and niece (my children), my wife, and my other brother (Carlo's twin) it is hard to avoid the difficulties and injustices this world holds. Life should not be this way!

Does this way of thinking coincide with the reality of life and what the Scriptures teach? For someone to feel betrayed means they expected or were promised that life would be different. The sense of betrayal reveals a way of thinking that underlies the expectation of good. At times like this we need to ask ourselves. "What is the mind of Christ regarding how life is supposed to be?"

It seems there are different generators of expectation. Some of our expectations are prompted by the specific declarations of others stated as promises. Take wedding vows, for example. We promise to love and cherish each other till death do us part. The fact that no one can perfectly live up to that promise doesn't seem to diminish our disappointment when our spouse is less than loving. We feel the same way when the abundant life Christ promises in John 10:10 doesn't turn out like we want it to.

Our expectations are one area where our thinking must be brought into alignment with reality. We forget that Jesus also said, "In this life you will have many tribulations" (John 16:33). Reality includes abundant life *and* tribulation. But we don't want to "groan" along with the rest of creation for the eventual restoration of God's rule (Romans 8:22-25).

Expectations color all our experiences. I was talking with a friend who is a successful businessman, very involved in his church, a committed Christian, happily married, and a great person to be around. Yet he spoke to me about a void that gnaws at him and how he struggles with his feelings.

I asked him, "What did you expect instead?"

He was visibly taken aback by the question. It was obvious that his expectation for a full and pleasant life hadn't been fully realized, and it left him frustrated.

This seems to be a normal response, especially when our expectations seem legitimate—within the boundaries of the will of God.

As my friend and I explored the question together it became obvious that there was something that tied his unmet, undefined expectation and frustration together. But the problem again arises when the expectation is illegitimate—beyond what God intended. What if the outcome we expect is one we have created to coincide with our self-serving preferences instead of God's promises? Would we not then be constantly dissatisfied?

Or the expectation may be fully legitimate, one that's even woven into our being but will not be realized until we are with Him in eternity. We are created longing for eternity and perfect love, yet for now we are stuck in a temporal world with imperfect people. This is also a set-up for disappointment.

I know many Christians, including myself, who at times expect that, because they know Christ, their experience this side of heaven should be one primarily of happiness. When they experience unfulfilled longing, as my friend did, they think there is something wrong with them or that perhaps they have missed God's plan.

It may be true that we sometimes add unnecessary, self-inflicted suffering to our experiences through our disobedience. But I can't ignore the many faithful and dedicated servants of God over the centuries who have experienced long seasons of winter and certainly "long nights of the soul." They were, in my opinion, in God's will, and yet they suffered horrible things not of their own doing. Believing in God neither means that we are immune from the world's pain nor that we long deeply for the peace of God's kingdom. We are foreigners here. We are not of this world. The peace and joy we receive is "not as the world gives" (John 14:27). We must explore our expectations and align our minds and expectations with what the Scriptures teach.

The other aspect of expectation is the effect it has on what you truly have, not what you wish or expect to have. A story found on a Down Syndrome website says it well as this mother describes her unmet expectation about what it would be to have a child:

> It's like planning a fabulous vacation trip to Italy. You buy a bunch of guidebooks and make your wonderful plans. The Coliseum. The Michelangelo David. The gondolas in Venice. You may learn some handy phrases in Italian. It's all very exciting. After months of eager anticipation, the day finally arrives. You pack your bags and off you go. Several hours later, the plane lands. The stewardess comes in and says, "Welcome to Holland." "Holland?!?" you say. "What do you mean Holland?? I signed up for Italy! I'm supposed to be in Italy. All my life I've dreamed of going to Italy."

But there's been a change in the flight plan. They've landed in Holland and there you must stay. The important thing is that they haven't taken you to a horrible, disgusting, filthy place, full of pestilence, famine and disease. It's just a different place.

So you must go out and buy new guidebooks. And you must learn a whole new language. And you will meet a whole new group of people you would never have met. It's just a different place. It's slower-paced than Italy, less flashy than Italy. But after you've been there for a while and you catch your breath, you look around...and you begin to notice that Holland has windmills...and Holland has tulips. Holland even has Rembrandts.

But everyone you know is busy coming and going from Italy... and they're all bragging about what a wonderful time they had there. And for the rest of your life, you will say "Yes, that's where I was supposed to go. That's what I had planned." And the pain of that will never, ever, ever, ever go away...because the loss of that dream is a very, very significant loss.

But...if you spend your life mourning the fact that you didn't get to Italy, you may never be free to enjoy the very special, the very lovely things... about Holland.[41]

Or think about it another way. The time for a long-awaited skiing vacation finally arrives. As the organizer, your hope was that your family would become more closely bonded, create lasting cherished memories, and find enjoyment. You've saved and planned to assure the vacation would turn out just right. You've taken lessons, bought new ski equipment and clothes, and imagined swishing down beautiful snow covered slopes with the family. Upon arriving at the location, instead of snow you find yourself in a consistent dreary rainfall. This is reality, and it is not the way it's supposed to be.

Resistance to reality would be to sit around complaining about the rain. Or you can get angry with the weather service which indicated that there is usually snow at this time of year. The whole family may spend the entire vacation sulking and you secretly resent even God because the scenario doesn't match what you imagined or wished for, one leaving everyone feeling shortchanged, grumpy, and even strained towards one another.

If the energy used in resisting would have been channeled in another direction, you may have been able to invent enjoyable times around the fireplace, playing games, having meaningful discussions, watching movies together, reviving nearly lost family cooking recipes, even learning how to be disappointed together in a constructive way by discussing how often life doesn't turn out the way we think it should.

There are times when we must adjust our expectations to reality. This is different from settling, as many expectations are not raised by any promise from God; they are creations of our own fantasy. It takes great faith and hope to find special and lovely things in places we never expected to. Joy is much bigger than circumstance. Many can't seem to find joy when circumstances would dictate misery. Joy is different from happiness because happiness is dependent on the circumstances (happiness comes from the word "happenstance") whereas joy supersedes circumstances. It is a fruit of the Spirit and can be present in the midst of terrible happenstances. As we allow this fruit to come forth we continue to be transformed.

In reference to changing a relationship dynamic, expectation can be a tremendous sabotage agent. Think about how often one person in a relationship has an internal expectation that the other person isn't fully aware of. A spouse may have an unspoken expectation that their loving partner should be able to intuit what the other person thinks or desires—a mind reader, if you will. Sometimes a spouse may have actually articulated his or her desires. Expectation in this case takes over something like this: "I told her what I want, and I believe she heard me. Since that is the case, if she really loved me she would do what I requested." Translation: "If you love me you will agree with what I say and go along with it."

I've seen many relationships break down around this dynamic. In marriage or other close relationships it is often the unspoken internal expectations, which undermines connection. Instead of taking responsibility to ensure that the appropriate need is communicated and then behaving responsibly with whatever results, often the person spurned withdraws in silent and resentful judgment. She resorts to being "right" about how her need was not responded to, and she cools in her love and ultimately becomes conditional, cold, and bitter.

The willingness to have reality conversations with the people in our lives will spur transformation on. These conversations may well be uncomfortable and cause both parties to face up to disappointments and hurts. They also leave us vulnerable because the need will probably not be met the way we think it should be or not met at all. And too often we're not even aware we have those expectations.

Transformation is often averted because we are not disciplined enough to know what we think and converse internally about regarding so many things. Unidentified forces imbedded in our belief system rule us, and until they are exposed for what they really are, we will remain stuck.

Choose Life

So the way I relate to any given person or circumstance *can* be altered. Depending on God and the hope He has opened in my heart, I can choose to sow seeds that will produce the best possibilities to usher in a future worth having. The way I relate to anything in my life no longer needs to be dictated to me because of decisions made in my past. If I see that how I'm relating isn't contributing to what I want and what I am committed to, I can shift and change the way I'm relating.

I can sow differently.

Staying stuck in relating a certain way, even though that way of relating helped me get through a difficult past event, gives the past control over my present and future. I am thus a victim or slave to the past. As such, I essentially deny my God-given freedom to choose and engage life with faith, hope, and love each day and in every circumstance. God calls Himself "I Am," not "I Was" or "I Will Be." He is now, current and present tense. Just as He is in the here and now, God calls us to live in the here in now, making daily decisions by relying on Him that lead to life. As we do, we will discover how He is redeeming our past to open up our future hope.

Deuteronomy 30:19 states, "I have set before you life and death, the blessing and the curse. So choose life in order that you may live, you and your descendants."

To me this suggests that in every situation, event, interaction, or choice, there is a way available to us that leads to life and blessing as well as a way that leads to curses and death. Our marching orders are this: *choose life!*

I have seen many radical real-life examples of this truth, but one of the most poignant is the story of Charlie Johnson, who I encountered through a Training I did. Charlie is a man who has been HIV/AIDS infected for ten years. While he was surviving, he would be the first to tell you that he wasn't *living with* but rather *dying of* AIDS for ten years.

Like so many others receiving what felt like a death sentence that came with the AIDS diagnosis, Charlie began to shut down to life. Life was no longer what he thought it would be. Hope drifted away and apathy settled in. The choices before him appeared inconsequential in light of the prognosis. The choice to give up beckoned him, and in many ways he did just that.

While at the training Charlie was convicted in a huge way that the life God had given him was being squandered, and that he was using his AIDS diagnosis as justification for doing so. He was upset at himself and God for contracting the disease, and he had shut down to life and its possibilities. The realization and conviction regarding giving up on life went so deep that he truly repented and began choosing differently.

Charlie began choosing life.

This daily, moment-by-moment decision to choose life has impacted not only Charlie but his family as well. They are thrilled to see Charlie thriving, and his witness is causing his family to be open to Christ. But it doesn't end there. Charlie's story of choosing life has touched hundreds of people, and I am convinced that God will use him to impact thousands if not millions. You see, Charlie has become a missionary to South Africa, beginning in the shantytown community of Kayamandi. His mission is to bring the message of hope and life to an area devastated by the plight of the AIDS epidemic.

With no credentials and no major contacts or backing, Charlie went to South Africa and gained a major toehold in the community simply by loving people. He has rescued people from certain death and has become a bridge to reach many. Quietly yet inspirationally, Charlie has activated a very big movement of Americans to consider how they can come alongside his vision. Already he has been instrumental in prompting two American doctors, Dr. Robert Sheneberger and Dr. Becky Kuhn— AIDS specialists—and five lay workers to travel to South Africa to help fulfill his vision. I had the privilege of meeting with him and others in this outreach and was awestruck at the scope of what is underway. And to think it all began with the decision to obey the Lord's very clear command, "Choose life!"

It's this simple yet profound decision to choose life that allows God to extract the precious from the vile and raise beauty from the ashes. God takes what the enemy intended to destroy and turns it into an avenue to bring life. Even though crawling away into a hole to escape my pain may feel like what I need and deserve to do, choosing the opposite brings me what I truly desire.

It is this tension that must be overcome because some of the life and blessing choices appear at first like choosing death. Frankly, it feels like a kind of death when I am called to enter a conflict I have no idea how to resolve. And in a way there *is* a dying that needs to happen: death to staying in control, staying comfortable, feeling good, looking good, and being right.

Ultimately, it seems to me that the choice of life and death is between one of choosing to follow what God requires or to revert to self-preservation, self-pity, self-loathing, and self-sufficiency. Matthew Henry comments on Deuteronomy 30:19: "Those that come short of life…die because they will die; that is, because they do not like the life promised upon the terms promised."

What are the terms promised? One of them is that, outside of what He offers, there is no provision that will ultimately deliver what we desire. We don't like that because it drives home that we are, in fact, dependent creatures. This is an insult to our conceited and lofty view of ourselves. But we are not the masters of our lives! In addition, other terms promised are that without Him we can do nothing. He alone is our fortress, our shield, our stronghold. If we love God we will keep His commands and die to self.

But choosing life is more than that. Choosing life beckons us to risk. Life calls to us from the areas we resist because we don't know what's on the other side. It calls to us from areas that seem just too big, too daunting, too uncertain, too...fill in the blank from your own experience.

Eddie Jacobs, a man who has coached me, says "Significance breeds resistance." The resistance to go into the great unknown actually reveals how significant we see ourselves. This idea seems counter-intuitive. I believe it reveals our self-significance because we lose sight of the One calling us. In light of Him, what is daunting? We must choose. Again, what will determine us: our God or our circumstance?

It is ironic that non-religious people oftentimes seem to grasp the power of God-given choice more readily than believers. Perhaps this is because they take the attitude, "If it's to be, it's up to me." Tragically, non-religious people do this because they don't know they have a God they can rely on. The opposite should be true. Knowing we have a God who is for us, behind us, working through our weakness, and who redeems should lead us to a wholehearted, abandoned way of living that drinks deeply from the cup of life and takes risks—no matter what is before us! "I can do all things through Christ who strengthens me" (Philippians 4:13 NKJV).

Dawna Markova writes a beautiful poem, *Fully Awake,* which captures the spirit of a person who has made this choice to grab life with gusto.

> I will not die an unlived life.
> I will not live in fear
> of falling or catching fire.
> I choose to inhabit my days,
> to allow my living to open to me,
> to make me less afraid
> more accessible,
> to loosen my heart
> until it becomes a wing,
> a torch, a promise.
> I choose to risk my significance;
> to live so that which came to me as seed
> goes to the next as blossom
> and that which came to me as blossom,
> goes on as fruit.

Charlie Johnson is undergoing a radical transformation as a result of deciding to choose life and love. One way of choosing death happens when we close ourselves off in bitterness, resentment, and entitlement when life doesn't turn out the way it "should". Then we go a step further and justify doing so because of the perceived injustice of God (who supposedly has given us more than we can handle.)

Choosing life will again bring us into confronting the smallness of how we think, believe, behave, relate, and every other aspect of life. Changing the way we think and the way we relate to people and circumstances will lead us quickly into a confrontation with the deepest aspects of core change.

As God reveals our iniquity and draws us in to face reality, this level of change is something we can only respond to. It's at this level we begin to lose ourselves (the selves we've made up) and therefore find our true selves (the selves God created us to be).

It is here that I believe it's appropriate to apply one of the paradoxes found in the Bible: "Whoever finds his life will lose it, and whoever loses his life for my sake will find it" (Matthew 10:39 NIV). At some level God is out to kill the "me" or "you" we have constructed outside of Him—for our own good.

TWELVE

Abandoning Ourselves to God

*When I say "I" I mean a thing absolutely unique,
not to be confused with any other*

Ugo Betti

Now, with God's help, I shall become myself.

Soren Kierkegaard

Who am I? When God formed me in my mothers' womb, what inherent gifts and abilities did He set in me? What purpose did He design for me? What unique "soul print"[42] did He create when He created me? Are these the elements that define my identity? What is my identity and is that all there is to me? And what is my role in answering these questions?

When I reflect on the potential of losing ourselves in order to find our true selves, I think of the disparity between who God created me to be and who I've become. I think about all the belief systems I've established and based my identity upon as a result of my self-protectionist way of living. I also wonder how much of my unlimited self I've exchanged for the one who just gets by? While such reflection makes me sad, I also long to leave behind the man I have limited myself to be and realize the man God created me to be.

Keeping the Change

So how do we partner with God in actually accomplishing such a sustainable change, so that we actually *change who we are?* I'm referring to a deep and fundamental transformation at our core. The word "core" comes from the Latin *cordis*; this is the same root for *heart*. The proverb reads, "As a man thinks in his heart, so is he." What if transformation into Christ's image is a complete alignment between what He has written into our hearts, with all the potential realized, and how we actually engage and subsequently impact others? I'm talking about complete integrity between the internal intention and external living out of that intention, all the while depending on God.

Some people get very confused when the internal intention and how they live it out don't line up. They say things like, "That's not the real me." I think they mean that the way they are being isn't in keeping with the way they desire to be. But in a very real way, the way we are living is the only true indicator of the "real" us. In some way, the way we impact others in any moment is "who we are"—at least for the persons we impact. This does not mean that we are *only* that identity. In a very real sense, however, we are our impact. I can declare I am a loving husband (as I say I am), but if the impact Dawn receives is that I'm just placating her, then which identity is the real one? Who am I, really, for her? Is not the "real" me for her a "placater"?

In Chapter Nine I pointed out that changing at our core does not mean the change is permanent. I say this because I believe the way we are constituted is dynamic in nature, as opposed to static. This is freeing because, as in the example I just gave, when I notice my impact on Dawn does not align with my declaration of being a loving husband, rather than getting stuck on a conversation of "I'm bad" or "I'm inadequate" or other similar identity conversations I can shift. We often refer to ourselves using terms such as "That's the way I am." We defend our limitations by using the same terms. It is these internal conversations about ourselves that first establish our beliefs, and continued engagement in these conversations reinforces our internal belief systems. Out of these belief systems we act, behave, and become.

Who we are is *who we are being*. Who we are being—*consistently*—determines who we are.

So when we talk about core transformation, if we are not talking about a change that does not need to be maintained, what are we referring to? We are being transformed into Christ's image. Jesus has always been "streaming forth from the Father, like light from a lamp, or heat from a fire, or thoughts from a mind. He is the self-expression of the Father-what the Father has to say. And there was never a time He was not saying it."[43]

I believe transformation is a complete alignment of ourselves to the Father's will, such a total integration between what we say we believe and how we actually comport ourselves that the flow is unimpaired. Jesus said, "I only do what I see the Father doing" (John 5:19; 8:28; 12:50). This transformation is not us trying to "be like Jesus" but rather a complete surrender of our will to the Father. In other words there is integrity, which is the quality or condition of being whole or undivided—completeness. This is the end goal of our transformation: to be presented whole and complete in Christ's image (Ephesians 5:27, Colossians 1:22, Philippians 1:6). This wholeness and completeness is evidenced by keeping His commands, the supreme one being loving God with all my heart, soul, mind and strength, and my neighbor as myself.[44]

So what role, if any, do we have in changing who we are at the core? On the one hand it would appear we have no power, and on the other it seems we have the final say. The ultimate paradox about us is that we are creatures who would not even exist if not for God's sustaining power, and yet He has given us free will which gives us the power to not choose Him.

This kind of change is spoken about in 2 Corinthians 3:18: "But we all, with unveiled face, beholding as in a mirror the glory of the Lord, are being transformed unto the same image, from glory to glory, just as by the Spirit of the Lord" (NKJV). The word used here for transformed is *metamorhoo,* from which we derive our English word "metamorphosis."

We are most familiar with metamorphosis in regards to butterflies. Butterflies become themselves through metamorphosis, but the only path for a caterpillar's transformation is through a type of death. I believe that the path to Christian transformation and the full realization of ourselves is through death also—death to the way I think life should be, the way I think others should be—and arising to the life of God, the life of love.[45]

This is what Christ demonstrated. He died to the way He preferred it to be and then literally died for the sake of love. This is most poignantly demonstrated in the Garden of Gethsemane where Jesus clearly didn't want to die, as evidenced by the torment, sweating blood, and His three requests of the Father to let the cup pass. Faced with the choices between His human will (escape the suffering) or the Father's will (dying in order to love), He chose love: Not My will but Yours be done (Luke 22:42). He presented Himself to the Father, endured the cross, and despised the shame for the joy set before Him. What was the joy set before Him? Relationship. He always enjoyed relationship in the Godhead and wanted the same with us.

When we present ourselves as lumps of clay into the hands of the Potter, we can expect Him to transform these earthen vessels into vessels of honor.[46]

> We carry this precious Message around in the unadorned clay pots of our ordinary lives …We've been surrounded and battered by troubles, but we're not demoralized; we're not sure what to do, but we know that God knows what to do; we've been spiritually terrorized, but God hasn't left our side; we've been thrown down, but we haven't broken. What they did to Jesus, they do to us — trial and torture, mockery and murder; what Jesus did among them, he does in us — he lives! Our lives are at constant risk for Jesus' sake, which makes Jesus' life all the more evident in us (2 Corinthians 4:7-11, Eugene Peterson, *The Message*).

Why did Paul put himself at stake this way? He answers it in 2 Corinthians 5:14: "For the love of Christ compels [me]." Yes, he had his eyes on eternity, just like Jesus, and like Jesus the eternity he must have imagined was one of relationship both with God and others. He was clear that the way to this transformation was dying to self and living through Christ. To Paul the death and resurrection of Christ was the possibility and path for living the life Christ called him to. And so it is for us.

We "are being transformed into the same image." This can connote passivity on our part, as if we are recipients of a work God undertakes in us while we are inert. I believe there is truth in this thinking. Nothing happens in us if not for God moving in His grace toward us. Even so, it is God Himself who has invited us to participate with Him, and at some level He restricts Himself according to our invitation. As C.S. Lewis says, "There are only two kind of people in the end, those who say to God 'Thy will be done' or those to whom God says in the end 'thy will be done.'" Adam Clark comments on 2 Corinthians 3:18:

> By *earnestly contemplating* the Gospel of Jesus, and believing on him who is its Author, the soul becomes illuminated with His divine splendor, for this sacred mirror reflects back on the believing soul the image of Him whose perfections it exhibits; and thus we see the glorious form after which our minds are to be fashioned; and by *believing* and receiving *the influence of his Spirit...* our form is changed [47]

It is clear that, even though we are recipients of God's transforming work, we are also active by earnestly contemplating, believing, and receiving the influence of the Spirit. This is active work and we are partners with Him. The transformation He invites us to participate in is deep, real, and sustainable. So how does this kind of change happen? How can God transform us from normal lumps of clay to vessels displaying increasing stages of His glory? How do we facilitate the process? How do we impede it?

The question that arises here is: With what faculty of our being do we believe? How is it we actually receive the influence of the Spirit? The usual answer is, "With our hearts." But this is a metaphor. It refers to that deep inner part of us, the core, but how is this core activated or accessed?

I believe this heart function involves the internal dialogue we engage regarding the truths God reveals to us. Receiving the living God is a work done by the Holy Spirit, and I don't purport to know how He functions. What I have noticed is that the actual "believing" in me happens by *receiving* the Logos, the active dynamic conversation emanating within the Godhead, to me and about me. Jesus is the Word, the Logos. Logos is not just a static "word" but a dynamic "conversation"[48]—alive, dynamic, and active. It was out of the conversation within the Godhead that we were created and again out of the conversation or Logos that we are born again (John 1:1 and John 1:12-13).

In Acts 17:11, the word "receive" means to give ear to, embrace, make one's own, approve, not to reject.[49] Matthew 13:19 says, "When anyone hears the word of the kingdom, and does not understand it, then wicked one comes and snatches away what was sown in his heart" (NKJV). The word "understand," sometimes translated "receive," means literally "to put the perception with the thing perceived."[50] In other words it's one thing to hear the Word of God and what He has to say to us, and another thing to hear and actually *receive* it.

Oftentimes in Scripture the Word is used in connection with being sown like seed. The sense is that the seed comes in and ultimately, if received, bears fruit. Our conversion is even referred to as being born again: "having been born again, not of corruptible seed but incorruptible, through the word of God which lives and abides forever" (1 Peter 1:23 NKJV).

I believe we have an important role in perceiving the thing being received.

This role involves old time practices such as exercising faith in, believing, and appropriating the truths spoken to and about us. This is how we participate in the transforming work of Logos. As it says in Acts 17:11, "They received the word with all readiness."

Christ Incarnate exemplifies the proper hearing, receiving, and response to God's Word. Christ, Logos, did not resist what God the Father said to Him or about Him, on earth or in Heaven. How often I do!

The process begins with a foundational core conviction which gives rise to a belief system, which in turn influences all we think and do. This core conviction is formed by the conversation we engage in. Essential to real, full, and sustainable change is a fundamental shift in a core conviction, which impacts every sphere of how we view and comport ourselves in life. At this foundational level we must deal with who we are in essence. We will never change *in essence* until we come face to face with and trust "I Am," who is the essence of all.

Moving Out of Your Comfort Zone

But how can we choose a fundamental core change when we've disciplined ourselves so long to choose a safe, pain-free life? If we are so stuck in self-preservation, how can we ever trade in our all too familiar preferences in life for ones that feel so unnatural and threatening?

After all, isn't that why we make the decisions we make? They feel natural and they help us survive? I mean, why do anything different— especially anything risky—when we've been able to get by doing what we've been doing?

Through trial and error we have learned that protecting ourselves means others cannot hurt us as easily. Doing a quick yet thorough assessment prior to taking any risk diminishes the chances that things will get out of my control. I determine how far and how fast I will proceed into new territory.

Make no mistake about it: The choices we make are clearly the most life-preserving choices we see. We normally choose the least threatening, least painful options, even if the only choices at hand are "horrible" and "even worse." We are quite adept at discerning the lesser of any two evils. As Derek Watson, a former mentor of mine, used to say, "Your chooser is perfect!"

Rejection in a relationship or social setting often feels like death, so we are experts at opting for anything but rejection. For example, if someone has many past experiences of being rejected and is presented with the choice of risking rejection again or being alone and lonely (which would prevent rejection) they would probably choose isolation. Even though isolation is horrible, rejection is even worse, so we will go for isolation because it appears less painful.

I believe people generally make the best choices they see available to them, and what we see available to us is always colored by our drive to survive. Survival is a desperate mindset. Thriving doesn't seem to be one of the options. It's either horrible (surviving) or even worse (which to us equals pain).

We have all learned to navigate through life avoiding (as best we can) all the possible painful experiences life thrusts upon us. I remember vividly how, as a young boy, I experienced much teasing by my schoolmates. My "chooser" mastered the art of self-preservation at a very young age.

My family and I moved to this country from Italy when I was five years old, and I was placed immediately in school. I didn't know the language, I was not familiar with baseball or other popular American games, and I certainly did not dress like the other kids or eat the same kind of lunches (things I grew proud of as I got older!). But at that time all of this drew a lot of unwanted attention to me, and I felt totally rejected at school.

On top of that, the environment at home was not much safer. There was often anger and chaos. It was a place where I quickly learned to walk on eggshells and not do anything wrong. But as careful as I tried to be, I could not preempt every explosion. To be sure, there were times of love, nurture and connection as well- especially by my mother and at times by my father- but too often it appeared unsafe to me.

In those times that it did appear dangerous at home and at school I saw only two choices. I could continue to take risks, thereby inviting the rejection and abuse that came with any misstep. Or I could play it safe, not rock the boat, and settle for shallow, acceptable behaviors that dared little but provided safety from rejection.

You can probably guess that my "natural" response was for safety and survival. While some choose to rebel by taking the opposite strategy, my way was to become very guarded and cautious and to attempt to disappear. I also became a conformist and tried to figure out ways I thought would get people to like me. As I've gotten older, even though I know I'm not under the domination of survival strategies, the natural tendency to survive by employing self-preserving strategies is still there.

For example, in order to avoid possible rejection, I often revert to being the nice guy—no argument, no opposition, no wave. These time-honored strategies of mine seem to assure me, at least for a while, that I will avoid painful rejection.

Any time I get into a situation that touches my areas of insecurity, my practiced mode of surviving all those years is automatically triggered. Before I even cognitively process what's happening, I often revert to a knee-jerk reaction which is anchored in a tried and true self-survival strategy that allowed me to get by in the past.

So as we talk about making a fundamental shift at the core of your being, be aware that your self-preserving tendencies will fight you every step of the way.

Shifting From Trusting in Self to Trusting in God

When we talk about a core shift, what are we shifting *from* and what are we shifting *to?* This shift centers on a fundamental principle of Christian life, namely the shift from self-survival to God-survival. We must go to trusting God enough to abide by His principles of honesty, humility, and love for others even when we are frightened at the prospect of being rejected or hurt.

Self-survival is the cancer that must be cut out. Consider, for instance, the penchant most of us have to cover up our failures, mistakes, and sin. This tendency toward self-survival permeates every sphere of our lives. It shows up in the most inconspicuous ways and is triggered even by seemingly small things.

I remember when I broke a simple promise to Dawn regarding being home at a certain time. I was going to a meeting and told her I would be home by 2:00 P.M. Due to certain situations that arose, I chose to stay beyond 2:00. My conscience alerted me to the discrepancy, but I quieted the alarm by justifying my need to stay longer. Besides, Dawn and I didn't really have any plans anyway.

I ended up coming home around 3:30, and when my wife asked had happened, a feeling of insecurity was triggered. Automatically I employed time-tested strategies to deflect what felt like her rejection. It came too close to those feelings I remembered from my early years.

Attempting to avert those feelings, my defenses were unleashed. I minimized my tardiness by saying it was no big deal. I attempted to confuse the issue by arguing that I didn't say *precisely* when I would be home. I blame-shifted my lateness onto the person who said we'd be done earlier. I got defensive as Dawn continued to close all my back doors. Ultimately I got very angry with my wife. All of this happened in a matter of seconds, and it wasn't until it was all over that I realized what my reactions were all about.

What it was all about, of course, was my attempt to avert the rejection I anticipated. I thought I had changed and that my past propensity for self-protection from someone I love so much no longer had that kind of hold on me. What an amazing and painful discovery.

What makes this more puzzling is that I know Dawn is not an unreasonable woman. If I had been honest with her, or even considerate enough to call, I know the breakdown could have been averted. The truth is that I didn't want to open myself to the vulnerability required by requesting release from my promise, so I attempted to weasel around what I had done. I wanted to maintain control.

We are strongly pulled to attempt to provide for ourselves and do things our way. There are many expressions of these attempts to manage what only God can manage. For example, when we sin, we are often reluctant to appropriate God's provision for being released from sin, which is confession and asking forgiveness. We prefer to utilize one of many strategies for managing it ourselves.

Most of these strategies are a cover-up of some kind.

One dynamic I work within the Impact Trainings is our proclivity to keep secrets. Keeping secrets is one way we deal with pain and sin in our lives. We tend to hide the stuff we don't want others to see for fear that exposing it will lead to rejection. It's another method of self-survival. You've heard people say, "If anyone knew about this I would just die!" So we trust in our own devices and cover up instead of trusting what God says, which is that confession leads to true fellowship or life!

Trusting in these strategies to cover sin will inhibit change. In his book, *The Perils of Power,* Richard Exley cites Dietrich Bonhoffer's view of trusting in our own devices to deal with sin. Bonhoffer writes that as long as we pretend we are without sin (by hypocrisy and denial) we remain bound:

> Freedom from sin does not come through denying our sinfulness, but in confessing it to each other and to God. In the transparent fellowship, sin is deprived of both its strength and its power. *Its strength is its secrecy.* As long as it is not exposed to the power of true Christian fellowship it can continue to dominate us, but once it is exposed to the light, its hold is broken. Sin's power is its ability to isolate us from the fellowship, *to make us feel that we are the only person who has ever been tempted this way.* Alone we are no match for its subtle temptations, but together with the fellowship we can defeat it".[51]

How sad! The very strategy we use trying to prevent rejection and its ensuing loneliness actually *assures* that we will be lonely.

When it's all said and done, the reason change is so hard to come by is that we fight so hard to maintain what we've set up and practiced for so long. Namely, we long to be the directors of our lives and we refuse to fully yield to God. We resist the reality that we are derivative and dependant creatures, relying on our manmade strategies, and therefore undermine the transformation God wants to work in us.

Furthermore, we suspect that God really isn't out for our best interest and that He will allow us to be hurt—which at times He does. We believe looking out for ourselves is the *only* surefire way to survive.

The only way to experience true core transformation is to abandon ourselves to God and lay down all the ways we strive to make it on our own. Our strategies involve what we think, what we believe, how we relate, how we comport ourselves, and how we look at life, God, and others.

It is at this point specifically that all three areas of change we have been looking at converge, incorporating elements of thinking, believing, and relating into a new attitude toward God, others, life, and ourselves.

Perhaps you have noticed how the way we think impacts our attitudes, which in turn alters the way we relate, which in turn affects the core aspect of what needs to change: who we rely on. As we move into this area we are coming close to discovering what it will take for real transformation. The question has to do with dying *to* and living *for*. The question we must answer in order to partner with God in our transformation is this:

Who is on the throne of our lives?

THIRTEEN

Shifting Trust from Self to God

It's the one who won't be taken
that cannot seem to give, and the soul afraid of dying
that never learns to live.
It's the heart afraid of breaking that never learns to dance.
It's the dream afraid of waking that never takes the chance.

Bette Midler, *The Rose*

Let us examine our ways and test them and let us return to the
Lord

Lamentations 3:40

What Is It That We Can Change?

The shift from trusting self (*self*-survival, *self*-preservation, *self*-protection, *self*-fulfillment) to trusting God (*self* abandonment, *self*-denial, dying to *self, losing our false self* as we are consummated by God) is the most important and significant step toward transformation. Could this simple and yet most challenging shift be a key to solving the conundrum of transformation?

In Ephesians 4:23-24 we are instructed to "put off our old self, which is being corrupted by its deceitful desires; to be made new in the attitude of our minds; and put on our new self, created to be like God in true righteousness."

Put off our old self, put on our new self. This is a command and definitely implies that we have a choice as to which self we may put on. Notice: The fact that we have a new self is not in dispute. Nor is the fact that we still possess an old self with its "deceitful desires" in dispute. To what extent does our choosing carry the day when it comes to which self we "wear"?[52]

Just what is the old self with its deceitful desires? I suggest that one deceitful desire is our endeavor to provide for ourselves what only God can in eternity, and when that endeavor fails we blame others and God for the results.

Sound familiar? It should. Adam and Eve lived in an ideal state and yet rebelled against God. They attempted to become "as God" themselves. Why they did so we can only speculate. Could it be they didn't want to be dependant on Him? Yet when questioned by God about their rebellion they proceeded to accuse Him and others for choosing as they did. Adam said, "It was the woman You gave me." Eve asserted, "The serpent gave me of the fruit."

How similar this refrain sounds to some of my own excuses. Unwilling to trust that God will supply my needs, I provide for myself by engaging my many survival mechanisms. Then when I reap what I've sown, I get disappointed in God and others because my life is not working. This blame of God is very subtle and shows up more like a self-pitying internal whine or a general discontent with my life. I conclude, "I guess I'm just not good enough, lucky enough, loved enough, holy enough, *enough* period." As a result of trying to be enough on my own, I feel shame.

So many of our illusions, delusions, strategies, and ways of relating are simply frantic efforts to make life be different than it really is because underneath it all, life is ultimately a mystery and a state of longing. Any glimpse of beauty is simply a fleeting foretaste, and we often cannot bear to live in the tension of waiting for the day when we will once again live in the state of complete fellowship with God and others.

I wonder how you, faithful reader, have sung Adam and Eve's refrain? I believe it is a universal proclivity of humankind to minimize the impact of refusing to trust God's provision.

The battle between reality and resistance again rears its head here. The reality is that we are completely dependent on God. The resistance is that we don't want to be dependent on God. Resisting the reality of God's sufficiency will hinder the transformation we want.

I must tread carefully on this point because I am aware of the sense of guilt so many Christians carry. Feeling they have not surrendered enough (i.e., are not spiritual enough), they keep trying harder to surrender in hopes that the desired change will ensue. The result is more frustration.

Be that as it may, we need to come to an understanding that God isn't on our timetable and isn't interested in temporary relief and immediate gratification. In fact, He rebukes these shallow efforts to deal with problems (Jeremiah 6:14). Instead, He relentlessly pursues us like a determined surgeon resolute in removing the cancer that threatens to kill us. In this case, cancer is the idea that we can manage life without God.

Abandoning Ourselves to God

In C.S. Lewis's *Chronicles of Narnia*, Lucy, when first learning about Aslan (the lion who is the Christ figure in the story), inquires, "Then he isn't safe?"... "Safe?" said Mr. Beaver; "don't you hear what Mrs. Beaver tells you? Who said anything about safe? 'Course he isn't safe. But he's good." Lewis pictures Aslan the Lion peeling off, with his claws, dragon-like scales that have formed on Eustace as a result of his theft of a dragon's treasure. It is scary and painful for Eustace.[53] We need not walk long with the Lion of Judah to understand that much of what He needs to work in us can be scary and even painful.

This abandonment, this letting ourselves completely go into God's hands, while the only reasonable path feels nonetheless like a kind of death. Repentance, then, is a turning away from our strategies and abandoning ourselves to the dangerous but good God we believe in faith exists.

It is much like the story about a man who stumbles over a cliff but avoids a deadly fall by grabbing a small branch protruding from the cliff face. Holding on for dear life as his strength ebbs away, he cries out, "Help! Help! Is anyone up there?"

He hears a booming voice above him but he can't see who it is. "Yes, I'll help you."

"Who are you?" asks the man.

"I'm God. Let go of the branch and I'll catch you."

After several anxious seconds, the man cries out again, "Is anyone *else* up there?"

Reality is that oftentimes we are unable to see how we can be extricated from our situation; we can't even see how it can be different. We'd rather hang onto the little bit of security we have than to let go of own devices and apparently have nothing. Change will only happen as we let go of what we hold onto and turn back to the One who will continue to work in us until He presents us without spot or wrinkle, transformed into the image of His Son.

Repentance Is At the Core of Change

The one major component I have consistently noticed leading to possibilities for real change in *essence* is repentance. The reason should be self-evident to anyone giving even a cursory look at what keeps us operating in the same manner we always have. That reason is *self-protection*. Self-protection is a way we usurp the role of God in our lives and attempt to supply for ourselves what only He can provide, replacing trust in Him with strategies we control.

Self-protection is what keeps us repeating the patterns we do. For whatever reason, at some point in our development and based on seemingly incontrovertible evidence, we decide that certain actions or ways of being are more dangerous than others. We deem them dangerous because they do cause *pain*—the pain of rejection, betrayal, failure, etc. It seems we conclude early in life that trusting others and even God leads to pain. Therefore self-protection (trusting in self) appears to be a better option.

As my colleague Jean-Marie Jobs points out, self-protection isn't just a harmless way to keep from getting hurt, it's actually an *aggressive* action, buffeting others away from you, creating distance and separation. Self-protection, self-preservation, and self-survival are at the base of all life's real problems, and possibly even at the root of all continuing sin.

This is in stark contrast to the pop-psychology mindset which asserts that damaging experiences in our formative years are the root of our problems.[54] While I agree these experiences open the door to our dysfunctional ways of relating (in this context, self-protection), it's our refusal to trust God's provision that digs the pit we are desperate to climb out of that causes the problem.

These tendencies also keep people from experiencing transformation. People who are not experiencing spiritual and relational vitality rely on themselves and not God. I make this assertion according to Scripture for, "He who loses his life for my sake shall find it" (Matthew 16: 25-26).

If all law can be summarized by the command to love God with all your heart, mind and strength, *and* love your neighbor as yourself, then self-protection, self-preservation, and self-survival are violators of the supreme law of the universe. It is impossible to love others fully while clinging to self-survival strategies for avoiding pain. Consider the possibility that *pain in life* is not the problem keeping us from experiencing real change, but rather it is our *insistence that pain be avoided* that is keeping us stuck.

While most Christian readers will assert this observation as truth, there is much more to this shift than theological acknowledgement. Laying down these strategies often feels like a form of suicide. If I make myself vulnerable without the self-protection I've lived with for so long, how can I be assured that I won't be devastated again? We've had so many painful experiences with being vulnerable that exposing our hearts in this way seems foolish. So we silently and sometimes ceremoniously vow never to repeat this stupidity. The Who said it well in their song, "We won't get fooled again!"

Here is the dilemma: Do you revert to self-protection and live a reduced life without the true comfort of God, or do you love, risk, and experience pain in the arms of God? God never promises to prevent us from pains or sorrows; He promises to be with us in them. He is not safe, but He *is* good.

I'm suggesting that real core change coincides with the transformation of our character from egocentric self-love to loving others freely. As we do, we trust God to provide for us as we inevitably experience rejection, betrayal, and hurt in the process of living so passionately. This is a life worth living!

Being made new in the attitude of our minds is tantamount to shifting from a self-providing way of life to surrendering to the way He provides and commands. This is what it means to be rightly related to Him (righteousness). We are, after all, derivative beings. In Him we move, breathe, and have our being (Acts 17:28).

I assert that it is our self-providing mindset that inhibits true transformation. Self-providence is idolatry. And to the extent that we serve idols we are hampered at being transformed into what God created us to be.

Perhaps the assertion that idolatry hampers change appears farfetched to most modern day Christians. But if the heart of Christianity is true transformation then why is it that so many do not exhibit this kind of change?

Do You Worship Idols?

Christians know the evil of idolatry. It violates one of the Ten Commandments,[55] and idol worship is forbidden throughout the Bible. Thank God we live in a civilized, technologically advanced society and have moved past primitive practices of bowing down to manmade images of humanly devised deities.

Or have we?

The word "idolatry" comes from the Greek word *eidololateria,* derived from two root words: *eidos* and *latreia.* Together they mean roughly "to worship or serve an appearance."[56] In an earlier chapter I asserted that preoccupation with looking good, feeling good (staying comfortable), being in control, and being right were key to undermining God's transformative process in us. One reason is because serving these idols keeps us from answering the call to love, the love that effects great transformation.

We practice idolatry when we serve our own image, or the appearance that we project, rather than serving God. I am talking about answering the great call of serving God, which is love. Jesus said, "If you love me, you will keep my commands." And His commands are summarized in the Great Commandments: "Love the Lord your God with all your heart and with all your soul and with all your strength and with all your mind" and "Love your neighbor as yourself" (Luke 10:27 NIV).

Look at the two contrasting charts below. The chart on the left, headed Idolatry, represents attitudes or strategies we often rely on to get us through life. The chart on the right, Kingdom Living, represents attitudes required of us when we are relying on God to redeem and deliver us. I assert that we are primarily either serving our idols (Idolatry) or God (Kingdom Living). Furthermore, we are *always* primarily serving one or the other—ourselves or God. The two charts represent attitudes that are constantly in competition with one another. They are attitudes that drive us in one of two directions: either trusting God with all we are or trusting in our own might.

Idolatry	Kingdom Living
Looking Good	Humility
Feeling Good	Gift of Pain/Suffering
Staying Comfortable	Dying to Self
Being in Control	Surrender
Being Right	Right Relationship (Righteousness)
Self-Serving	Servanthood
Taking	Giving
Happiness	Joy
Doing	Being
Fear Driven	Love Driven

Now, I understand that there is no altruism in the sense that we can love and serve God and others perfectly at all times. What I am referring to is who is our primary love focus: ourselves or God/others?

As Bob Dylan noted in song, "You gotta serve somebody."

In the idolatry mindset, fear is the driver because, in our insatiable desire to *take* and *have*, we shrink our world to a size we can manage. We shrink our relationships down to those which benefit us and somehow intuit that we will never get enough. So we *must* continue to take by taking care of ourselves. On this side, giving selflessly feels much like suicide. Jack Hayford notes that experience has taught us that if we give *at all* we won't have enough and if we give *it all* we won't have anything (or so we fear).

Putting on the kingdom mindset moves us to be love driven. It takes our focus off what we may lose and directs it to what we can give to others. Scripture says that perfect love casts out fear (1 John 4:18). The contrasts are between a life committed to being self-sufficient and self-reliant (idolatry) versus relying on Jehovah-Jirah (God the Provider).

Let's look at each contrast and identify the differences.

Looking Good vs. Humility

Let's say that I am in a situation with someone where obeying the law of love runs counter to the human drive to look good. For example, in order to clear up a misunderstanding I need to confess a fault, exposing the disparity between my projected image of perfection and the reality of my failure. If I am serving my image instead of God, then I *sacrifice* what love requires for the sake of maintaining that image. This is as much idolatry as when pagan people sacrifice animals or even human victims to their invented gods.

Loving God and others more than my own image necessitates an attitude of humility. *Humility is the willingness to be known for who I really am.* I can only have a true, intimate relationship when I'm not concerned about how I look and am willing to be authentic about what's true about me, even if it's unpleasant. It takes humility to allow people to see the real me—the good, the bad, and the ugly. And it certainly requires humility to trust that God will show up for me in those times when I want so much to resort to a fabricated image to carry me through a hard time.

Feeling Good/Staying Comfortable vs. Suffering/Dying to Self

What am I willing to go through in order to connect with people? What am I willing to pay to have authentic, vulnerable, and intimate relationships? How often is the command to love forfeited to accommodate my desire to feel good and stay comfortable?

Real relationship demands being willing to be uncomfortable and die to self-interests, even on a daily basis. Don't we have to die to self in order to interact with people meaningfully when what we really want is to "veg out" for the evening? Very closely related to humility, dying to self also means laying down our pride and allowing uncomfortable feedback to pierce our self-perception.

In contrast to staying comfortable, being in relationship requires a willingness to enter into the struggles of life. Since suffering is inevitable in this life, engaging in relationship with another human will unavoidably compound the suffering. Allowing their pain to touch me causes me to get in touch my own- which invites suffering.

Being in Control vs. Surrender

While we have been given full responsibility by our Creator to govern our lives, we are not to exercise that right when doing so undermines our call to serve God. In fact, we are commanded to surrender our will to His and to do so as an act *of* our will, which reflects our love. John 14:20-21 says, "Whoever has my commands and obeys them, he is the one who loves me" (NIV). Yet many times I have used my desire to control or mitigate the pain or discomfort of certain situations as a license to withhold what love would have me do.

When I was first married, there were times when Dawn was upset with me for one reason or another. I remember how uncomfortable and out of control I felt when I looked at her and realized she was angry at me! I just didn't like it.

I remember walking up to her in those times, embracing her, and playfully holding her tight while trying to make her laugh. She resisted my attempts, but I persisted until she finally began laughing, and then I felt better.

Whew! The crisis was over.

The last thing I wanted was to acknowledge that I had upset her, ask her what I had done or said, and work toward reconciliation. Instead,

I felt like I had to control the situation by controlling her in some way. As I resisted entering an area where I felt I would be out of control, the transformation I desired remained elusive.

Surrendering ourselves into the hands of our God is a scary thing for many of us. The question that plagues is, "Will He *really* come through?"

Being Right vs. Having Right Relationships

Am I willing to give up my "right to be right" for the sake of the relationship? How threatening it can be to admit that I am wrong, especially if that means being wrong about how bad I am! It saddens me to think of how many of my relationships have been sacrificed on the altar of "I'm right."

I am a detailed thinker and sometimes this trait borders on splitting hairs over technicalities. For example, when Dawn and I are having a disagreement, she may get one of the details wrong. It may be as simple as where the offending incident or conversation happened. She says it happened when we were in such and such a place, and I'm positive it happened elsewhere (or at least I'm convinced I'm right!). Notice, I am not arguing about the incident happening, just where it happened. Instead of listening to her side of the disagreement, I start arguing about the meaningless technicality of where it happened. I so desperately don't want to be wrong that I'll make Dawn crazy insisting on what I *am* right about.

I'm not saying we need to go along with whatever someone says. I am saying this: Is the relationship more important than our need to be right? Many times, the relationship is sacrificed when we are *technically right*. I'm right about the fact that you hurt me, so therefore, "You're outta here!" I'm right about how ridiculous my situation with you is and I'm tired of it, so, "I'm not going to take it anymore!"

In relationship, trying to decide who's right and who's wrong usually leads to a dead end. It is seldom the case that one is completely right and the other is completely wrong. Focusing on having a right relationship will usher in forgiveness, responsibility, understanding, and love. "Love covers a multitude of sins" (1 Peter 4:8). Love doesn't pretend sin isn't there; rather love sets aside being right for the sake of keeping the relationship alive. A sense of justice may insist we have a right to treat someone with distance, but love moves beyond justice to mercy.

If our lives and our relationships are going to be transformed, our insistence on being right must die.

Self-serving vs. Servanthood (Self-giving)

Self-giving is the essence of love and heaven. We can truly have a taste of heaven here and now. In his powerful book, *The Problem of Pain*, C.S. Lewis gives us an exquisite picture of the self-giving aspect of love that has always been:

> Each soul... will be eternally engaged in giving away to all the rest that which it receives... For in self-giving, if anywhere, we touch a rhythm not only of all creation but of all being. For the Eternal Word also gives Himself in sacrifice; and that not only on Calvary... From before the foundations of the world He surrenders begotten Deity back to begetting Deity in obedience. And as the Son glorifies the Father, so also the Father glorifies the Son... From the highest to the lowest, self exists to be abdicated, and by that abdication, becomes the more truly self, to be thereupon yet the more abdicated, and so forever. This is not a heavenly law which we can escape by remaining earthly, nor an earthly law which we can escape by being saved. What is outside the system of self giving is... simply and solely Hell... the fierce imprisonment in the self is but the obverse of the self giving which is absolute reality...

A wonderful old parable really drives home this point. This story is found in many different cultures and has also been ascribed to the poet Virgil. It is a contrast between the heavenly way of living, focused on others, and hell, where people are only self-serving:

> There was a man who died and was being taken to heaven by angels. The angels said to him, "We are going to take you to heaven, but first we will show you hell." The angels then took him to a place where there was a great table which held a great bowl, so great that it was as big as a lake. The bowl was filled with a nutritious stew. All the way around the sides of this table, seated around the bowl were people. Emaciated, starving, miserable people. These people had spoons to eat the stew with, and the spoons were long enough to reach the stew (about 12 feet). The trouble was, while they could

scoop up the stew into the spoon, they could not get it into their mouths because the spoons were too long. When they would try to turn the spoons around to eat off of the other end, the handle of the spoon would hit someone else in the face and cause them to spill the stew. So here were all these pathetic people, suffering and moaning in agony, constantly trying to eat the food that was abundantly in front of them, all in vain. They were continuously striving for self fulfillment and never finding it. Next, the angels took the man to heaven. To his surprise, he saw the same scene! There it was, a giant table and lake-like bowl of the same stew, surrounded by people with 12 foot long spoons. Yet something was different here - all these people were smiling, happy, and healthy looking! "Why? What is the difference here that these people are happy and well fed?" the man said to the angels. They relied, "Have you not eyes to see?" The man looked more carefully, and observed that one person would scoop the stew, and bring it to the mouth of another. Then someone else would scoop up stew and feed it to the other. The angels smiled and said, "Here the people feed each other. Here are the people that learned the way of Love."

Transformation in its fullest sense is when we become like Jesus. Serving others in love and giving up what we hold precious in order to become Christ-like is evidence that transformation is happening. Christ uses strong words in reference to our servant hood: "Whoever wants to become great among you must be your servant, whoever wants to be first must be your slave- just as the Son of Man did not come to be served, but to serve, and to give his life as a ransom for many." (Matthew 20:26-28 NIV).

Serving oneself is to resist the reality of how life is supposed to be and will keep us from transforming.

Taking vs. Giving

The taking-versus-giving dynamic is evident in the familiar biblical phrases, "It is better to give than to receive," "If you lose your life you will find it," and "The last shall be first." The difficulty in fully believing these concepts arises from our bent to have life work without trusting God to provide. It's only if we trust Him that we dare let go of what we hold onto.

For the sake of argument, let's say that we can condense every interaction with someone down to two *primary* motivations: giving or taking. When we do, each act, conversation, and interchange can reveal significant attitudes regarding who we are, how we rely on God, how we see others, and who we really love. This assessment reveals what is driving us: fear or love. Let's be clear, however, that no one is always either giving or taking; no one is only a *giver* or a *taker.*

Taking and giving are mindsets or heart attitudes, and each produces different fruit. To distinguish what fruit is produced by either, consider how you feel when people are either taking from or giving to you.

When someone takes from me, I experience the "rotten fruit" of anxiety, anger, pain, bitterness, disappointment, powerlessness, frustration, sadness, disillusionment, loneliness, despair, apathy, regret, loss, betrayal, upset, worthless, fearful, conditional, confusion, irritability, and the sense of being cheated, ripped off, devalued, used, duped, and deprived. And when I am taking from others in my relationships this is the type of fruit I leave with them.

When someone gives to me I experience an entirely different crop of fruit. I receive value, worth, joy, love, peace, freedom, honesty, fellowship, intimacy, sharing, reciprocity, hope, commitment, openness, support, unity, connection, and other desirable qualities. When I am giving in my relationships, this kind of fruit will abound.

I have met people who mistakenly believed they reaped rotten fruit because they were giving too much. This, according to Scripture, is a lie. We reap what we sow (Galatians 6:7) and we cannot out-give God. Only our selfish giving, when we give with the intent to gain, will produce rotten fruit. The beneficiary of the taking mindset is self; the beneficiaries of the giving mindset are God and others. That's why when we have a heart attitude of giving even receiving from another is a giving act. We offer the humility to accept gratefully and graciously what another has to give. In the taking attitude, pride reigns and tells others they can make it on their own.

I put taking under the Idolatry heading because a taking attitude stems from the lie that God will not provide. Therefore, if I don't have what I want and am unwilling to give what is required to produce what I desire, my only option is to take. Taking comes from a poverty mindset. It is the epitome of self-sufficiency. It is desperate and lonely.

Consummate selfishness leads to consummate loneliness. Transformation is always hamstrung when selfishness is operating.

Happiness vs. Joy

There is nothing wrong with happiness per se. But happiness comes short of Kingdom living when it is tied to circumstances. As mentioned earlier, the word happiness is derived from "happenstance," suggesting that happiness is contingent upon what happens. We are happy when things happen to go well, and we are unhappy when they don't. If we are only happy when all's right with the world, we are subject to forces outside ourselves instead of Christ in us. When happiness is thought of in this manner we then serve the "idol" of circumstances and tie our experience of life to it. Then when we answer "who or what is in control" we can't answer God but rather circumstances. Remember who the "prince of the air" is. Happiness is good, but restricting our happiness to our circumstances sells short an aspect of the Good News of the Gospel: "In the world you will have tribulation; but be of good *cheer*, I have overcome the world."[57]

Joy transcends happiness and is not at all dependent on circumstances. We need abiding joy, not circumstantial happiness, to carry us through. It is the lack of true joy that causes people to chase after elusive and ultimately disappointing endeavors to be happy.

Like many of God's people throughout the centuries, we can live with joy even in the face of the storms of life. The joy of the Lord is our strength to persevere and overcome and transform. Experiencing His joy in the midst of turmoil is a possibility that does not compute too easily in our human practice. We so easily slip into the mindset that equates joy with how well things are going and how we feel about life. I assert that joy is so much bigger than we've made it. Joy has more to do with our vision than our internal subjective feelings.

When our own happiness is our main focus we will resist entering the difficult areas necessary to have transformation happen.

Doing vs. Being

The contrast between doing and being is perhaps the most revealing about our conviction of who we are. In the doing mindset, we derive our meaning from what we *do*. Doing, in the way I'm using it, is a mindset from which actions are generated *from*. There are generators within us or contexts we *come from* which set the stage for our actions. This dynamic alone will affect the outcomes. In the doing mindset, who we are (our sense of worth) is derived from what we do. But if what we do determines who we are, we can *never stop doing,* because then we will *stop being.*

The fruit produced by doing in order to derive life is also rotten: exhaustion, frustration, envy, drudgery, fear, loneliness, anger, failure, shame, limiting, selfishness, performance envy, chaos, comparing, controlling, bitterness, trying, paranoia, competition, suspicion, striving, defeat, insecurity, manipulation, rage, and caretaking. This fruit emerges because every human effort flows out of a belief that we must do something to actually live.

On the other hand, if we derive our meaning from who we *are* (our being that is connected and reconciled to God) and from whom God has created us to *be,* we reap different fruit. Life is filled with excitement, joy, fulfillment, peace, purpose, energy, flexibility, giving, acceptance, unity, contentment, passion, hope, cooperation, community, and love. Instead of the paranoia that views people as threats we can see people as mentors and resources because who we are is not threatened.

Galatians 5:10-23 is a beautiful contrast of the acts of a doing mindset and the fruit of a being mindset:

> The acts of the sinful nature are obvious: sexual immorality, impurity and debauchery; idolatry and witchcraft; hatred, discord, jealousy, fits of rage, selfish ambition, dissensions, factions and envy; drunkenness, orgies, and the like. I warn you, as I did before, that those who live like this will not inherit the Kingdom of God. But the fruit of the Spirit is love, joy, peace, patience, kindness, goodness, faithfulness, gentleness and self-control (NIV).

The fruit of the spirit is proof that transformation into Christ's image is happening. The reality of the fruit testifies to what's really going on.

The flow of the Idolatry chart is *inward*, from everything else to me. It's as if I am a black hole, sucking everything dry. Kingdom living, on the other side, flows *outward.* We become conduits of living water to everyone around us. We are truly connected to the Source of Life, and out of that connection we *do* certain things.

When employed, all of the idolatrous strategies keep us from fully loving God and others; and that is sin. These forms of idolatry keep us from fulfilling His command to love, which is consistent with His transforming work in us, for God is Love. C.S. Lewis says, "We might think that God wanted simply obedience to a set of rules, whereas He really wants people of a particular sort." He wants people conformed to the image of His Son.

This is why we are called to serve by loving with our whole heart, mind, and strength. Serving ourselves instead of the Lord of the universe *is* idolatry. If coming face to face with God ushers us into facing reality, then idolatry keeps us from that encounter. The only cure for idolatry is repentance, and there can be no real change without repentance.

So I pose the question: What best ushers us towards repentance?

FOURTEEN

Turning Away from Self Survival

It takes infinite power for God to create the universe out of
nothing. But it takes even greater power to make saints out of
sinners. For the nothingness out of which God created the universe
did not resist Him; but sinners do.

Peter Kreeft

Isn't it amazing how we simultaneously desire God's transformation
of us into the image of His Son and resist what is required for it
to happen? This resistance is grounded in our propensity to serve
ourselves (idolatry) instead of God. Idolatry calls for repentance, yet our
long-held misconceptions about repentance contribute to our resistance
and keep us from the freedom reality offers. Let's contrast the reality of
repentance with the less resourceful views we have invented.

Repentance

What do you think of when you hear the word repentance? Do medieval
images of self-flagellation flash through your mind? Does guilt figure
prominently? What role does penitence play in your view of repentance?
What about kindness? True repentance leads to change: turning from self-
reliance and self-survival strategies to a full reliance on God, and obeying
His commands, which leads to the elusive transformation we seek.

Yet many Christians associate repentance with suffering for their
sin. This concept is vividly illustrated in the 1986 movie *The Mission*.
Robert DeNiro plays Rodrigo Mendoza, a man racked by guilt as a result
of having killed his own brother. Seeking to repent and find redemption,
Mendoza joins a group of missionaries in the hostile jungles of Brazil and,
as an act of penitence, carries his renounced weapons and armor (symbols
of his pre-repentant state) up the perilous cliffs. Painstakingly, Mendoza

climbs through the rugged terrain lugging his load, making the arduous trek much more difficult and perilous. Finally, weary and exhausted from self-imposed suffering, Mendoza accepts release from his burden from the people he used to oppress. It is a poignant and powerful scene and yet begs an important question: Does repentance include an *earning* of forgiveness through self-imposed guilt and punishment?

If I suffer from my sin then can I find peace? Is this what repentance is like?

If your concept of repentance is similar to that of Rodrigo Mendoza, I want to challenge you to shift your perspective of repentance from that of a chore or ordeal to something good and life-giving. Repentance leads to true life and joy, not death and misery.

What Leads to Repentance?

The Scriptures teach us that godly sorrow leads to repentance (2 Corinthians 7:10). But what does this mean? What is godly sorrow? It sounds like something spiritual: looking sorrowful, feeling extremely pious and compassionate. But to understand godly sorrow you must see it as a sorrow which is like God's sorrow. So instead of focusing on what godly sorrow should look like for us, it is helpful to learn what causes God to be sorrowful. Just whom does God sorrow for anyway? Does He ever feel sorrow for Himself?

It is evident from Scripture that God sorrows over people who are lost, hurting, oppressed, and so on. Nowhere in Scripture can we find instances of God feeling sorry for Himself. Just the opposite is true. Out of His great love for us God feels sorrow and sacrifices His own comfort for our sake.

Godly sorrow, then, is allowing ourselves to feel the sorrow we have caused others through our behavior and attitudes. When we get in touch with how badly we have hurt others, and realize that our sinfulness and selfishness is the cause of that pain, it will lead us to repentance.

Sorrow is not the same as self-pity. Sorrow prompts tears for others; the tears of self-pity are for self. Self-pity is interwoven with blame and shame. We say things like, "How could I be so stupid," "I should know better," "I can't seem to do anything right" and other self-blaming statements. These feelings are born out of conceit; godly sorrow is rooted in humility. Self-pity reflects a disconnect from the reality that we are sinners; godly sorrow embraces that reality.

The Catholic Church uses a term that hasn't found its way into most Protestant circles: compunction. Compunction can be described as a piercing sense of sorrow one feels when they fully realize the impact of their sin on God and others. Compunction is not the same as guilt. Guilt still has self as its main focus. Guilt is essentially feeling bad for *me*. Francis Frangipane says, "Guilt is inauthentic repentance." Compunction is godly sorrow because it describes feeling bad for others. This kind of sorrow can lead to repentance that "leaves no regret" (2 Corinthians 7:10 NIV), meaning the repentance is genuine and lasting.

True repentance is a 180-degree turn. You are turning away from the thoughts, words, or deeds which have elicited compunction. Christians who "repent" but continue in the same hurtful, disobedient way of life have not really repented. True repentance results in repositioning, turning your face and your attention in another direction.

I suggest that what we most need to turn *from* are all the self-survival strategies we use that keep us from loving God and others passionately. What we must turn *to* is a deep trust in God that embraces whatever comes our way and prompts us to love the way He has commanded us to love, *loving as if we have never been hurt*.

Since we are made in God's image and born to love others, we will experience sadness when we hurt others by living in a self-serving, self-protecting manner. This sadness can lead us to godly sorrow and repentance. Dan Allender writes in the *Wounded Heart*:

> Sorrow accepts sadness and grief but adds a new dimension: recognition of damage done to others. Sorrow over the harmful impact of one's life on others is unto life. It is the core of repentance. Biblical sorrow acknowledges and moves beyond the loss of oneself and enters the wounds in others, perpetrated by one's own capacity to abuse through defensive hostile behaviors.

> Sadness opens the heart to what was meant to be and is not. Grief opens the heart to what was meant to be and is. Sorrow breaks

the heart as it exposes the damage we've done to others as a result of our unwillingness to rely solely on the grace and truth of God.

In this passage, Allender says damage is caused to others as a result of our reluctance to "rely solely on the grace and truth of God." We trust our strategies instead of trusting God. For example, we cover our sin instead of confess it. I wonder how often we see self-protection, self-preservation, and self-survival as sins from which we must turn in repentance. It often seems rational, normal, and necessary to employ these strategies in a world full of betrayal, rejection, pain, and hurt. It seems silly—even dangerous—to make ourselves vulnerable. Yet we fail to realize how these self-protecting actions are actually hostile and hurtful to others. These actions play out in various ways, such as not allowing yourself to get connected with others and in some way leave them or hurt them before they leave or hurt you.

Anytime there is a healing shift in a person's attitude and consequently in the way they relate to others, it always involves coming to the painful realization that the old way of relating has wreaked havoc and pain on others. Of course, this person also experiences pain from the consequences of self-centered living. Having alienated others, he or she suffers the pain of relationships that are not vibrant, passionate, intimate, and thriving. Who would not feel remorse at the realization that their legacy in the lives of others was negative instead of positive?

When this individual's heart is pierced with sorrow over how they have hurt others, he or she is ready for repentance.

In the New Testament, the Greek word for repentance also means a change of mind.[58] The Scriptures consistently depict repentance as renewing the mind so it aligns with God's commands.

Our role in repentance includes a willingness to honestly pay attention to the fruit that is present in our lives. We must interrupt our conceited view of ourselves, which tends to let us off the hook, and allow ourselves to feel godly sorrow instead of attempting to numb it. We must invite the Spirit to search our heart, and we must believe Scripture to be true and admit we are the liars. Then we must engage in self-examination by the Spirit's leading, earnestly explore the feedback from others, and trust that the Lord will sift us as we endeavor to love Him and others.

In my own life, I have noticed that when I get my eyes off myself long enough to notice how I have impacted my world, I begin to sorrow over the neglect and hurt I have contributed. As I acknowledge my sinful behavior, I begin to lament what has been lost and to long for the healing that is possible.

Godly sorrow is so much more powerful for change than feeling bad, guilt, regret, or shame, which only keep us stuck in a sense of failure. Being bogged down in shame divulges that we are not yet trusting in God. Wallowing in guilt and shame over things we've done and that have been done to us reveals our self-sufficiency. Godly sorrow breaks your heart and prompts a commitment to alter the behaviors that hurt you and others.

Dr. Dan Allender and Dr. Tremper Longman III speak about shame in their book, *The Cry of the Soul*. They contend, "Shame exposes what we worship...(Psalm 97:7; Isaiah 42:17)." The authors state that when one of their patients feels shame over past abuse and pain, inevitably it is because they disdain the weakness that made them vulnerable to hurt and that causes them to desire connection enough to risk being hurt. When their way of dealing with the horror of past abuse inevitably fails, they feel shame for not being able to provide for themselves instead of the sorrow that would be the normal reaction.[59]

People feel shame, Allender and Longman assert, because they attempt to do for themselves what only God can do. True and final comfort and relief from life's pain come only from God. People endeavoring to navigate life without suffering and pain are attempting to provide what only God can. When one engages true repentance and turns to God for forgiveness, the result is not guilt or shame but freedom and cleansing. Remaining in guilt and shame reveals that we are trying to provide for ourselves, which is a form of idolatry.

Any attempt to provide for ourselves that which only God can provide means we are setting ourselves up as gods. This is idolatry and will inevitably lead to failure, frustration, guilt, and shame. The other dynamic that produces these negative feelings is the sense that we should, after an unspecified time, arrive at a place where we don't struggle with sin anymore. This is another manifestation of a fallible and imperfect being who is unwilling to accept the reality of being a sinner who needs God's mercies daily.

The other changing of mind and turning away involves decisions we have made about ourselves that are contrary to God's declarations towards us. He says that with Him all things are possible for us. We contradict that declaration with our own, saying things like our history, our circumstances, our failures, and even our personalities determine what is possible for us. These declarations, sustained by the conversations we continue to have about the lies we've chosen to believe, then define our reality. Is this not also a form of rebellion, where what we say trumps what God says?

It is also a statement of unbelief that says God won't really provide.

Receiving Grace vs. Extending Effort

I would now like to address another paradox involved in repentance. While godly sorrow is essential to repentance, it is something that can only be accessed as we receive God's grace. If sorrow and compunction are the only motivators to repentance, we may end up serving another idol: the desire to live a good life on our own power in an effort to please God. Once people realize they have hurt others, they can easily slip into a desire not to do that anymore, moving them into striving to not sin.

Motivated by good intentions for pleasing God and not hurting others replace relying on grace with relying on effort.

When we fully believe that God's goodness and kindness is directed toward us, and that His grace is sufficient, we will be open to turn to Him, accessing mercy, humbly sharing our struggles with others, and living in a community of love and openness.[60] If we are not truly relying on God's grace, we can come to rely on our own effort. And self-reliance leads to shame because, having been designed by God to live in dependence on him, we instead rely on our own strategies.

Desiring to be done with the struggles of sin and pain, we can actually perpetuate the struggle by refusing to believe that God will meet us as we trust Him enough to share those struggles with other people in a fellowship of openness and honesty. Too often, we fashion masks in an effort to convince ourselves and others that we have arrived spiritually when we have not.

All too often we move into shame and self-condemnation about facing the same struggles over and over again, concluding that no ground has been taken in our transformation. Or we give up in despair and conclude that somehow we are not meant to take dominion over our lives. Our idea of lasting change is that we no longer struggle in areas where we previously struggled. Or if we do encounter struggles, we feel they should be insignificant scrapes that we quickly overcome. This view is partly the result of our frustration about not yet overcoming our weaknesses and partly from our mistaken expectation that maturity is equated with an end of struggles.

We do not wish to allow for the paradox that Christian growth and transformation can occur in the midst of our imperfection. Having been reborn of God and received His nature, we still have a sin nature battling within us. How both can be true is beyond me; so many of life's truths are paradoxes.

Let's look at some other paradoxes because, if paradox is reality for the Christian, then embracing it leads to transformation while resisting it does not.

PART FOUR

INVITING AND EFFECTING TRANSFORMATION

FIFTEEN

Who or What is in Control?

We see things not as they are, we see them as we are

Morrie Camhi

The meaning of things lies not in the things themselves,
but in our attitude towards them.

Antoine de Saint Exupery

Our opinion of the world shows up in our attitude and reveals our character. Ralph Waldo Emerson once said, "People don't seem to see that their opinion of the world is also a confession of character." Opinions, according to Webster, are judgments "the mind forms of any proposition, statement, theory or event, the truth or falsehood of which is supported by a degree of evidence that renders it probably, but does not produce absolute knowledge or certainty... From circumstances we form opinions respecting future events."[61] This seems like the antithesis of forming opinions based on what God says but rather allowing circumstances to form them. Thus we can have strong beliefs or opinions about life that are not necessarily true but which nevertheless cause us to see future events in the light shed by our opinion! This fits in with that dynamic spoken of several times where we have a way we believe life should be.

Attitude is also a key in developing our character because it works as a filter through which we see life, a filter that colors all our experiences.

Attitude

Attitude is looked upon in some Christian circles as a sales-enhancing or athletic performance pep talk at a motivational seminar. There's an association with the human potential movement attached to it that says essentially "I can accomplish anything I set my mind to." Attitude has been so assimilated into secular leadership courses that in some Christians' minds it is somehow apart from spirituality. Thus many do not pay attention to this very important aspect of our heart. How we interpret things and our attitude about things has profound impact on both our experience and the outcome.

From there we can easily move to a place where our attitudes actually undermine what we want the most. The longer I read the Bible and walk the Christian path, the more I realize that most of God's dealings with us have to do with our heart attitudes. It appears clear to me that change is also an attitude issue. It's significant that Jesus' Sermon on the Mount contains the beatitudes, ways of relating to God, man, and life that are quite paradoxical to our way of thinking.

In the beatitudes, Jesus confronts our view of how life should work with some very hard paradoxical sayings. "Blessed are the poor in spirit... Blessed are the meek... Blessed are the ones who are persecuted for the sake of righteousness." Huh? Being poor, meek, and persecuted doesn't sound like a blessing in my book. It sounds more like a curse.

So what can these sayings by the Author of Life be referring to? I believe they refer to how our attitudes towards these areas open up the possibility to be blessed by both God and others as we permit Him to provide for us even though we know that we will face lack and hurt over and over again.

An example of this is found in C.S. Lewis's book, *The Four Loves*. Lewis writes about different types of love and the attitude (heart posture) that goes along with them. The first distinction he writes about is between Need-love and Gift-love. He says, "Divine-love is Gift-love." He does not say that Need-love is necessarily selfish. "A tyrannous and gluttonous demand for affection can be a horrible thing. But in ordinary life no one calls a child selfish because it turns for comfort to its mother; nor an adult who turns to a fellow 'for company'."[62]

The attitude of being poor in spirit makes us aware of our need. We are poor in the sense we have need. Someone in poverty is aware of his or her need. Need-love makes us aware that we lack. In reference to poverty, Lewis makes the statement that our "Need love cries to God from our poverty,"[63] and although our Need-love for God can never end in this life or the next, our awareness of it *can*. While this attitude is a great first step, if we stay in the Need Love attitude we will only hold it until the need is met; it is the "short lived piety of those whose religion fades away once they have emerged from 'danger, necessity, or tribulation.'"[64] Once awareness of the need fades and the crisis is past, the attitude toward whatever or whoever was meeting the need is quite different. The appreciation may quickly fade.

For example, Lewis likens Need-love to a thirsty man's desire for a glass of water (*Four Loves* pp.28-33). He says the same glass of water that seems so vital from a dying-of-thirst perspective is the very same glass of water we ignore and even disdain when we've met our immediate need, have all the water we need, and are no longer thirsty.

We certainly lose sight of our "poverty of spirit" and don't live in the be-attitude advocated by our Lord: "Blessed are those who are poor in spirit... for they shall inherit the Kingdom of Heaven." This awareness is a discipline that must be undertaken daily. It is obvious that we can soon forget that we have need for others and God; because relationship with God and others is what the Kingdom of Heaven is comprised of. Need-love can quickly move to entitlement- a sense that whoever is meeting the need actually *owes* me.

This sense of entitlement permeates most of our life. We take things for granted and easily slip into a mindset of having a *right* to have what we have until one day we wake up and discover we've lost what we had. This is partly because we lose the discipline of being poor in spirit, keeping aware of our need, which involves an attitude of our hearts.

This awareness leads to Appreciative-love, which is a more mature love.[65] Appreciative-love is loving not because of what others can *do for me*, but rather a love for *who they are*. I can still appreciate what they offer (which will always be a part of who they are), but I can now look beyond that and appreciate even aspects of their person I find challenging.

In The Art of Marriage Workshop seminar that my wife and I conduct in through Reinvent Ministries, one of the first dynamics addressed is attitude. What is the prevailing attitude we hold toward our spouse, the person we chose to be the provision for our need for relationship, belonging, companionship, and sexual connection?

Too often our attitude toward our spouse is akin to the previously mentioned attitude toward water: Once satisfied we easily forget that a great need has been met. We forget the "poverty" of being unable to provide these needs for ourselves, nor were we intended to meet these needs ourselves! The very nature of what we want most in life is interwoven and connected to others. Or we just take both the gift and the giver for granted and we move into an entitlement attitude toward them. At its worst, our forgetting turns to resentment or scorn toward the one who met our need.

For example, an attribute of Dawn's that I've always admired is her incredible sensitivity to and care for detail, which translates into an effective love for others. This characteristic is one that attracted me to her, one that I also knew was underdeveloped in me.

As we began married life, Dawn's attention to detail produced changes in my life and the life of my family. Then one day, when Dawn exercised her gift to help shape my character, all of a sudden this "gift" seemed more like a curse. I appreciated it when it was directed toward others and I wanted her input, but I often resented it when she continued to operate in it naturally and it forced me to face things I'd rather not.

Attitude of Entitlement

I believe an attitude of entitlement is evil! It is arrogant and self-focused. Entitlement causes people to treat others as things and not as unique beings of value. An attitude of entitlement looks to people and God for what they can give. Ironically, when the entitled person extracts what they want from another, they often come to disdain the person who met the need. Any sense of gratitude is overpowered by feelings that the person meeting the need didn't do it well enough or with the right attitude.

Entitlement is about what we think we deserve. Webster defines "deserve" as what I merit or am worthy of. We are sinners! So what do we *really* deserve? If we truly got what we deserve, it would be death.

Nothing like a shot of reality to shake up our attitude!

Entitlement attitudes carry a sense of being owed. There is no humility or appreciation that goes along with that attitude. Relationships that operate from entitlement mindsets are transactional as opposed to true giving and receiving. Attitude has everything to do with what we see and how we respond in any given circumstance. Consider this statement by Charles Swindoll:

> The longer I live, the more I realize the impact of attitude on life. Attitude, to me is more important than facts. It is more important than the past, than education, than money, than circumstances, than failure, than successes, than what people think or say or do. It is more important than appearance, giftedness, or skill. It will make or break a company, a family, a church, a home. The remarkable thing is we have a choice everyday regarding the attitude we will embrace for that day. We cannot change our past… we cannot change the inevitable. The only thing we can do is play on the one string we have, and that is our attitude. I am convinced that life is 10% what happens to me and 90% how I react to it. And so it is with you…we are in charge of our attitudes.

Here is another interesting attitude check: why is it we always ask "why me?" when bad things happen but fail to ask the same question in regards to our blessings? How quickly I ask "why did I get cancer?" but not wonder with gratefulness, "why did I get to grow up in America instead of the poorest area of sub-Sahara Africa?" I mean, think about your blessings- do you ask God "why me?" from an attitude of gratitude (with-out false guilt)? If not, how come? What do you think this reveals about what you feel you're entitled to and where did you get that notion?

Our attitudes have much to do with how we respond to, and what results come out of, whatever happens to us. Attitudes affect how we engage the elements God uses to effect transformation in us. Attitude can either encourage or discourage facing reality, which in turn opens or closes the possibility of transformation happening. As we examine the following situations, the influence of attitude will become evident. Attitude impacts each and every aspect of life. And, paradoxically, many things we don't like and at times are taught to do away with can actually be used by God to transform us if engaged in with the right attitude.

Let's look together specifically at how.

Attitude Towards Pain and Suffering

Suffering reveals clearly how our attitude affects and transforms our experiences. Attitude coincides with and is connected to expectation, and what we expect affects what we experience. There are two extremes and many in between points in this statement. If we expect life should always be easy and pleasant, then any slight pain or imposition will feel like devastation. If we take Christ at His Word that life is often difficulty, then no amount of pain and suffering will sway us.

Suffering and pain are undoubtedly the most challenging of the philosophical and theological discussions. The purpose of this book is not to undertake that challenge but to specifically hone in on God's use of suffering and pain in transforming us.[66]

There is a strong case to be made for the wrongness of pain. After the fall of Adam and Eve we hear God saying, in Genesis 3:16 that their pains would be *increased* and that even tending the garden would become painful toil. Many take this to mean that if it weren't for sin there would be no pain. Most people seem to believe that pain is evil. While I agree that sin introduced *unnecessary* pain, suffering, toil, and death, I wonder if it's true there was no pain prior to sin.

Did Adam have the freedom to stub his toe? If so, would he feel pain? When he looked at Eve and experienced the wonder and mystery of her, did he not feel a beautiful ache? Have you never experienced a kind of pain from too much beauty, even too much pleasure? To use an example from C.S. Lewis, does not a certain amount of pain even bring pleasure as in the slight ache of worked out muscles from a vigorous climb? If pain was in and of itself bad, why do we even have nerves and the capacity to feel pain?

Gift of Pain

During Jesus' time on earth He healed lepers on several occasions. Leprosy is a disease where the nerve endings die. Imagine you had this problem and developed a blister on your foot. If you weren't diligent to thoroughly check for problems, you would never know anything was wrong because you wouldn't be able to feel any pain. Being unaware of the problem, you would be vulnerable to infection. Eventually, gangrene would set in, ultimately resulting in the decay and death of the extremity. All the while you would remain ignorant that something was wrong.

So along comes Jesus and, seeing the predicament of the lepers, is moved by mercy and compassion to heal them. What is His healing gift to the lepers? The last thing on earth you might expect: *the ability to feel pain!*

And for this they were extremely grateful!

We all know pain that alerts us when something is wrong. Both emotional pain as well as physical pain point to something needing to be addressed. Of course, the same nerve endings that enable us to feel pain allow us to feel pleasure. You can't enjoy the warmth of the sun on your face without the possibility that you may also feel the sting of sunburn. And you can't enjoy the pleasure of passionate relationships without the distinct probability that you will also feel the pain of conflict or betrayal. We will be hurt in relationships because the world and the people that populate it are sinful. Sin is the culprit, not pain. Peter Kreeft puts it this way in *Christianity for Modern Pagans:*

> God does not cause pain; sin causes pain. But the juxtaposition of God and sin also cause pain. The surgeon who does not cut out the cancer is not kind but cruel. The God of mere kindness whom we long for, the Grandfather God who leaves us alone to enjoy ourselves rather than the Father God who constantly interrupts us and interferes with our lives is really not kind but cruel... The "cruel" God of the Bible is a God of battles. He fights a spiritual war for us against the demons of sin in us. This God is not cruel but kind, as kind as He can possibly be.

Whether pain is or isn't necessary is not really the question. The real question is: Does God use pain to transform us? I believe the answer is a resounding yes! He is so committed to transforming us into people who passionately love Him and others that He allows pain to bring us back from the exile of self-love. C.S. Lewis, a man who knew self-love, love of God and others, joy and pain, wrote this poem:

All this is flashy rhetoric about loving you.
I never had a selfless thought since I was born.
I am mercenary and self-seeking through and through:
I want God, you, all friends, merely to serve my turn.

Peace, re-assurance, pleasure, are the goals I seek,
I cannot crawl one inch outside my proper skin:
I talk of love —a scholar's parrot may talk Greek—
But, self-imprisoned, always end where I begin.

Only that now you have taught me (but how late) my lack.
I see the chasm. And everything you are was making
My heart into a bridge by which I might get back
From exile, and grow a man. And now the bridge is breaking.

For this I bless you as the ruin falls. The pains
You give me are more precious than all other gains.[67]

Yes, God will allow the ruin to fall, and He will use pain if necessary. C.S. Lewis also says, "God whispers in our pleasures, but shouts in our pains."[68] He shouts to us that something is wrong, needs to be addressed, and probably needs to be changed.

In addition, the very pains of our life, things we prefer not be there, are the elements He uses to bring beauty to our souls. We often refer to these experiences as one that "stink" or we use worse terms, and refer to them (to use King James language) as "dung". You know what I mean. Amazingly, the international symbol of transformation, the butterfly, exemplifies how God creates beauty from "stuff that stinks" in a most striking way. I understand that it is the excrement of the caterpillar, the "frass", which serves to give the color to the butterfly's wings. And then there is the well known dynamic that if an emerging butterfly does not go through the struggle and fight to break out of it's cocoon (for instance if some well meaning soul tries to make it easier and opens up the cocoon) then that butterfly will never have the strength to fly and will die prematurely. Conflict that brings life and "crap" that brings beauty- only a magnificent God can accomplish that. Wow, is there a message there for us or what?

Attitude in Suffering Either Opens or Closes Possibilities

One thing that distinguishes a person who is refined and sanctified through difficult and horrific circumstances from someone who is embittered and corrupted by the same circumstances is the attitude they take toward what is happening. A person's attitude affects how he or she relates to God, people, and circumstances. In relationship to God, our attitude reveals how deeply we trust Him, how dependant we are on Him, and how sold out we are to the idea that He will really come through no matter how bad things look.

Charles Swindoll says, "We are in charge of our attitudes." This is not something God does for us. Persuaded that God is sovereign and will work out our circumstances, we adjust our attitude to be consistent with what we say we believe. An attitude that allows that God is God and we are not will usher in changes in our thinking which will lead to further transformation. Perhaps an analogy will help picture this.

Mosaic Analogy

I have likened God's handiwork in us to a work of art. I had the privilege of visiting St. Peter's Cathedral in Rome, Italy. Standing at the base of the cathedral and looking up into the domed ceiling, you notice the beautiful images of art. The pictures are striking and moving. It is not until you make the arduous trek to the top of the interior and stand on the catwalk around the dome that you realize that the beautiful images are done in mosaic. There are multiplied thousands if not millions of small fragments of ceramic tile carefully arranged to form a picture.

The striking aspect of a mosaic is that, until all the pieces are in place, they are just random fragments of broken colored tile. The individual pieces, and even small clusters of assembled pieces, are incomplete.

I wonder how much of our life experience is like a mosaic. Small, separate incidents in life don't make sense before they are set into place in the big picture. We don't have the perspective the Artist has. Since God is Sovereign and committed to our good, we must also allow Him to do His work even though we don't know how all the seemingly mismatched pieces of our experience will fit together into something beautiful. We don't know (and can't see) how the raw material will emerge as the finished product. But the Master Artist knows what He is doing.

No one would question Michelangelo's assertion that within the massive block of marble a David is waiting to emerge, especially when you've seen any of his other works of art. Why then should we question God's artistry?

Our doubts in this area reveal another foundational level where our repentance is required. How can we, the clay, dare to dictate to the Potter what kind of vessel he should make of us (Romans 9:21) or when He's kneaded us too hard?

Attitudes clearly reflect what we believe and affect how we relate.

Think of Joseph, sold into slavery in Egypt. After the prophetic dreams about his prominence in the family, he found himself further from that reality than he could have imagined. His own envious brothers sold him into slavery, and his master's wife had him thrown into prison. What was Joseph's attitude toward these horrible events? Obviously, Joseph did not hold an attitude of entitlement or bitterness, for this would have assured him of staying stuck in his circumstances.

Victor Frankl, the Jewish psychiatrist who authored *Man's Search for Meaning*, survived the Nazi concentration camp at Auschwitz. He is another profound example of how someone's attitude can transform a horrific experience into a work of art that blesses and inspires many.

Frankl adopted an attitude of hope and maintained a semblance of dignity in the midst of his horrendous circumstances. Imprisoned at age 26, he watched as his entire family was wiped out by the Nazi killing machine. Everything he had was stripped from him, including his clothes. Standing naked while being interrogated and humiliated, he recognized that the only thing they could not take from him was how he would interpret his circumstances. He could choose his attitude. He went so far as sharing his meager rations of food with those who needed it more. Obviously, an attitude that maintains concern and generosity towards others somehow translates to life-giving possibilities.

Or consider Paul and Silas in prison (Acts 16:22-25). Severely flogged and beaten, these two men maintained an attitude that allowed them to sing songs of praise to their Lord and ultimately lead their jailer to salvation.

The other dynamic Frankl, Paul and Silas, Joseph, and others like them all had in common was vision. Yes, their vision helped them *survive,* but it also enabled them to *derive* something precious from their vile circumstances. Victor Frankl said that a person can survive any *what* if they have a *why*.

Our attitudes permeate all our experiences of life. The stance of our heart toward anything that happens in life transforms what could be meant for bad into something fruitful. A positive attitude sees a valuable source of fertilizer in a common pile of manure. So it's through our attitude that we see possibilities in life's many obstacles.

We don't get to decide the point at which God is finished working something out in us. That's the prerogative of the Master Potter. We should not be surprised when we face repeated, familiar struggles in the same area of our lives. If nothing else, these continuing challenges will help us appreciate how far God has brought us!

Your Altitude Determines Your Attitude

In fact, I believe Scripture suggests that we *will* face the same things over and over. Proverbs 15:24 says: "The way of life winds upward" (NKJV). What happens when you wind your way up a mountain? My friend Hendre Coetzee suggests that even though you frequently circle back to a side of the mountain you have already visited, if you continue to gain altitude you should have an increasingly better perspective on that side. Each new and hopefully clearer perspective of a familiar old challenge should help you reach a better outcome than the last time.

One side of the mountain I visit repeatedly in my upward journey of transformation in the Master's hands relates to times when I perceive that others are rejecting me or my ideas (and often it is only the *perception* of rejection). I have feared rejection for as long as I can remember, and in the past that fear has immobilized me. But one incident not too long ago gave me new perspective on the good work God has already completed in me.

I was on stage facilitating a new seminar in front of about a hundred people sitting in theater style rows. My mentor, who was coaching me in this seminar, sat at a table at the back of the room. In the middle of the presentation, my mentor suddenly grabbed his head with his hands and lowered his forehead to the table, an action that communicated to me, "What are you doing?!" No one else in the room saw him except me.

In that instant, the pain of being rejected in the past coursed through me and left me reeling. The old tapes started playing a familiar theme in my head: "I'm not adequate." I wondered what in the world I did wrong to elicit such a reaction.

It wasn't too long ago that a scenario like this would have sent me spinning in a cycle of internal debate as one side of me tried to disarm the perceived attack while the other side argued for its validity.

But this time I decided to set aside those internal conversations and forge ahead with what I was doing. I decided to take on the perspective that my "I" (my essential being) was not being called into doubt, but rather that something I was doing was off and I would get clear about it later. So in a matter of seconds, without understanding what my mentor was communicating, I shifted and continued the presentation.

The perspective opened up by the altitude I took on the situation helped me maintain an attitude that allowed me to complete the lecture and provide value to the seminar.

The changing perspective and attitude I take when faced with these stirrings in my soul actually determine what I see as possible. As I have become more intimate with this part of my inner machinery, a new dynamic has opened up. Instead of allowing the fear of revisiting the same haunting dictate to me, causing me to retreat into my playing-it-safe mode, I can face these fears while allowing a different result than what happened in the past.

I can come to a place where I have my struggles instead of my struggles having me.

This is a powerful stage of maturation that recognizes the reality of life's struggles and accepts that, while we are not where we want to be, we are also not where we used to be.

Defined By Circumstances or By Christ

Here's another way of looking at how we face the paradox of our struggles: Are we defined by our circumstances or by Christ? Do our circumstances dictate what we become or do we engage our struggles in such a way that who we are is impacted in a life-giving way? Do we really believe that "God works all things for good to those who love God, that are called according to His purpose" (Romans 8:28)? Are we victims or victors in life?

There's no doubt circumstances and events of our life influence and can sway us into a way of being and relating that doesn't often feel like our choice—certainly *not* our preference. We may feel at times that we have no choice in the matter, but God's Word says we *do* have a choice. Deuteronomy 30:19 states that God has set before us "life and death, blessings and curses. Now choose life, so that you and your children may live" (NIV). These choices, some that lead to life and others that lead to death, are present in every option we face. No matter what circumstance, situation, or event we find ourselves in, we have choices present that will add value to our life.

I suggest that the only way we can even see the options that lead to life is to first face the reality we are in without using any strategies to make it better in our own strength. Facing reality frees us to see the true choices before us. Face to face with what is really so and trusting God to be our protector and redeemer, we continue to act and choose in a way that is consistent with His commands.

Consider how our attitude impacts what people communicate to us. Depending on how we decide to view the person we are in relationship with, we can have very different reactions to things they do or say. Whether we've decided the person a friend or foe, our attitude will color our conclusion. Our attitude can alter our perception of a comment from criticism (negative) to feedback (positive).

Attitude Towards Feedback

One of the most underutilized gifts God has given people is the gift of feedback. Feedback is vital and necessary. Feedback is a vital cog in the wheel of transformation. Feedback gives us a perspective outside of our own egocentric, subjective, and sometimes conceited view of ourselves. We suffer greatly when we go without feedback or turn a deaf ear to it.

Every one of God's creatures survives life best when they pay attention to feedback. Bats, blind as they are, have highly developed radar that helps them navigate and find food. Dolphins have sonar that alerts them to what is around them to the point that they can sense if an approaching shark has eaten or has an empty stomach. All animals have a keen sense of smell or hearing or sight. These help keep the creatures alive, or they become part of the food chain!

While humans are definitely physical beings, we often find more important the state of our relational lives. That's why many can't eat or sleep when a relational issue is undone. More than once I've stayed up all night talking through difficult issues with my wife, even though sleep sounded much better. This is because I didn't want the relationship to die, if you will, and I needed to pay attention to the feedback that was coming my way.

While I believe that most people have experienced this dynamic, many times we neglect one of the most effective instruments God has given us to assure that our relationships don't die a slow death. That instrument is feedback.

Feedback which is intended to hurt someone is prohibited in Scripture. Paradoxically, even negative feedback can be useful if received with an attitude of allowing God to show us any truth contained in the feedback. Some of the most honest and helpful feedback I have received came from people wanting to hurt me. I am not encouraging this way of interacting. I am only pointing out that even something intended for bad can be used by God for good in my transformation. How often is valuable feedback unconsidered because it isn't given the way I prefer or because it makes me uncomfortable?

Feedback comes to us in so many ways when we are in relationship. The most obvious is direct verbal feedback. If we care to listen, people will tell us what about us isn't working for them. We often don't like what we hear or that it doesn't match up with what we want to believe, so our avoidance mechanisms often spring into action in response to verbal feedback.

There are many other forms of feedback going on in our relationships. We have all noticed nonverbal signs from our loved ones that something about us isn't working for them. We sense it when they pull away physically or emotionally, when they are less responsive or even cold. This kind of feedback waves a red flag and invites us into investigation.

God has placed people in my life to provide feedback for me. However, its value is often negated because I choose to ignore it. In my conceit, I reject anything that contradicts what I prefer to believe about myself, and my reluctance to face reality will sabotage the very transformation I want in my relationships and myself.

I find it both understandable and mystifying when people withhold hard feedback from loved ones. Understandable because hard feedback causes pain and who willingly wants to hurt anyone? Mystifying because when someone is stuck and unaware of their self-destructive behavior, and we withhold helpful feedback about it, in the end it hurts them even more. It is not uncommon that the person from whom we withhold feedback feels betrayed when our reluctance finally comes out. I've heard people say, "If you saw what was really happening, why didn't you tell me?"

I don't think we withhold feedback because it hurts others; I think we hold back because it will hurt to have these difficult conversations. It's a risk to tell people the hard truth. I know I weigh the possible misunderstandings that may ensue. The person I'm talking to may get upset or they may point out the same flaw in me. Who wants that? So I withhold feedback because I'm more concerned with myself than I am about the other. We must become lovers of truth and God more than lovers of ourselves. To embrace truth and enter into difficult conversations for the sake of someone else, no matter what the cost to us, is a true expression of love for God and others.

Truly loving God and others brings about transformation because we cannot remain self-centered and shallow when we give ourselves over fully to Him *in* love and *for* love. Giving ourselves fully moves us to engage all life has to offer. When loving God and others is our focus, we'll do what's required, even if it means engaging uncomfortable situations, risking vulnerability, or anything else that is called for to let your commitment to love come through. We will even give up our ideas of how it's supposed to look and deeply drink in all He has for us.

Let's now consider some other aspects of life that are crucial in the role of transformation but are sometimes misunderstood or used both for good or ill, and therefore are avoided.

SIXTEEN

The Role of Conflict, Vision, and Surrender in Transformation

Consider it a sheer gift, friends, when tests and challenges
come at you from all sides. You know that under pressure,
your faith-life is forced into the open and shows its true colors.
So don't try to get out of anything prematurely. Let it do its
work...

James 1: 2-3, The Message

Conflict is Our Ally

We often view conflict as an enemy, the same way most of us view pain. But in reality, conflict, like pain, can be another friend. In it we are sifted and refined. I believe love and conflict, just like love and transformation, go hand in hand. True Christian love of necessity points us toward areas that are in breakdown and compels us to move into the conflict for the purpose of restoration. The need for reconciliation presupposes there currently is or soon will be conflict to resolve.

I'm not suggesting that we go out of our way to look for conflict. As much as possible, we are to live in peace with all men (Romans 12:18). At the same time, we don't have to go far into a typical day to find ourselves in conflict of some kind! It reminds me of a humorous, insightful prayer that goes something like, "God, I thank you that today I have not been mean or selfish or angry or rude or self-serving. But I am ready to get up now, so I will really need your help!"

Conflict is always ready to infiltrate our days because people and problems infiltrate our days. We should not find this surprising because 2 Corinthians 5:18 says that God has given us the ministry of reconciliation. Reconcile means to "call back into union."[69] Our ministry of reconciliation presupposes that there are conflicts to resolve. When we commit ourselves to become reconcilers, we can no longer ignore the conflicts in us or around us because we'd rather not be bothered.

Conflict can range from a knock-down drag-out fight to a husband and wife who are emotionally cool to each other to any relationship marked by distance or indifference. It may be a relationship that was intended to be close and loving but has never been good. For example, a parent/child relationship should be close and loving, but many parent/child relationships have never experienced this connection, so we can say there is conflict in this relationship. Whenever the state of a relationship is less than the ideal purpose or vision inherent in the relationship, conflict exists.

Thinking about conflict in this way, you can easily see that conflict is a part of everyone's life in some way or other. So how can we make conflict our ally instead of our enemy? Attitude, expectation, and possibility-thinking come into play here. Shifting our attitude from "This shouldn't be happening" to "What does this conflict tell me about what is missing in the relationship" is the first and most vital step. Once you make this shift, expectations change and new possibilities open up. When resistance turns into surrender—acknowledging reality—circumstances can become a doorway to reconciliation and restoration.

Here's an example. Let's say I'm in relationship with a person and we began our association committed to being honest, connected, and intimate. Instead of what we intended, we find ourselves being dishonest, separate, and distant. Releasing our resistance to conflict may take many forms. It could be as simple as changing from pretending that all is well to acknowledging that something is off. It could mean that I stop blaming (myself, the other person, lack of money, other circumstances, etc.) and take a responsible stand which says, "We are in breakdown, and that's not what we're about. I'm committed to do whatever it takes and go through the struggle to restore the vision for our relationship."

In this way conflict becomes an instrument and an opportunity to bring about what we desire in the relationship. It turns from being something we avoid into a vehicle to help bring forth our vision.

One of the mindsets I endeavor to communicate in life coaching is to reframe the concept of conflict and confrontation. What if our view of conflict/confrontation shifts from something we avoid at all costs to something we welcome to help us explore and find new possibilities? Can a simple shift in thinking begin to transform some things? I believe so.

Consider Webster's definition of confrontation: "The act of bringing two persons into the presence of each other for examination and discovery of truth." Wow, that's a different frame. In some ways this mindset, frame, or way of looking at confrontation makes me actually excited about opening it up.

I have begun to live out this response to conflict in my marriage. Mind you, the shift still doesn't make conflict and confrontation more appealing or any easier. What changes is my experience in the conflict and the fruit produced. When Dawn and I are in a breakdown and we engage in the conflict to fight *for* each other instead of *against* each other, just about everything changes. How we speak to each other, how we listen, how we move forward, and even the tactics we use are altered when we make conflict our ally and make the good of the relationship (love) our purpose.

Conflict can be our ally for far more than transforming our relationships and circumstances. God can use conflict to transform *us*. Perhaps a couple of examples from the movies can help us picture this better.

In *Lord of the Rings: The Two Towers,* the wizard Gandalf is compelled to confront the Balrog, a fiery demon-type creature. He tries to avoid facing this enemy he knows and fears, and only faces it in order to save the lives of his companions (another function of vision). As the Balrog closes in on Gandalf's companions, Gandalf takes a stand between the enemy and his friends, putting himself at stake for them. As a result, Gandalf is pulled into an abyss by the Balrog and seems doomed. Instead of resisting the reality, Gandalf throws himself headlong into the battle as he falls with the fiery Balrog.

The battle is long, furious, and exhausting, but Gandalf finally triumphs and defeats the Balrog. As a result, he is transformed from Gandalf the Gray into Gandalf the White, who is far more powerful than ever and even luminous in his appearance, so much so he must cloak his brilliance.

What a wonderful metaphor for the potential effects of the battles of our lives. Those who inspire us the most are those who face tough battles (even their own demons), refuse to become embittered and hard, and allow God to transform their character through the trials. As we throw ourselves into the battle for the sake of love, we too are transformed by God, who uses our trials to prove and mature us.

"Consider it pure joy, my brothers, whenever you face trials of many kinds, because you know that the testing of your faith develops perseverance. Perseverance must finish its work so that you may be mature and complete, not lacking anything" (James 1:2-4 NIV).

The word "mature" is the Greek word *teleios*; meaning complete (in various applications of labor, growth, mental and moral character, etc.). The word is translated "perfect" in the King James Version. The word "complete" is the Greek word *holokleros,* meaning complete in every part, perfectly sound, entire, whole.[70]

As *The Matrix* opens, Thomas Anderson is a "nobody-special" type person just surviving life. But that's not the end of the story. Thomas Anderson also goes through a transformation. Through many intense battles, including internal ones of disbelief, he begins to transform into Neo, a man destined to bring liberation to many. He's no longer nobody special; he is unique, causing people to say, "He is the one."

A crucial turning point in Anderson's identity happens when he is fighting the evil Agent Smith. No one has ever been able to defeat an Agent, and as Agent Smith pummels him, Anderson appears ready to suffer the same fate. As he is ready to dispatch the human, the Agent sneeringly refers to him as "Mr. Anderson" in a mocking tone, inferring "You *are* nobody." Suddenly, as if driven by his vision to interrupt the mediocrity that is killing off his race, Thomas Anderson answers back, "My name is Neo!" Then he rises to the fight and defeats the Agent.

We too are destined to be liberators. We are destined to be given a new name and move from being nobody special to become sons and daughters of the Living God. There is no doubt that God uses the trials and battles of our life to transform us. If only we would give our energy to align ourselves with that reality rather than waste energy resisting Him!

It is this kind of attitude that ultimately allows God to turn an Abram into Abraham, a Simon into Peter, a Saul into Paul, and you into a new creation.

When we surrender to God's purposes in conflict, we allow Him to refine us by taking us through the fire. Refining and fire are inseparable. I believe there is no refining crucible as effective as the one of human relationships. Proverbs 27:17 states, "As iron sharpens iron, so one man sharpens another" (NIV). God does some of His most extensive transforming through others: our spouses, our parents, our children, our siblings, our associates, fellow churchgoers—even the driver who cuts us off on the highway. Everywhere we go people are there to help file off our rough edges!

Bringing Order to Chaos and Releasing Beauty

Conflict often includes chaos. Many of my struggles appear at times to be a chaotic mess. I often would rather get far away from what's undone in my life and relationships. Questions of my adequacy, hauntings from the past, fears, and dread rear their ugly heads when I am faced with the chaos of conflict. And yet ordering chaos is part of what we were created for. Look at the Scriptures below:

> Genesis 1:2: Now the earth was formless and empty, darkness was over the surface of the deep, and the Spirit of God was hovering over the waters.
> Genesis 2:5-6: And no shrub of the field had yet appeared on the earth and no plant of the field had yet sprung up... there was no man to work the ground...
> Genesis 2:15-16: The Lord God took the man and put him in the Garden of Eden to work it and take care of it.

In the beginning the earth was formless and void. There was chaos. Then God's Spirit began to work and bring order. I believe being created in God's image includes us having a similar creative aspect residing in us. In fact, the above Scriptures make it clear that we have that nature in us. This has always been so.

All through human history men and women have entered into wild chaos and brought order. Wilderness has been tamed. Scientific breakthroughs continue to be achieved. When not abandoned to cynicism, humans have an insatiable drive to create, order, and release potential. In some way our lives and relationships feel like the most chaotic of wildernesses. Things can certainly become messy! As children of Creator God, we have the calling to enter into the turmoil of life and exercise our faith and vision to bring order and release beauty.

If you are a husband, what beauty are you called to release in your wife? If you are a wife, what has God created your husband to be that you are called to draw out? If you are parents, what ordering and releasing are you called to do in your children? No matter who you are, what were you created to bring forth in the garden of relationships God has set you to tend?

Entering chaos with the purpose of bringing forth fruit is the noble work we have been created for. As we do this, God's work of transformation continues in us. In order to release the beauty inherent in our relationship, we must encounter and overcome the struggles in us and in others we are laboring for. This takes character and a willingness to stay in the fray.

But we get tired of facing the same challenges over and over, and we are tempted not to go on. We want to be done with it! We must release our unrealistic expectation that we can ever be done with something until God lifts it from us.

Avoiding suffering is not really an option. Jesus said, "In this life you will have tribulations." In light of this reality, our refusal to embrace God's purposes for allowing suffering in our lives leaves us with a sense of emptiness, which brings further suffering. People willfully and even joyfully (at some level) go through suffering when they know there is a purpose for it. The pain of childbirth is just one poignant example.

Vision

In the Impact Training we have a sign on the wall that reads: "Have a vision that can call you through the pain of transformation." Change always involves pain—the pain of laying down what strategies we've held for a long time. The fact that we hold onto something indicates it is very dear to us. Laying down or giving up something near, dear, or familiar is painful. Holding onto things is a type of control. We like to be in control and resent the fact we can't dictate life on our requisites.

By its very nature vision places demands on us, including the demand that we give up control and develop self-control, a fruit of the Spirit. Vision becomes the controlling driver as we align our will with the vision. Vision restrains and constrains us. The Scriptures teach that where there is "no vision, people cast off restraint" (Proverbs 29:28 NASU).

Bringing a child into the world helps us understand what it's like to bring forth a vision. There is conception, gestation, delivery, and finally nurturing the newborn. Take any experience from life and you will readily see that all vision requires these elements.

Anything you give yourself to fully will require the process mentioned above. Committed athletes go through the pain it takes to "buffet their bodies." They discipline themselves to eat healthy foods, get sufficient sleep, and push themselves when they would rather coast. They endure the pain of working out for the reward of achieving victory. Other people earnestly go through the pain of working out for the reward of looking a certain way or being physically fit.

People committed to a degree in education must go through rigors to complete the coursework and achieve the degree. They may need to say no to going out or watching T.V. and study instead.

Couples committed to marriage must submit to the demands inherent in the most intimate of human relationships. They must get into difficult conversations when necessary to keep the relationship healthy when they would rather avoid conflict. They must close down other intimate relationships they could pursue. People who desire an early retirement discipline themselves in their spending and saving habits and deny themselves the freedom to spend whatever they want whenever they want.

Any vision will draw you into going through some things that are not fun. I remember sitting in tepid baths late at night with my screaming three-year-old son as his mother and I tried to cool his fever. This was a natural outworking of our vision to provide for and care for our son. While this is just a small example of suffering for a vision, I can tell you that the inconvenience of the experience was dwarfed in significance by the purpose. In other words, vision will constrain us and draw us into going through even pain if necessary.

What Was My Vision???

Only day three; it was going to be another long week in the infusion center. I had to receive chemotherapy for five days at a time and there I was stuck (both by location and the needle in my vein) in a room full of people in similar predicaments. The combination of the effect of the chemo agents and the IV poles made it unappealing for us to move about freely, so we just sat in quasi uncomfortable recliners and watched the nurses work and assess how each other were doing.

"What am I doing here?" I queried myself. "I should be on my way to another training and instead I'm locked up in this place." Once again life was not the way it should be and I was resisting it and consequently feeling myself get in a bigger and deeper funk.

As I thought about this and felt sorry for myself I had another thought invade my mind: "Why do you want to be at a training?" The thought was an intrusion and an interruption.

"Why to be with people and minister to them of course, it's what I love to do!" Even before I finished having the response I realized how incongruent my stance was. This was mostly about how I wanted it to look and not really about ministering to people. Why, I was in a room full of a captive audience who was facing some of life's biggest challenges and I was complaining the scenario didn't fit in with my declared life vision of "ministering to people and having them see possibilities where they may be losing hope!"

As I realized all this and interrupted my preference I asked myself other questions: "How can I live out my vision in these present circumstances? What if this was a provision from God to really make a difference?"

These questions caused me to open my eyes in a new way and as I did I saw Thuy. Thuy was a young wife and mother who had a very aggressive cancer. Her English, while sufficient, carried a heavy Asian accent–she was Vietnamese.

As I engaged her I found out a whole bunch. Her five year old daughter was awkward around her since Thuy lost her hair. Her husband had a very high pressure job that didn't make provision for him to take a leave of absence and that precluded him from being with her as she received her chemo. Her family was back in Vietnam. She was scared and alone.

I decided to befriend her if she would allow it- God knows we both needed each other. It wasn't long before my heart was fully connected with her and we began looking forward to the times we would be in the infusion center together. We became friends who shared deeply about our fears, hopes, histories, and futures.

Vision is never held hostage by circumstances.

The amazing thing about vision is that at first we *form it*, and then it begins to *form us*. Vision will call us into trans*form*ation, and most of the time vision dictates the terms. Our vision, not our natural desires, will order what is required. When vision is the focus, how we get where we are called to go is secondary to actually getting there. The vision continues to draw us, to constrain us.

The frustration with not knowing *how* to get there is acknowledged but is not permitted to dictate an abandonment of *getting* there.

It's amazing how some people seem to resent the requirements the *vision itself* puts on them. What confuses me about this is that if the vision I say is important has attached to it certain necessities then railing against those requisites is really showing antipathy towards my own vision. For example, if part of my vision is to have a faithful, intimate, exclusive relationship with my wife then that vision requires me to be honest, present, open, exclusive, etc. So if I then resent the fact that I cannot be with other women or can't be vague when my wife asks me questions, or "have to" participate in uncomfortable conversations, what I am upset about are the very things that will actually open up what I say I want. This is, of course, incongruent.

I'm not suggesting these things become fun when looked at in this light, I'm asserting this recognition can transform these experiences from things I resent to them becoming opportunities to realizing my vision.

Vision is not the same as a goal; it is something bigger that encompasses goals. In fact, vision encompasses everything, including circumstances that could derail it. In this mindset whatever circumstances come up can be opportunities for our vision to be fostered not hindered. Vision is the focal point in the midst of our experiences. Imagine yourself on a hike in the wilderness using the North Star as your focal point. It's not your goal to reach the North Star; but using the North Star as a focal point will guide you in the direction you want to go and help you get back on course when you get sidetracked. You may need to change direction many times to get over mountains and around lakes. We may need to shift many times in order to readjust the direction. But by keeping the

North Star in sight, you will always know where you're going even if you don't know exactly how you're going to get there.

At the same time, you will be completely ineffective if your only focus is on the North Star and you fail to navigate the path below your feet. You may be moving in the right direction but if you fall into a gorge because you are not paying attention to where you currently are you will never get where you envision. There is a continual flow between using the directional guide of the star and then looking at the path to avoid the pitfalls, crevasses, and obstacles on the path. As you are on the path your focus naturally goes from big picture (the directional aspect of the North Star) to details (the practical step by step on the path as you move forward).

If we're honest what most of us really want from God is a *map* that will detail every step we "should" take in order for us to navigate through life and have it be the way we prefer. "Just tell me what I'm supposed to do Lord and I'll do it." Except for the rare times He actually directs this specifically (rare in my experience and in many others I know) all He seems to provide most often is something more like a compass as we make our way through the murkiness.

When the circumstances of life throws us curves and knock us off course our vision can have us see how we could walk out our vision *now* and not wait until life starts looking the way we think it should and then live out our vision.

Often, when working with individuals they readily seem to know what they don't want and have a harder time identifying what they really long for. "I *don't* want to be like my father." "I *don't* want to be alone." "I *don't* want to be overweight." People are crystal clear about what they don't want.

This is a set-up for mischief.

When your focus is on what you don't want, you channel your energy towards the very thing you want to avoid. Remember when you were learning to ride and steer a bike and you started veering towards a tree? "Don't hit that tree! Don't hit that tree! Don't hit that trreeee…!" You know what happened—you hit the tree. Why? It's what you focused on.

We have more power than we realize to achieve what we focus on and when that translates into focusing on a negative we mysteriously accomplish the very thing we don't want. Or we become the way we don't want. I have worked with many men and women who were so focused on not becoming like their own father or mother and were shocked to discover they became exactly like them.

It's critical to create a vision for what you *do* want. Dream big. Make it something that requires you to be all in. Make it something that will necessitate you to fully rely on God.

Vision is our North Star for the journey of life. Goals serve as intermediate steps along the way. A vision that compellingly draws us through life will dwarf our need to have our experiences play out a certain way. We will comply with whatever terms are required and step into what God is ordering. This too will bring more change.

Give Me a Reason

Until recently, one of my real struggles was getting in shape physically and depriving myself of whatever foods I craved. It's amazing how insignificant cutting out unhealthy foods and taking up exercise became as I measured those things against walking my daughter down the aisle on her wedding day or watching my son raise his own family. This may seem like a no-brainer: when faced with this kind of choice who wouldn't make the necessary corrections? Well, I think all of us can readily bring to mind many people who have refused to do all they could and instead continued to have their addictions chose for them. Incredibly, many people with emphysema go on smoking until their condition deteriorates further culminating into lung cancer.

It's as if the temporary pain that may be required in order to give up the gratification received by the destructive behavior is not weighed against the ultimate payoff. This principle holds true for the big and little things we choose in life. I assert that without vision, there is no reason to deny ourselves anything.

This is essentially what Christ did as He measured the pain His vision called Him into versus the glory of redeeming us. Yes, the pain was tremendous but insignificant when measured against what He would gain.

Now, you may say the cancer brought me face to face with that kind of choice and that is true. But the reality is everyone can decide to make their choices just as gripping.

In addition, vision can be the most compelling reason to do what we don't want to do or stop doing what we should not do. Think about all of the things you struggle with, such as eating too much chocolate and indulging in addictive behaviors. We do those things *because we like them!* This is true for people addicted to drugs, sex, slothfulness, eating, whatever. We are drawn to them because we like some aspect of how they make us feel in the moment, even when the aftertaste is bitter. But if our vision, for example, is a healthy, productive life, we can step away from these behaviors because they are not on course with our focal point.

Having a reality conversation regarding these struggles is a huge first step to changing them. Just like the alcoholic admitting he is an alcoholic, acknowledging that you like something which is not in harmony with your vision can be a helpful slap in the face. Getting real about where you are with something can give you great freedom for finding the way out.

How can vision help? Think about it this way. Let's say I'm addicted to over-indulging my sweet tooth. I can think of many reasons why I shouldn't overindulge, such as how the excess negatively impacts my weight. Even more powerful is finding a reason more compelling than how it's hurting me. Yes, I may like the temporary high or comfort I receive from pigging out on sweets, but what is the bigger reason for being more disciplined in what I eat?

If the reason I want to quit overindulging my sweet tooth is to lose weight, then I need to ask why I want to lose weight. What would it mean for me if I shed the pounds I have gained? What would be a *compelling* reason to lose weight? For me it may be because I want to live a longer, healthier life. If so, then my focal point for cutting back on sweets is the quality of life I really want to live and how my healthier life will affect others.

An example of a compelling vision in this area might be stated this way: "If I don't cut back on sweets and lose weight, my health will be negatively affected and I may not be around to see my children married and enjoy and positively influence my grandchildren. I love sweet snacks and desserts, but in light of my vision for enjoying healthy interactions with my grandchildren, I can cut back even though I'd rather not."

Or similarly, let's say you like to stay in bed a little longer in the morning and have pastries and lounge around much more than walking or jogging or going to the gym. But suppose you create a vision for your life to be fit enough to do outdoor activities like skiing with your kids as you get older. It's not that you enjoy skiing more than anything else, but the vision is more about time together that will generate family closeness and memories. Envision laughing together and building memories you can savor for years to come. This, if you make it real enough for you, could be reason enough to forego the unhealthful practices and undergo the disciplines required to have the vision come to pass.

Imagination

Imagination is vital to keeping your vision in "sight." Imagination is God given. The ancients used their imagination to "see" reality that didn't yet exist. But on the strength of God-energized imagination, they acted as if it was a reality. It just needed to be brought to the physical realm. I've heard that Einstein imagined what it would be like to travel on a light beam, then imagined someone else traveling on one going the opposite direction, giving rise to his theory of relativity.

There came a time in my cancer journey when I was admitted into the hospital with highly elevated liver enzymes. It turns out one of the medications I was on to combat infection had actually had a negative effect on my liver: the situation was bad. Imagination was running amuck during that time. Here is something I wrote in the middle of the night while at the hospital:

"My oncologist showed up at 1:40 AM. He is obviously concerned since my fever continues to be elevated and/or rise in spite of the antibiotics. For me, I find there is much to ponder and most of it does not contribute to peacefulness.

It's amazing how easily I can let the thoughts and fears run rampant. Many would say this is "normal" in the sense of "who wouldn't be concerned?" But I'm questioning why that's normal. What is this predisposition to default to this? For me, obviously, it has to do with history. In other words, many things have happened in my life that I would have preferred not happening. I have been disappointed many times and know that life is like that. On the other hand, I am reminded of that saying which goes something like "I have experienced many frightening situations- most of which never really happened." My imagination has caused me to "experience" so many hard things that never actually came to pass. I just let myself go there.

That's where I find myself currently at 5:00 AM. I have determined to arrest the negative thoughts and "what-ifs" and replace them with prayer and affirmations. Like the fears, these may not actually pan out either, but I guarantee my experience is different energizing those thoughts. I'll reserve the energy squandered to fearful imagination in order to marshal the appropriate response once we figure out what's up. Imagination is a wonderful God given tool, and I suggest that in and of itself is neutral. I can determine what it fuels."

Yes, imagination is always going, and the main choice we have is in directing it.

I have worked with many men and women who struggle with sexual addiction. These addictive behaviors provide a temporary sense of control, relief, and pleasure, and imagination is a large part of the delusion. But imagination can be used positively as well as negatively. Why not use imagination to see a real relationship that is more fulfilling than a fantasy?

A compelling vision for calling a sexual addict through the painful steps of transformation is a totally satisfying, gratifying, and intimate relationship with the right person. This is a much more powerful motivator than guilt-laden self-talk like, "I shouldn't do this" or "This is a shameful sin." If you dare to imagine a healthy, loving, and intimate relationship and to believe it is possible, and you see the addiction as a hindrance to the vision, the means for getting there will probably be grasped and sustained. The vision becomes big enough to push people to do what they would rather not do; including getting whatever help they need to get them through confession, repentance, and accountability.

With an imaginative vision clearly in view, we can throw ourselves fully on the grace of God which is our only real possibility for true freedom. I am fully aware that most addictive behavior is anything but rational. But I have also found that until people have a persuasive vision for *why* they want to change, the pattern won't be broken.

Whatever the struggle, it can be viewed as two attractive choices. Yes, there is attraction for the behavior that is keeping me stuck. But I like the attraction to an alternative, healthy choice even better. So, since my chooser is perfect and I have a choice between temporary relief and long-lasting joy, I am more inclined to choose the latter. The other element that helps this choice is having a clear awareness of the consequences of both choices. Each choice comes with payoffs and prices. Weighing them honestly and counting the cost and rewards for each will help tremendously to make the right one.

Obviously, in every moment of decision we are presented with a choice. As we contemplate the choices before us, standing in the present moment, we can make the decision from one of two perspectives. We can make the choice in the moment based on a future worth having, or we can make the choice based on the past. A choice based on the past can be driven by fear of wanting to avoid a breakdown, fear that nothing will change or fear of being inadequate to rise above the temptation. And, what about the hauntings of our choice not working out the way we hope because at times in the past it didn't work out? When fear of the past is the driver, it shuts down going to God again in faith and opening a possibility for things to be different this time around. It's as if every new event is only looked at through the perspective of the past and we decide how the future will be based on that evidence alone.

A choice based on a future hope can generate much more energy. Faith, hope, and love are the pillars of life. Hope for a God-ordained future can carry us through many trials, temptations, and setbacks.

Todd is a man who is on a valiant mission to rescue his marriage. Unfortunately, the mission became necessary because Todd sabotaged the relationship himself. He betrayed his wife and for years sowed neglect and nonphysical abuse. His encounter with God at the Impact Training brought him to repentance and fanned his desire for God to redeem his marriage. It happened because Todd caught a vision of a future worth having and a passion to leave a legacy that would bless his wife and children.

Upon returning home from the training, Todd began the process of repenting, repairing, restoring, and reclaiming. The years of sowing destruction had a deeply negative effect and impact. As of this writing

Todd's wife has not been persuaded that their marriage is worth the risk of trusting Todd again.

I have seen many people throw in the towel at this point and say, "Well, I have done all I can." Not Todd. As we talked, he explained that he is committed and will do what it takes. When I asked what keeps him going, his answer was twofold. First, he recognizes that he the primary reason for the disintegration of the relationship. In a spirit of humility, he is sowing differently now and trusting in God to bring about the different fruit. Second, he attributes his energy and sustenance to his vision for a healthy relationship. He is making choices in the present from a hopeful future, not a failed past. If he was solely focusing on the past, he would be a guilt-ridden, cautious man rather than the energetically loving man he is today.

Where Are You Coming *From?*

When we begin to consider the vision we will set before us as our North Star, the context we operate *from* makes a tremendous difference. When most of us consider what is possible for us in the future we often reference the past in some way. Think about it: When you consider what is possible for you, don't you automatically scan through references from the past to identify what you're good at or not good at with statements like, "I've been able to accomplish such and such before, I can do it again" or "I tried that before and it didn't go well; I'm just not good at such and such." If the past is the context we access to determine what's possible, and then we operate *from* that context in the present, we can pretty much guess what our future will be. Our future becomes some variation of the past: the words *more, better,* or *different* all have the past as a point of reference. More than I already have, better than I already have, different than I already have. When we look to the future *from* this orientation, the unprecedented future is not one we commit to. We only commit to some modification of something we've already had. In this way the past is the framework within which we paint our future.

Hence, when I consider what kind of relationship I can have with my wife, I'm drawn to the options of better than we've had, more than we've had, and different than we've had. This is not to say it's good or bad; it's just not *unprecedented*: new, unparalleled, exceptional, and extraordinary.

Operating from the context of the future gives rise to possibilities never before considered or engaged because we have nothing in our past that informs us it's possible for us. "Up until now" and "from now on" are resourceful statements to move us into unprecedented territory. The Scripture teaches that with God all things are possible. I assert that to access and stand for things we currently see as impossible necessitates that we disengage from the past as a jump off point for our future. Instead of an incremental step we can take a quantum leap and imagine a future that, based on evidence from the past, we may think is impossible for us. We can envision something we've never even come close to having and rely on God that it is possible, not because we've had it before, but because it's a declaration of faith.

Once we fully develop the picture of an unprecedented future we then begin to act in the *present* in ways that are congruent with that future vision. For example, in my coaching I sometimes ask, "If you were already intimate with your husband, how would you relate to him right now? How would you talk to him, be with him, share with him?" Too often people allow what they've had or currently have to set the frame or context for what is possible or impossible in their future. I call this *coming from* the past.

Envision yourself fully living in an unprecedented future. Allow yourself to experience it so it feels real and palatable. What's it like to live this way? How are you relating, how does it feel, how are you choosing? Then come back to the present moment and act congruently with that future. If it's about how you relate, it doesn't matter what others in the relationship are doing. You are making your choices *now* consistent with a future that you say is important, that you desire, and that you're standing for.

In addition to being more resourceful for taking on new ways of being, coming from the future can be useful to transform current breakdowns. When in the midst of a tough time in life you can imagine looking back on this present moment three months from now, or even thirty years from now. What will you have learned by then? How will this current challenge contribute to your overall character and wisdom when integrated with the other lessons and experiences of life?

Isn't this idea just as valid as any other conversation we may be having about our current circumstance?

Calibrating Where We Are Versus Where We're Committed to Be

Coming from the future is not some kind of pixie dust that magically transforms the present in and of itself. It is an important element, but there is a distinction between envisioning a future worth having (and living in the present *from* that future) and living in fantasy. The difference lies in how we live in the present and give ourselves in order to have it turn out. When we set a vision for the future, what crystallizes very quickly is what's missing between where we are and where we want to be. The more real the vision, the clearer the disparity.

The present then becomes a place where I contribute in order to bring about the envisioned future. I call this calibrating, and three questions must be asked.

1. What's the reality?

This is where you calibrate what's happening now, become aware of the disparity, and basically notice where you are in relation to the declared future.

2. What's missing?

Not *in* me, as in what's wrong with me, but what am I not *giving* in order to have my vision turn out.

3. What's next?

Meaning: What can I give now that will bring the vision to which I'm committed into reality?

We are in a constant dance with these questions, continuously calibrating, assessing, shifting, and failing our way towards our vision.

When we come from the future as a context, we will see new possibilities because the future is unfettered from the past. We will dare great things because we don't need evidence from the past that it's possible. We are free to invent a future we never considered before and allow God to transform us into the person required to live it out.

So, vision is a big part of allowing God the access He needs to transform us. Vision will move us to give up our terms and accept His. I believe real change will never happen until we allow the Lord to fully expose our inner petulant child who constantly demands life be lived on our terms, without responsibility and consequences.

Surrender

Surrendering to what *really is* is vital to the transformation process. Surrender has a way of sobering us up and giving us the best chance to deal effectively with our problems. It's at the point of surrender we can begin to see the true choices we need to make. I dare say that up to that point all choices that present themselves will not get to the heart of the problem. It is a Band-Aid approach to a cancer within.

This kind of surrender doesn't mean throwing in the proverbial towel. It's the beginning of true freedom. When one surrenders to reality and stops pretending things aren't what they really are in an effort to stay the chaos of their world, the way to proceed becomes clearer.

When I surrendered to the reality I had cancer in the sense I'm talking about, and gave up my complaint that it shouldn't be the way it was, that I shouldn't have it, that it wasn't fair, etc. I began asking: "Now what? What can I choose, right now, that will provide the biggest possibility to me having the future I say I want? What is within my ability to choose that will be congruent with that future vision?"

Out of those questions came clarity about undergoing treatments I'd rather not, and eating in ways I'd rather not, and exercising at times I'd rather not.

When a swimmer caught in riptide surrenders to the reality that he can't overcome the current, only then can he see clearly what must be done to get back to shore. In the same way that surrendering to the riptide is the means to a safe return to shore; surrendering to the reality of our situations is the means to transforming our lives. It may seem like certain death at first, allowing yourself to be swept further from shore. And it will also mean a longer swim once you drift out of the riptide's grip. But in life as well as riptides, sometimes you have to go out of your way to reach your goal.

There is another aspect of surrender which redirects wasted energy to achieve more effective change. Energy useful in our transformation is wasted when it is used trying to control life and make it turn out the way we want. But pouring our energy into the struggle of transformation, while acknowledging that the effort may be painful and costly, will help get us where God wants us to be.

The story is told of a practice Samurai warriors engaged in before a battle.[71] The practice was referred to as dying before going into battle. The practice involved the warriors acknowledging the prospect and probability that they could die in the battle. Until they acknowledged this reality, the warriors tended to fight defensively and with hesitancy. The defensive posture, adopted to prevent injury or death, resulted in ineffectiveness and often brought about the very outcome they feared. But when they surrendered to the possibility of dying, the net result was a nothing-to-lose attitude which motivated them to fight with abandon and win many victories against overwhelming odds.

We face battles and difficulties too. We know that life won't always turn out exactly as we prefer and people and situations won't always match up with our expectations. When we resist these realities we are like the tentative Samurai warrior who just wants to avoid getting hurt. But when we acknowledge our readiness to "die" by accepting that life won't turn always out the way we prefer, we are free to divert our energy to the process of vision and creativity.

Strength in Weakness

Misapplied resistance paradoxically saps strength from us while surrender invites potency: the power of God! Think about it this way. In Romans 7, Paul says he is a slave of sin in the sense that "the good I want to do I do not and the evil I do not want to do, that I do."[72] This is a type of surrender. He realizes he has this sinful nature living in him. As he acknowledges his weakness, he also declares his victory in Christ when he exclaims, "O, wretched man that I am, Who will save me from this body of death? Thank God through Jesus Christ our Lord!" Paul evidently understood paradox!

He also understood that his only hope to overcome his wretchedness was the transformative power of Jesus Christ. Bending the knee and surrendering to Him is the only possibility for salvation and transformation. In 2 Corinthians, Paul expands on a concept that doesn't compute to the modern, self-sufficient American mind, another of God's mysterious paradoxes.

Namely, His strength is perfected in weakness. In 2 Corinthians 12:9-10 Paul states:

"And He has said to me, 'My grace is sufficient for you, for power is perfected in weakness.' Most gladly, therefore, I will rather boast about my weaknesses, so that the power of Christ may dwell in me. Therefore I am well content with weaknesses, with insults, with distresses, with persecutions, with difficulties, for Christ's sake; for when I am weak, then I am strong" (NASU).

We humans can easily fool ourselves into thinking we can handle life on our own. When all appears well, it's easier to continue this lie. Calamity, infirmity, and weakness bring us back to reality. It's again paradoxical that when we feel strong in ourselves we actually undermine our true strength, which comes from being connected to and utterly dependent upon God.[73]

Jamieson, Fausset, and Brown comment on this verse: "The Lord more needs our weakness than our strength: our strength is often His rival; our weakness, His servant, drawing on His resources, and showing forth His glory. Man's extremity is God's opportunity; man's security, Satan's opportunity. God's way is not to take His children out of, but to give them strength to bear up against trial (John 17:15)."[74]

As a result, we hear Paul saying, "Most gladly, therefore, I will rather boast about my weaknesses." He literally embraces and surrenders to his weakness and "thorns" for the sake of finding his true strength and purpose.

So we really don't have to arrive in order to minister!

When we intimately know our weakness and persevere through our trials, we become much more effective, empathetic, and energized in serving others.

I have seen many of these dynamics relegated to the passive category of "God will do it all" if I only pray and wait on Him. This view reduces our responsibility to a level that stunts change. Don't get me wrong; I believe that prayer is essential. But after the prayers it takes congruent action to see things happen. I believe this is yet another area where reality is misunderstood and displays some element of paradox.

Let's delve into this question and try to untangle the truth from the myth. Of course, as with everything else offered in this book, I only offer the truth as I have seen it in regard to the effectiveness of bringing about transformation.

SEVENTEEN

God's Role, Your Role

Dear friends, now we are children of God, and what we will be has not yet been made known. But we know that when he appears, we shall be like him, for we shall see him as he is. *Everyone who has this hope in him purifies himself*, just as he is pure.

1 John 3:2-3 NIV (Emphasis Mine)

Do-it-yourself sanctity is an oxymoron.

Peter Kreeft

Who Is It Up To?

There has been a long-running debate in the Christian community regarding who effects change. The Bible is very clear that humanity is helpless to bring about the kind of regeneration that God, through faith in Christ and the power of His Holy Spirit, brings about. But once we are saved, much is still left up to us. If not, why are we commanded to obey? Why are we asked to repent when we disobey? Could it be that the changing into new views and feelings is up to us? Read Romans 12:2 again: "Be transformed by the renewing of your mind." Who is being asked to act here? The implication of us asserting our authority is clear. The choice to implement change is *ours*.

The word used in 1 John 3 for "purify" means to consecrate. Consecrate means to set ourselves apart. *We* are to set ourselves apart, as we participate in God's sanctifying, transforming work. Over and over again the commands are clear: put on the new self; turn away from sinful ways; put on the mind of Christ; etc. We *can't* sanctify ourselves without God, and He *won't* sanctify us without our participation.

I concur with the following view that we as Christians have a secondary role in what we refer to as sanctification:

> Sanctification is defined as 'a progressive work of God and man that makes us more and more free from sin and like Christ in our actual lives'[75]

Sanctification is a joint venture between God and us. The roles that God plays and we play in sanctification are by no means equal, yet we cooperate with God in ways that are appropriate to our status as God's creatures. All the moral commands of the New Testament emphasize the role that we play in sanctification. If our will wasn't involved in the process, God would not have needed to command us to act in certain ways. Our role in sanctification is both a passive role in which we depend on God to sanctify us and an active one in which we strive to obey God and take steps that will further our sanctification.

Primarily, our role is passive. We are encouraged to trust God and ask Him to sanctify us. Paul tells us, "Yield yourselves to God as men who have been brought from death to life" (Romans 6:13), and he says to the Roman Church, "Present your bodies as a living sacrifice, holy and acceptable to God" (Romans 12:1). Paul is clear that we depend on the Holy Spirit's work to grow in sanctification, because he says, "If by the spirit you put to death the deeds of the body you will live" (Romans 8:13).

One great misconception about sanctification in the church today is that our passive role (the idea of yielding to God and trusting him to work in us) is the only component. Many times the idea of our active responsibility in our own sanctification is met with fear and accusation. The popular phrase, "Let go and let God," is used to summarize how to live the Christian life. However, this is a tragic distortion of the doctrine of sanctification.

The active role which we are called to play is indicated in Romans 8:13, where Paul writes, "If by the Spirit you put to death the deeds of the body, you will live." Here Paul acknowledges that it is "by the Spirit" that we are able to be sanctified. But he also says *we* must do it! The Holy Spirit is not the one commanded to put to death the deeds of the flesh; Christians are! Similarly, Paul tells the Philippians, "Therefore my beloved, as you have always obeyed, so now, not only as in my presence but much more in my absence, work out your own salvation with fear and trembling; for God is at work in you, both to will and to work for his good pleasure" (Philippians 2:12-13). Paul encourages them to obey even more than they did when he was present. Only through obedience can we "work out" the further realization of the benefits of salvation in our Christian lives.[76]

God's immanence, the reality that He resides within us, gives surety that we are part of the process, albeit under His power. It's clear that if we don't say "Yes, Lord" the work does not take place. Perhaps this is no more beautifully portrayed than in Mary's response to the angel's announcement that she was to conceive the Christ: "Be it done to me according to your word" (Luke 1:38). What a poignant example of Christ being "formed" in someone!

At the same time, our Lord is not a tyrant. He pursues and persuades and calls. Our God is also transcendent, wholly apart from His creation. He is the King of heaven, earth, and the universe. From that place of reign He commands us and lovingly awaits the response from our freewill.

Dr. Gerald May, in his book *Addiction and Grace,* explains it this way: "Obviously, we cannot 'conduct' spiritual growth. At bottom, it is God's work. It is grace. But neither is it something we can be quietistic about. The immanence of God involves us of necessity, and the transcendence of God calls forth a response from our freewill."

Throughout His dealings with people in the Scriptures, we see God moving at times in sovereignty and at other times waiting on His people to move forward in faith. Let's consider an example that may shed some light on how our roles and God's role may change.

My former pastor, Doug Richardson, gave a message about the exodus of Israel from Egypt and the subsequent inheritance of the Promised Land that illuminates this well.

As you recall, the Jews found themselves in captivity to Egypt, the most powerful kingdom on earth at the time. Four hundred years earlier

Jacob and his family had migrated to Egypt, where Joseph was second in command, to survive a famine in their homeland. Egypt, at first, was a place of protection for Israel. There came a time when the stronghold of protection became a prison.

In the same way, our humanly devised strategies are a means to protect ourselves, yet they ensnare us and keep us stuck in repeating old patterns. The Jews were powerless to extricate themselves from the powerful forces that held them. It took God's sovereign intervention through a deliverer—Moses—to bring them from bondage to freedom. God took them from the living death they were surviving to the possibility of the fullness of life that freedom brings.

The Jews played a passive role in their deliverance from Egypt. They had only to respond to God's deliverance by packing up their spoils and following His lead. God moved by His mighty hand and amazing miracles and set them free! God's people were primarily grateful spectators during the ten plagues and the parting of the Red Sea and the destruction of Pharaoh's army and the provision of manna from heaven.

Then God began to deal with Israel differently. As they sojourned to their Promised Land, God, while never withdrawing His hand or abandoning them to fend for themselves, required a different level of participation from them. He still made it clear the He would fight the battles, but they had to play a more active role. They had to actively confront their own fears, enter the conflict, and take the land God had already given to them!

God didn't zap the Canaanites with a lightning bolt so the Israelites could move in uncontested. No, He called His people to risk and to fight, and some of them died in the process. Yet the outcome was clear: The land was theirs for the taking. He called them to a new level of trust, maturity, and responsibility in the process of claiming their inheritance.

I see our journey of transformation similar to the Jews passage from Egypt to the Promised Land. Until we are released from bondage into freedom and delivered from death into life by God's sovereign act, we are hopelessly imprisoned in the stronghold of our sin. Our role at this stage is simply to respond to Christ's offer.

However, as we mature and begin to move into our inheritance, God requires a different level of participation. He calls us to actually enter battles we would rather avoid, ones that seem insurmountable and feel risky. It seems He will not just unilaterally win them while we watch, mouths agape, His marvelous miracle-working power. We want the full freedom He offers without paying the price required and certainly without having to fight for it.

Frederick Douglas describes the fight for reform (change) this way:

> Let me give you a word on the philosophy of reform. The whole history of the progress of human liberty shows that all concessions yet made to her august claims have been born of earnest struggle. The conflict has been exciting, agitating, all absorbing, and for the time being, putting all other tumults to silence. It must do this or it does nothing. If there is no struggle there is no progress. Those who profess to favor freedom, and yet depreciate agitation are men who want crops without plowing up the ground. They want rain without thunder and lightning. They want the ocean without the awful roar of its many waters. This struggle may be a moral one; or it may be a physical one; or it may be both moral and physical; but it must be a struggle. Power concedes nothing without a demand. It never did and it never will. Find out just what people will submit to and you have found the exact amount of injustice and wrong which will be imposed upon them; and these will continue until they are resisted with either words or blows, or with both. The limits of tyrants are prescribed by the endurance of those whom they oppress.[77]

We *do* have a role; that is clear. So why are people so reluctant to accept responsibility for this role when it's apparent that responsible action gives us the most freedom?

The opposite of responsibility is victim-hood, the sense that things are beyond your ability to command. In a sense, when we're victimized, we have no choice in the matter.

I believe that our resistance to exercise the full power of choice given to us by God is few-fold.

First, if we acknowledge that we have a choice of actions in all life situations, then we become accountable for the state our life is in. We can no longer blame others for the shape of our life. Yes, some awful things happen to us. Life gives us lemons, but we have the choice of making lemonade of our difficulties or becoming soured by life.

Second, if God gives us choices, we must relinquish the idea that we are right about how bad we've had it instead of eliciting the sympathy we crave for our plight.

Third, it just plain feels good to be able to blame someone else for how bad our life is. At the same time it temporarily relieves us of the ache of dealing with how wrongly we were treated by turning that energy into blaming. The problem is that here can be no freedom without responsibility. And to most people, true freedom is frightening.

Peter Koestenbaum writes, "Some people are permanently angry or in a constant state of feeling sorry for themselves. The explanation? It's a common way to avoid the anxiety of freedom, the fear of responsibility, the resistance against owning one's choices. The result? It keeps them infantilized forever, and none of the rewards of mature leadership will be available to them."[78]

In many ways we are Peter Pans, lost boys and girls living in Never-Never Land singing, "I won't grow up"! And when that is what we *will*, that is what we'll *have*.

We Choose What We Want.

One of the most confronting realities in life is personally *owning* that we have designed our lives to be the way they are. I am talking about acknowledging and realizing that we have what we want, even though we recognize in our more clear-headed moments that what we have stinks. What incredible freedom and what sobering responsibility comes with the idea that we really are co-architects with God in constructing our lives!

This is an idea that needs careful exploration and consideration, because what I am *not* saying is that we are responsible for everything that happens to us. We are, however, fully responsible for what we *do with* and what happens to us and for perpetuating the effects of these happenings. During the Impact Training, we thoroughly explore how we frame communication to others. How we present anything to another person is not an accident. I believe just about everything we do is "purposed." This purpose points to what we want to elicit from the person we're interacting with. This desired response affects what we say and how we say it.

For example, during an exercise in the training, how we tell others the "story" of our lives is explored (the narrative we tell others regarding how our lives became the way they are). Essentially, we frame our stories in order to persuade people that we are justified in having the limitations we do, all the while drawing sympathy for our plight. We are very accomplished at doing this, and it's with great finesse that we communicate to gain the desired response. It's manipulation. The "victim" in us is especially good at this.

The reasons we give may be psychological, emotional, or circumstantial. But the bottom line is that we are the way we are and act the way we act because something outside ourselves caused it. We use our persuasive stories to influence our listeners and elicit the response that best serves us in the moment. I have used this method to minimize anger I may have sparked in my wife by certain actions. I've told her a true story but with a twist that will soften her response. It may not be evil, but it is manipulative. It's just another attempt on my part not to feel pain or pay consequences. When we come to understand that we craft our tales to achieve a desired outcome, we can begin to allow God to reveal our heart's desire to get by as often as possible without having to change.

While this storytelling gift is often misused, it also offers an incredible possibility for freedom from past horrific events. What our training participants come to realize is that, although they cannot alter past events, they *can* in fact alter the effect these events have on them. In other words, as creatures with the God-given power to chose, we have the ability to interpret what kind of power or control anything that has happened to us holds over us. Put yet another way, we have the ability to reframe what these past events mean.

For example, a child may decide that he is the cause of his parents' fighting and painful divorce. Interpreting his home this way, he comes to believe he is unlovable or bad or wrong or unwanted. This conclusion, invented by a child and left unchallenged, traps him as an adult in a prison of his own making. This person has the freedom to reinterpret and reframe his faulty belief. This is a fundamental component of our makeup. We are free to choose the interpretation and we are commanded to choose one that leads to life (Deuteronomy 30:19).

This is why it's imperative that we surround ourselves with people who are committed to challenge our natural disposition toward making life easier by blaming. If we are only committed to comfort, we will inevitably find ourselves in apathy, compromise, and a sense of helplessness. As a result, we will gather around us co-conspirators who allow us to continue in our victim-hood rather than friends whose "wounds are faithful" (Proverbs 27:6). We really do have a big say in the composition of our life. We have what we want because we have the God-given ability to choose.

St. Augustine writes that he didn't have the grace he needed to overcome his temptations because he didn't really want it fully with his whole heart.[79] In the Eighth Book of *The Confessions of St. Augustine,* he says, "I still did not reach or touch or grasp the goal, because I hesitated to die to death and live to life." In other words, at some level he liked the life he had, even its struggles, more than what he perceived it would cost him to die to his chosen sin. He demonstrated this ambivalence by crying out, "Lord, give me chastity... but not yet."

Modern speech has lost some of the words that imply responsibility for the state of our obedience. One of them is "temperance," otherwise known as self-control. It is one of the fruits of the Spirit (Galatians 5:23). The Greek word is *engkrateia,* meaning self-government.[80] It indicates being strong in a thing, mastering something. People were said to be intemperate when they were swayed or controlled by their desires in regard to appetite or sensual matters.

Clearly, temperance entails our freedom through Christ to obey (Romans 13:14). The question is do we want to? I assert that we as Christians choose how we live, how much freedom from sin we experience, how much love we exhibit in our relationships, and so on.

People who do whatever their appetites dictate are not really free. They are in a sense slaves to their desires. It takes real freedom to exhibit self-control, to say no to our impulses. If we are not living as saints, it is because we choose not to live as saints.

The prophet Jeremiah wrote, "You will seek me and find me when you seek me with all your heart" (Jeremiah 29:13 NIV). There are abundant examples in the Bible and church history of God's children seeking Him wholeheartedly and finding Him. When we cast ourselves entirely upon His mercy we find the grace we need. When we come to Him in our weakness He makes up what we lack. A broken and contrite heart He will not turn away (Psalm 51:17).

Along with our freedom comes the possibility to become a bond-slave to God and partner with Him in His commitment to transform us. As C.S. Lewis says, "I was not born to be free. I was born to adore and obey." Mary's response to the Word of the Lord in Luke 1 contains a beautiful picture of the mysterious interweaving of God's sovereign power with our participation. Her reply was simple and yet profound: "May it be done to me according to your word" (v. 38). I believe that Mary's determination came from purity of heart. Soren Kierkegaard writes, "Purity of heart is to will one thing."

What if Mary's response would have been double-minded, hesitant, equivocating? How much of God's working is impeded when we fail to sell out to His call to have Christ formed in us? Mary's full statement in Luke 1:38 reveals her full commitment: "Behold, the bondslave of the Lord; may it be done to me according to your word" (NASU).

Mary obviously didn't consider her life to be her own. She was God's bondslave, sold out to Him. *True* freedom is another paradox: Freedom is achieved by selling out to God as His bondslave. Only through radical surrender can Christ be fully formed in us. Mary's surrender to God is exactly what is required from us to experience the transformation we desire. Conformity to the image of Christ will take purity of heart: willing transformation with all we are and surrendering to His working in us.

When we respond with a simple, complete, pure of heart declaration of commitment—"Let it be done," God will bring forth our transformation into the image of His Son. "For nothing will be impossible with God" (Luke 1:37-38 NASU). It's when we are ambivalent about commitment that change is slow to occur.

Augustine explores this ambivalence in *The Confessions*. He points out that when the will fully intends a command, there is response. When there is no response, we may assume that the command is not given with the full will. Why does this happen? Because there are two wills in us and neither by itself is the whole will.[81]

By God's grace we have authority over our will. Choosing falls under our authority. This is yet another paradox, because I am not saying we can *will* to become saints by ourselves; [82] I am saying that *without us willing* it, God won't come and enable us by His Spirit to overcome what needs to overcome so that it happens. He does not override our freewill. At the same time, without God's grace we don't even have the fortitude to will with our entire will.

Getting on the road to transformation is only possible as God calls us and we respond. Once we do respond the journey of life takes on a whole new meaning. Answering that call also demands a constant willingness to hold to the narrow road.

EIGHTEEN

Moving from Glory to Glory

*But we all, with unveiled face, beholding as in a mirror the glory of
the Lord, are being transformed into the same image from glory to
glory, just as by the Spirit of the Lord.*

2 Corinthians 3:18 (NKJV)

The Path of Transformation

Paul describes the process of transformation into Christ's image as
"moving from glory to glory" (2 Corinthians 3:18 NKJV). The reality of
what this process entails makes me think of perseverance. I know that
moving from glory to glory is a journey. The verse indicates movement
and implies a willingness to stay on the path. I love the definition of
perseverance found in Webster's 1828 Dictionary: "Continuing in a state
of grace until reaching a state of glory."

Moving from glory to glory not only takes perseverance, it involves
living in a state of grace toward others and ourselves. Perseverance entails
giving each other and ourselves unmerited favor that springs not from
what we deserve but from love. It certainly takes grace to move forward
at all. It's grace that keeps us alive and grace that keeps hope alive in
us. Grace is unmerited favor, and not something we deserve. In fact, it's
God's mercy that stays the judgment we do deserve.

Perseverance is closely affiliated with the old English word
longsuffering, also found in the King James Bible. Love is longsuffering.
Love requires passion, and passion comes from the Latin word *passio*, from
patior, to suffer.[83] In Acts 1:3, Jesus' death is referred to as His *passion*
(Greek *pathein*). Any reflection of life and relationship clearly shows that
to passionately love life and others ensures a great dose of suffering.

Traveling versus Arriving

One of our greatest frustrations is our inability to "arrive" at complete change. Permanent change, constant happiness, and lasting victory seem just out of our reach. As a result, many of us fall into an all-or-nothing mindset. We say, "I haven't arrived and I haven't really gotten anywhere. I have struggled for so long, I must be all bad." This mindset is incapable or unwilling to embrace life's paradox. This paradox is found in aspects of ourselves and our experience of life. Paradox can certainly impact how we construe our circumstances, our life, and ourselves.

One of my favorite books is the great novel, *The Brothers Karamazov* by Fyodor Dostoevsky. One of the characters, Father Zosima, exhorts a distraught mother who has just lost a child. His statement is a brilliant and profound example of embracing God's call to live a life of love and how our attitude towards life enables us to persevere. Father Zosima says:

> If you do not attain happiness, always remember that you are on a good path, and try not to leave it... Never be frightened at your own faintheartedness in attaining love, and meanwhile do not even be very frightened by your own bad acts. I am sorry that I cannot say anything more comforting, for active love is a harsh and fearful thing compared with love in dreams. Love in dreams thirsts for immediate action, quickly performed, and with everyone watching. Indeed, it will go as far as the giving even of one's life, provided it does not take long but is soon over, as on stage, and everyone is looking on and praising. Whereas active love is labor and perseverance, and for some people, perhaps, a whole science. But I predict that even in that very moment when you see with horror that despite all your efforts, you not only have not come nearer your goal but seem to have gotten farther from it, at that very moment - I predict this to you - you will suddenly reach your goal and will clearly behold over you the wonder - working power of the Lord, who all the while has been loving you, and all the while has been mysteriously guiding you.

It often feels in our journey like we are not getting anywhere. In fact, many times it seems the more we work at something, the farther away we appear to be. But when we move in confidence that He will redeem and transform us, and relinquish the illusion of how we think it's supposed to look, we will prevail.

Sometimes, in order to get closer to our destination, we must temporarily move away from it. There is the analogy (C.S. Lewis *The Four Loves* pg. 15) about a person trying to get home who comes to the precipice of a sheer cliff which is, in space, very close to his destination. However, he cannot reach his home from that precipice; in order to find a safe path he must temporarily move farther away from what seems so close. Even if it seems like you are going out of your way, if you are on God's path, you are still moving from glory to glory.

I would like now to return to the story of John. As I mentioned earlier, John was discouraged because he had so much more ground to take in his spiritual journey than what he had gained. His greatest desire was to be done with his struggles; his greatest frustration was that the end was nowhere in sight.

As John began to accept the reality that life was not going to turn out the way he thought it should, he began to re-channel his energy toward what really mattered to him. Instead of attempting to reach Christian perfection, he began concentrating on lovingly accepting his struggles and the struggles of others, use them as points of connection, and enter into true fellowship with others on the same journey.

This shift alone has altered his experience substantially. John still experiences frustration. But as he accepts the reality of his circumstances and stops insisting that his life shouldn't be this way, he can channel his energy into what matters most to him: love, connection, and intimacy, to name a few. And when he's hurting, he asks, "How can I use this hurt to become more vulnerable and intimate with others?"

John now recognizes that he is not stuck in who he is, and he consistently challenges long held notions that have limited what he could do and handle. As a result, he has seen his influence increase as he steps into new areas of leadership. He is regarded as an approachable man who loves and cares and can identify with others' struggles without judgment or cynicism.

John relates differently to his past experiences and no longer assigns them the meaning he invented as a child trying to survive. By changing his reaction cycle, which dictated how he related to others, John has altered many aggravating, recurring interchanges with people.

The events of his life, good and bad, are interpreted inside the bigger frame of his vision for loving God, his family, and others. In the next chapter, I will share a very practical example of how John transformed a hurt into a life-giving experience.

All of these on-going shifts are contributing to John's transformation, with the added benefit of him experiencing more joy and fulfillment than when he lived in resistance.

In Between and Not Yet

And even so, the changes don't come as fully or as quickly as we prefer. Don't you often feel like you are just "not quite there"? Like you see a possibility but are unable to fully grasp it, or you are again frustrated in achieving a change you've sought/fought after, or that once again you find yourself in a place where life just isn't turning out the way you hoped?

What if this is by design? There is a word that helps describe this blueprint: liminal. Liminal means: "threshold" or "in between". It is rarely used but captures a powerful truth: Transformation always happens in the liminal spaces. It is always in the "in between" times that we are most open to change. It's the "space" between what was and is yet to be. It is the caterpillar in the cocoon and not yet a butterfly. It is a space of uncertainty where you don't know what will yet be.

As Richard Rohr says, "Liminal space is a unique spiritual position where human beings hate to be but where the biblical God is always leading them… It is when you are in between your old comfort zone and any possible new answer…It is no fun. Think of Israel in the desert, Joseph in the pit, Jonah in the belly, the three Marys tending the tomb. Everything genuinely new emerges in some kind of liminal space."

Dare we say that the liminal space is also a place of pain? It seems that pain often leads us into this unique place where something new can emerge. Not necessarily physical, emotional or even psychological pain, although God can and does use those, but perhaps the type of pain that can exist when things are not as we think or wish they should be.

For many humans, the in between time is resisted and therefore they do not hold in- hold in to the tension present when there is uncertainty. Our culture demands immediate answers, immediate remedies, and immediate relief.

Many won't surrender to the reality that God is working a process in them and that He seems unfazed to leave things undone for long periods of time. God often does not give answers, or, if you will, bring us to a place of certainty. Jesus didn't answer many of the questions asked of Him here on earth. He often leaves us to struggle with not knowing. This tendency of our God can lead to mischief if we don't accept the many paradoxes we find ourselves in: we are sinners *and* saints, wounded *and* healed, in communion *and* lonely.

The resistance to the "in between" time can show up in many ways. In my work, transformation, people often find themselves frustrated that they haven't permanently changed. Because of their great need to come to an answer, after many attempts to change, they conclude that something is <u>really</u> wrong with them. What's most tragic about this is that they therefore disqualify themselves from being used. Until they are "fixed" or "healed" or in some way arrive they count themselves as less than, as not worthy. Rohr says, liminal "is when you have left the "tried and true" but have not yet been able to replace it with anything else."

Again, it is imperative to remember that transformation is a process, not linearly but a journey in the sense that it's ongoing, and only God decides when we arrive. Like the metal worker who knows the metal has been purified when he can clearly see his reflection in it, God won't stop purifying us until He sees Christ fully formed in us. He is committed to the process, are we? Or are we always giving ourselves a back door to sneak out?

Commitment: Closing the back door

The back door in a house is another way out when a fire or another emergency necessitates a quick exit. In the context of transformation, back doors are a hindrance, not a help. Transformation can only happen in the blazing crucible of God's refining fire. If we're always looking for a way out, the change we want will be delayed or arrested altogether.

We create back doors in our lives as an easy excuse for why something can't happen. I have known people who leave themselves a back door (or a fire escape) when it comes to walking through the heat of a difficult process. Their backdoor thinking may even sound spiritual and contain some truth: "Oh, I'm so unworthy" or "I'll never be perfect." Or the excuse may sound cynical: "Most marriages end in divorce, so why should we get married?" Continually justifying why something hasn't happened yet also creates back doors. It's a matter of focus. I can look at why something hasn't happened and list the reasons why. They will sound valid, make sense, and be convincing (to me and those within earshot).

A good friend of mine named Beth recently confessed that she has for several years kept the option open that she might leave her husband of thirteen years. She was tired of the dynamic that was replayed constantly in the marriage. But as a Christian, she never pulled the trigger to end the union believing it was wrong to. Metaphorically, however, Beth did have one foot in and one foot out of the back door. As long as she kept this door open, transformation in her marriage was impossible. The one-foot-out part allowed her to gather more evidence against her husband, and she found herself more disconnected, unhappy, and resentful.

Lacking full commitment, Beth never bothered to recognize and interrupt what she was contributing to the unhappy relationship. To her credit, Beth stayed in the marriage, but the back door she created always beckoned her toward the escape from the rigorous road of forgiveness, accountability, necessary confrontation, reconciliation, and others disciplines required to make marriages work.

In addition, my friend had her radar tuned to all the things her husband wasn't doing right, hoping to validate the way she saw it. To use an earlier phrase, she was "listening for" the things that lined up with her assumptions for why she shouldn't be happy. And since she is married to an imperfect man, she found plenty of evidence!

It wasn't until she closed that back door that Beth could face the reality of what needed to happen. Her unequivocal commitment to the marriage forced her to focus on the future hope instead of the unwanted past and present. This focus and commitment even impacted the nature of their conflicts. In the midst of a recent argument, Beth yelled out, "And I'm committed to you for the rest of my life!" This unexpected declaration in the midst of the argument completely diffused her husband. It stopped him cold and invited him to engage a different possibility and to look at their interchange from a different perspective. Each of them began to own their contribution to the upset.

Beth's new commitment also caused her to realize that she had contributed much to the unhappy arrangement. As she accounted for these contributions, repented to God and to her husband, shifted how she acted and responded, an amazing transformation happened: She "fell" radically in love with her husband again. He also began to respond to her, account for his actions, and change his behavior.

Closing the back door changes our focus. Instead of trying to justify the way things are, all the our struggles become fodder, fuel, and feedback for discovering what it takes to experience what we desire. In some respect it boils down to trying harder. Is the vision big enough and important enough to generate this attitude in us? Closing the back door allows no way out and is the epitome of commitment.

Without vision, nothing of value gets fully developed. It's vision that elicits promises and establishes a commitment, and commitment is the soil that brings forth fruit. Commitment is instrumental in transformation because it's the glue that holds us on task when the going gets tough. A definition of commitment used in the Impact Training is by Shearson Leahman:

"Commitment is what transforms a promise into reality; it is the words that speak boldly of your intentions, and the actions which speak louder than your words. Commitment is the stuff character is made of; the power to change the face of things. It is the daily triumph of integrity over skepticism."

Skepticism undermines our lives and relationships. After repeated efforts fail to bring desired results, skepticism appears an easier option. Skepticism leads to cynicism. The doubt exhibited by an attitude of cynicism weakens the wherewithal needed to change things. A cynic, according to Benjamin Zander, is "a passionate person who does not want to be disappointed again."[84] When we commit to act despite the knowledge that we'll be disappointed again, and passionately stand for future hope, new possibilities come into view that could not be seen when skeptical, cynical reservation is in full operation.

Doubt opens up double-mindedness, and a "double-minded man is unstable in all his ways" (James 1:8). Being double-minded means our vision is divided. Instead of all our energy being focused on the outcome, some of it is diverted to justifying, cynicism, and surviving, dissipating our power. Being double-minded leads to double vision and brings *division* both internally and within the framework of what is being undertaken. Instead of a singular focus, which brings laser power to bear on our situation, double-mindedness is ineffective. Everything becomes blurred.

I believe part of our reluctance to make commitments is because, when we commit, we become vulnerable. Why? Because we are declaring that something is going to happen and we are on the line for the results, not just our intentions. When someone finally commits to act and puts it out there for everyone to see, his credibility is much more at stake than when he makes a silent, internal resolution.

You become accountable when you express a commitment. It's not that someone is holding you accountable, but rather you are accountable because others *know* about what you have committed to do. And if you fail to follow through, they will know that too when they ask you point blank, "So how's it going with...?"

Commitment also produces vulnerability because it stirs up questions of our adequacy. Can I really make this turn out? Am I really committed no matter what? Questions like this leave you with the realization that there is more to the equation than just you.

Without commitment, failure is almost assured. I think about people who are reluctant to get married and prefer to "test drive" their relationship, also called living together. I've worked with people in this situation who actually say to me they are committed.

"Committed to what?" is usually my question.

"The relationship," they respond.

"Then why not get married?"

"Because it's only a piece of paper."

"If it's only a piece of paper, then why not execute it?"

On and on it goes, and while the arguments are ridiculous, the point is clear: The *real* commitment being articulated is, "I'll stay with you as long as I feel good about it."

This relationship is undermined from the beginning. In every relationship there are days when we may not feel like living out our commitment. When one or both don't feel good about the relationship, without commitment, one or both of us may jump ship or compromise and settle. Commitment to each other and to the Lord is what sees us through times when good feelings aren't there.

Of course, just because two people commit marriage is no guarantee they will stay together. But this commitment is declared in a very public way and there are legal constraints added as well. Even though our society has developed no-fault divorce or dissolution of marriage, the dissolution of the marriage commitment is much more difficult than simply moving out.

For Christian couples not living together, the back door for their behavior may be expectation of a "burning bush" sign from God that they should marry. While I strongly advocate careful selection, prayer, and counseling prior to getting married, there comes a time when the final step feels like a leap into the unknown. It's normal for individuals to question, "Will our marriage make it?" and "Will God come through for us?"

There are two primary directional systems we can access when deciding which way to go in our situations. One I call our psychology: what we like or don't like, how we think life should be, what we feel at the time, and other subjective dynamics. The other directional option is vision. In this realm reside such qualities as promise, request, commitment, and declaration.

Consider Jesus' struggle in the Garden of Gethsemane. There, contemplating what would be required of Him to carry out His commitment to redeem the world, He engaged in an epic battle of will. His psychology pointed Him in one direction: He didn't like the prospect of the cross, He didn't feel good as He considered it, He preferred another way as evidenced by His request (three times!) to have this cup pass.

In the end, He subordinated His psychology to His vision. He didn't try to change how He felt about the cross or pretend He was looking forward to it. He deemed these less important than His vision for the future to which He was committed: reunion with us, regaining His potential bride.

Furthermore, He channeled all the energy His suffering stirred up to fulfill His vision. His death is referred to as the Passion. He became truly passionate about fulfilling His vision!

Here is a simple chart that contrasts our psychology with our vision. While the psychology was intact, Jesus subordinated it to His vision.

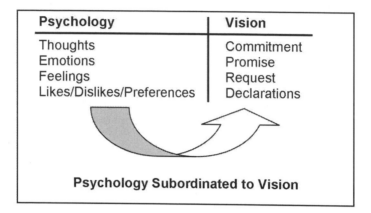

Psychology	Vision
Thoughts	Commitment
Emotions	Promise
Feelings	Request
Likes/Dislikes/Preferences	Declarations

Psychology Subordinated to Vision

If we allow our psychology to drive us, our lives will be aimless because we act on the whim of changing thoughts, likes, dislikes, preferences, etc...But when we subordinate our psychology to our scripturally based vision as Jesus did, our commitment will carry us through the changing winds of our thoughts and emotions.

Commitment reveals character. Commitment is the stuff character is made of, and our character is what God is out to transform.

Commitment is part and parcel of who we are. We are always committed to something. As C.S. Lewis points out, we were created to love and adore with all we are. So if we are not loving and adoring God, we will commit our affections elsewhere. We don't have a choice as to whether we will be committed or not; we only have a choice as to whom or what is the object of our commitment.

We may just be committed to our own comfort, image, desire to be right, or being in control. Or we may be committed to pleasure or power in the form of acquiring money or ruling others emotionally, sexually, or otherwise. Even the most slothful of people exhibit a full-blown commitment to staying comfortable. We human beings have an incredible capacity to commit and persevere and triumph. It is part of our character make-up.

Consider how our culture celebrates the truth of commitment and perseverance. One real life example is depicted in the movie *Rudy*. Rudy is an athletically average Midwest boy who dreams of playing football for Notre Dame. He didn't possess the size, speed, and talent to earn him a spot on the team's roster. But Rudy was not dissuaded because he was committed. He practiced with the team every day. He suffered setback after setback, was rejected, overlooked, and passed over many times, yet he persevered. Every time he was knocked down, figuratively and literally, he got back up. He did this until his courage and heart won the admiration of his team. Finally the demanding coach allowed him to play in a big game.

This is the kind of heart and commitment God is after. He isn't worried about our talent, He's after our *character*. He makes up for what we lack, perfecting His strength in weakness that is surrendered to Him.

All Things Work Together

Consider the possibility that when we are committed to God *we can't fail*. And even when we miss the mark it opens the door for correction and growth of character, which is the ultimate in success. This is another aspect of moving from glory to glory.

We make commitments and fall flat on our face. This fall can lead us to confess our failure, receive forgiveness, and recommit. This sequence actually moves us further into glory because we must deal with our pride, embrace humility, and depend on grace. In order to get going again we must not only accept grace but extend it to ourselves. We must push away cynicism and skepticism and resignation. This can be our daily triumph.

Missing the mark, if accepted as feedback, also serves to show us what doesn't work. If I shoot at a target and hit high and to the left, then I know I must aim lower and to the right.

The dynamic of diligently making and keeping promises and commitments, along with being held accountable, keeps us moving on from glory to glory. Not only will we enjoy achieving one accomplishment after another until we arrive in heaven, those who persevere will receive their due reward (cf. Rev. 3:10).

It's our responsibility to focus on what God has given *us* to do; He will do His part. It is not fruitful to be distracted by things that are out of our control.

"It's not in my boat"

One of my mentors, Dan Tocchini, tells the story of an Olympic rowing team that drew an unfavorable lane for a big race. They also faced the former champions, a formidable team who had been rowing together a good while and had won most of their races. The coach of the challengers was approached by journalists who asked about the obvious obstacles. "What are you going to do about the wake in the outside lane?" The coach responded, "It's not in my boat." "What about the champions?" Again he responded, "It's not in my boat." Everything that was brought up was met with the same response: "It's not in my boat."

The coach was focused only on what he was responsible for, namely his team and the effort they needed to put forth to accomplish their goal. Focusing on things that were beyond his control served only to diminish the influence on what was within his "boat." This concept, while simple, is critical. Some of the most challenging situations have been overcome in part because of this principle.

Take alcoholism for instance, an addiction that is tough to overcome. One key that Alcoholics Anonymous has found for overcoming this challenging addiction is to direct the alcoholic's focus to what is before him in each moment and in accepting reality. In, AA members pray the Serenity Prayer:

> GOD, grant me the serenity to accept the things I cannot change, Courage to change the things I can, and the wisdom to know the difference. Living ONE DAY AT A TIME; Enjoying one moment at a time; Accepting hardship as the pathway to peace. Taking, as He did, *this sinful world as it is, not as I would have it.* Trusting that He will make all things right if I surrender to His Will; That I may be reasonably happy in this life, and supremely happy with Him forever in the next. Amen."[85]

How often do we flail about on things over which we have no control and find our energies dissipated toward what we are responsible for? Keeping focused on what's in our boat will enable us be more effective in effecting change of any kind.

Delayed Obedience

There are seasons of growth. There are also seasons of severe dryness where not much growth seems to be happening. I've gone through times in the desert and the wilderness, and I'm positive I will again. It seems that God often leads His people to the desert. He led the Jews, Jesus, and many others there. Most of us can attest to the times of desert trial. The desert is a place of extremes. Hot and cold are the norms, mild is not. In the desert, the roots must go deep to find any water.

When God led the people of Israel to the desert, preparing them to come into their inheritance, one of the first lessons He taught them was obedience. Even their times to move and stop were set forth by Him. During the day a cloud led them, during the night a pillar of fire (Exodus. 13:21). They were to march as long as the covering moved, and rest when the covering stopped. I'm sure there were times when they would have rather rested while the cloud kept moving, and times they were ready to move when the cloud was still.

If the cloud moved and the people didn't, what did they miss out on? If the covering was still and they moved, what did they miss out on? How often do we miss what God wants to accomplish in us because of delayed obedience? We have so much information and teaching available to us today. Christians know more truth than ever before. But sadly, many Christians don't live out all the truth they know.

God reveals truth to us but only gives us more as we obey what He has already given. Oswald Chambers says, "Obey God in the thing He shows you, and instantly the next thing is opened up. God will never reveal more truth about Himself until you have obeyed what you know already." On the flip side, He will actually withhold from us growth until we grow into what He has revealed to us. Kierkegaard says if a man's mouth is so full of food that he can neither chew nor swallow, the kindest thing one can do for that man is to deprive him of the very food he thinks he needs.

I wonder how much of our lack of change stems from the fact that we are not true to what God has already given us. Delayed obedience undermines growth. When God moves or gives insight or truth to us, this is the time for us to move. One of the truths we need to fully embrace is that we are to live a disciplined life. Let's look at some of the daily disciplines that move us further on the path toward our goal of transformation.

NINETEEN

Disciplines of Transformation

*It is true that there is something painful in beginning to practice
piety, but this pain does not arise from the beginnings of piety
within us, but from the impiety that is still there... We only suffer
in so far as our natural vice resists supernatural grace: our heart
feels torn between these contrary forces...*

Blaise Pascal, *Pensee's*

We forgive to the extent that we love.

Francois de La Rochefoucauld

Engaging in Spiritual Disciplines

Why do many Christians shrink from the reality that God calls us
to a disciplined life? How easily it escapes us that we are called to be
disciples. It's as if we completely ignore the call of Jesus to lay down our
selfish ways of relating (die to them), pick up our cross, and follow Him
daily.

"Disciple" is from the Greek word *manthano,* meaning to learn by
thought accompanied by endeavor. A disciple is not only a pupil but an
adherent; hence disciples are spoken of as imitators of their teacher.[86]

Our endeavor as Christians is to be like Christ. The disciplines we
are to embrace include living authentically, forgiving others, confessing
sin, and communicating honestly even when it is frightening and risky,
all for the sake of others. Loving others more than ourselves means we
will enter into these disciplines in order to follow Christ's command to
love and to allow Him to transform us in the crucible of life, which is
hottest in the fires of suffering and relationship.

Confession

Confessing sin is a discipline. To confess is different than simply to admit we have sinned. True confession leads to cleansing. "If we confess our sins, He is faithful and just to forgive us our sins and to *cleanse* us from all unrighteousness" (1 John 1:9 NKJV emphasis added). The Greek word for cleanse is *katharo,* from which we get the English word catharsis. Catharsis can be hard, messy work.

Many Christians I work with confess secrets but do not experience catharsis and subsequent cleansing, freedom, and restoration of relationships. What kind of confession opens the door to healed relationships? I believe there are several aspects of the discipline of confession that are cathartic in human relationships.

First, there is a difference between *thinking* our confession and *speaking* it out loud, usually to another person. When we read about confessing in Scripture it involves confessing with the mouth. Speaking is an act of creating. When something is spoken out there is reality or substance to it that is missing when it is simply thought.

Second, authentic confession must be specific. When our confession gets into the details of our secrets, our emotions are stirred up. This is partly because the "gory details" begin to reveal the depth of the iniquity lodged in the heart. Iniquity is the heart attitude that produces the transgression. For instance, a man can confess acts of adultery and certainly feel badly about those acts. But as he confesses details such as scheming to seduce others, lying to his wife to cover up his sin, obsessing about the acts, and so on, it drives home the reality of what he is confessing. The stark reality of sin can serve to wake us up. Vague generalizations about sin, on the other hand, help hedge reality and thwart transformation.

Third, true confession involves feeling sorrow for transgressions. Allowing our emotions to be deeply touched brings gravity to the confession. We are more involved in the process and consequently our confession is more authentic. Please don't hear me saying that all confession must be an emotional mess. It's clear however that "godly sorrow leads to repentance." It's hard to truly sorrow without feeling anything.

When we confess in this way, transformation begins to take place. There is release from the past and from patterns that have held us. Confessing is another way to relinquish control and our attempt to handle what only God can.

In my own life as well as the people I work with, confession has opened new possibilities for change. The subsequent freedom that comes from authentic confession ushers in change. There is also the reality that going through the pain of confessing authentically changes our hearts, because pain is a powerful change agent.

Confession brings us into the light and into fellowship with God (God does not fellowship with darkness), and that fellowship changes us. It brings us into the light because the things we've held in dark secret and covered up are brought out into the open and uncovered. We can then be rightly related to both God and others (righteousness) and bridge the chasm of loneliness described in Chapter One of this book. God is out to transform us, and when our relationship with Him is healed we *do* change.

Forgiveness

Another spiritual discipline that needs to be practiced daily is forgiveness. Refusing to forgive is another reason we remain stuck in self-protective patterns which keep us from changing.

In Matthew 18:22, Peter, attempting to be magnanimous, asks Jesus how often he needs to forgive a brother who sins against him. He suggests seven times, which must have seemed to Peter to be extremely generous. Jesus' response must have shocked Peter: "I do not say to you up to seven times, but up to seventy times seven." Most commentators believe that this seemingly limitless forgiveness is to be extended for the same offense!

Why is it necessary to forgive someone repeatedly? If we truly forgive someone, doesn't it follow that we are done and don't need to revisit the offense? I believe this admonition is here because we are so quick to make someone pay for how they hurt us. It is truly a discipline to continue to forgive every time the memory of a transgression returns and brings with it the temptation to allow bitterness to take hold. Bitterness is "unfulfilled revenge," according to Francis Frangipane. Vengeance is not our job; it's God's (see Deuteronomy 32:35). Just like any other attempt to play God, our bitterness and resentment backfires. Peter Kreeft says resentment is like drinking poison and then waiting for the other person to die.

Why does refusing to forgive keep us stuck? It's very clear when you consider the nature of most hurts in relationships. We are hurt when a legitimate expectation between two people is not met. Promises are one way legitimate expectations are given rise to. When someone makes a promise, expectation is legitimately born. For example, when I say to Dawn, "I promise to be faithful," I give her the right to expect me to be faithful. When she receives the promise, she "owns" my fidelity because I freely gave it to her. I am indebted to her by virtue of my promise, and we are bound together by that vow. The vow is part of how we are connected and a foundation the relationship was built on. If I break that promise, we still remain bound together by the original vow in the sense Dawn still owns the debt I gave to her, even though the promise is broken. If she does not forgive the debt, holding onto the idea that infidelity cannot be forgiven because she has the right to expect it, the relationship will most likely be doomed. In order for us to be able to continue in intimate relationship she will need to release the debt the broken promise has left. If that debt is not forgiven the foundation will always be broken. Mysteriously, when forgiveness is extended, even though pain may remain, the relationship can be built on a new foundation.

Until the debt is released (forgiven) there is something between the two of us that continues to bind us. *Promise* originally bound us, now *"unforgiveness"* binds us. If we are bound to another person by virtue of an unreleased debt, the experience we had with that person will be a haunting in any new relationship. The specter of betrayal will haunt any new relationship where fidelity is desired. As I move into new relationships I will continue to find myself tied to the person who broke the promise to me and therefore find my willingness to trust again undermined.

This kind of unreleased bond can only lead to bitterness, withdrawal, anger, and resentment. The bond re-established once forgiveness is extended can lead to intimacy, connection, vulnerability, and love.

In their book, *Killing the Victim before the Victim Kills You*, Watson and Tocchini establish how promise and forgiveness are tied together even in their root meanings.

> The kinship between forgiveness and promise is displayed by the etymology of the words themselves… "promise" comes from a Latin word meaning "to send forth." This is similar to the Old English root meaning "to give forth" from which the English word "forgive" is derived. The Greek word for "forgive" [means] "to send from"… promise and forgiveness are reciprocal. Promise is sending

ourselves forth to another; forgiveness is releasing another from the debt we believe they owe us. Promise binds us, forgiveness releases others and ourselves as well. (pg. 121)

In some instances, the wounds inflicted on people are devastatingly deep. I have worked with many people seeking to get free of the anger and depression suffered from profound abuse and betrayal. And in some ways they had a right to be angry. As Charles H. Kraft puts it in his book *Deep Wounds, Deep Healing*: "You have a right to be angry, hate, and even seek revenge for what these people have done to you. But if you exert that right, there's a law in the universe that says you will be enslaved to those feelings... So Jesus says forgive them and get free."

When I am wronged and fail to forgive, my refusal to forgive imprisons me and doesn't allow for change. I could find myself stuck in many ways. Perhaps I refuse to completely open myself to receive a similar promise because I fear another heartbreak. Even if I can find someone different from the one who hurt me, I'll probably test them to see if they are trustworthy. Since I haven't forgiven, I will always be suspicious. When I am suspicious, I will be looking for proof that I am right to be suspicious. When the person I'm with feels my suspicion or testing, they will resist me. Their resistance may be all the "proof" I need that they can't be trusted. So I'll move on, not realizing that I had a big hand in undermining the potential relationship.

Another aspect tied to this refusal to forgive is judgment. When I harbor this attitude toward someone, it puts me in a place of judgment. We do not have the role of judge. "Vengeance is Mine, says the Lord" (Deuteronomy 32:35). When we usurp the role of judge, we set ourselves up to be judged the same way. We become both like the one we haven't forgiven and the judgments we judge people with are turned back on us. Jesus said, "For in the same way you judge others, you will be judged, and with the measure you use, it will be measured to you" (Matthew 7:2 NIV).

In the Impact Training, when working with someone regarding their unwillingness to forgive I will often have them state the judgments they have about the person. The person they haven't forgiven may be a parent, a spouse, or anyone else they were in relationship with. With their permission I'll actually write the judgments on a white board as they speak them out. Countless times I have noted their incredulity as

I ask them to circle the ones they see as true in their life—the traits are virtually the same in the person who hasn't forgiven. This is a mystery to be sure, but I have come to see this reality as one of God's mercies. By becoming like the one I haven't forgiven and having the judgments I use on others "be measured" to me, I have the opportunity to come face to face with what is undone in my life. If I want freedom and not have these judgments be measured to me the only path is through forgiveness.

Matthew 6:14-15 reads, "If you forgive others for their transgressions, your heavenly Father will also forgive you. *But* if you do not forgive others, then your Father will not forgive your transgressions" (NASU emphasis added). God loves us so much that He will allow us to suffer and stay stuck as long as we remain in refusal to forgive and judgment because He has dictated that He will not forgive us if we don't forgive! And He so wants to forgive us that He died to allow make it possible!

For years I stood in an attitude of refusing to forgive my father because of the abuse I received growing up. I remember vowing, "I will never be like him," and I moved on into judging him. In my thinking, my judgment was right. Ironically, as I became a father, I noticed that I interacted with my own children the way my father did with me. While I didn't act out in the same way my father did (physical beatings, ridicule), I abused in different ways; I've already mentioned sarcasm. My own failings have served me to see that no one is all good or all bad. This was certainly true of my father. While he was harsh by many standards, he also loved us greatly and worked tirelessly to better our life in the best way he could see at the time.

As I forgave my father another amazing transformation happened: I began to recall all the many times my father did many wonderful things for me. I saw with clearer eyes the sacrifices he made for our family and understood better his own challenges and aspects of his character he'd tried hard to change. I also began to be able to see the world through his filters and came to understand that his harsh treatment was in an effort to steer me in the way he thought best. Strange how I couldn't see that when I held onto "unforgiveness"! This deepened my forgiveness and love for him without needing to excuse the things that were wrong.

Whenever I take back my "right" to not forgive, I am again thrown towards those aspects of my character that I want to change.

Forgiveness is a discipline because it isn't just a once-and-done event. There are many times I recall hurts from past events and find it necessary to release those who hurt me again *for things I've already forgiven.* The word "forgive" comes from *remittere,* the same Latin root for our word "remit," meaning to "send back." [87] It's as though when an offense comes up, instead of engaging it, I send it away. It's an act of will where I purposely send myself away from the offense. It again drives me back to the Lord who alone can heal those hurts.

Many people, especially Christians, know that forgiveness is key to relational health, and therefore they take steps to do just that. So they go through the process of forgiving by telling God "I forgive them." Strangely though, the fruit that should accompany forgiveness does not emerge, fruit such as peace, release, trust, joy, love, etc. Instead they may remain guarded, conditional, angry, resentful, and bitter. Why? Many people I talk to are confused. When it becomes evident people are choosing self-protective behaviors we explore the dynamic of forgiveness. When we identify the person who is the object of their bitterness they say, "But I did forgive."

One reason for this dilemma is that many people mistake *forgiving* for *excusing.* Excusing can be easily confused with forgiving, especially because you can be excusing someone while using the words, "I forgive you." There is usually some stuff going on beneath the surface which dictates which one is exercised.

We choose to excuse instead of forgive when the process of true forgiveness stirs up too much pain. This may be because we have not truly released a major previous offense that caused significant hurt, or even if we have, we don't want to get near that pain again.

There are several distinctions when we compare excusing someone with forgiving someone. When we excuse, the foray into the offense stays on the surface. Perhaps you've seen or played out a scenario that goes something like this. Someone hurts me. The offender comes to me in an effort to account for the wrong. "Hey," he says, "I just want you to know I'm really sorry for doing that. I didn't mean to hurt you and I feel bad." My response is, "Oh yeah, it stung but no problem, I forgive you."

Notice: Neither the offender nor the offended gets very specific. The offense is not identified by either, and more importantly, the impact and consequences of the offense on me is not really considered. Excusing is attractive because we don't really have to delve into the messiness that is true forgiveness. Excusing allows us to stay in control, comfortable, insulated. By excusing, we really don't have to enter into the pain of the offense.

It also allows us to retain the debt, an attractive option because then we have a reason to withhold ourselves and stay safe. Even more pernicious and yet something that can make us feel good is that we can make the other person pay in subtle ways. We don't choose this because we are evil but because we want to avoid reliving the unpleasant memories of a similar theme, such as betrayal, abandonment, abuse, or rejection. So by excusing we turn people we are close to into surrogates, unwittingly taking out our revenge on them for things that happened long before we even met them. A major clue that this tactic is operating is when we respond disproportionately, such as making a huge deal out of a small infraction.

In addition, excusing just doesn't take as much work; it's easier. The underlying motives for the transgression do not need to be explored. So the knotty questions go unanswered, questions like, "Was the offender meaning to hurt me on purpose? If so, what is undone in our relationship? If not, what caused him to inflict damage to the relationship?"

In true forgiveness, however, there are no shortcuts. We are willing to acknowledge the pain to the offender and to ourselves. We will do the work to look beneath the surface and touch whatever may be there, including reliving and re-forgiving an even bigger offense in our history. We'll get specific. We'll allow ourselves to feel the full brunt of the offense, without minimizing, rationalizing, or justifying, and then consciously choose to release the debt.

Perhaps two contrasting charts will help fully delineate some differences.

Excusing	Forgiving
– Allows you to retain debt	– Fully releases debt
– Holds onto your "right"	– Gives up "right"
– Can still make the other pay (Revenge)	– Extends grace (Mercy)
– Is vague or general	– Is specific
– Does not need to fully feel pain	– Feels all the pain
– Maintains control	– Gives up control
– Is easier	– Willing to do hard work
– Stays safe (doesn't need to be vulnerable)	– Makes one vulnerable again
– Allows me to be right	– Looks for how I contributed to breakdown
– I get to blame	– I take responsibility to reconcile
	– Is humble

In forgiveness, as with every other virtue and grace, Christ is the prime example. If you remember, He spoke forgiveness to us on the cross.

What was happening on the cross? Jesus was in excruciating physical, emotional, and spiritual pain. He was betrayed, mocked, abandoned, derided, jeered, spat upon, rejected, humiliated, alone, innocent, misunderstood. He watched His mother and a few loved ones hurt for Him, and God only knows what else He was suffering. In the midst of all that, He forgave.

We want to forgive when we feel good.

Bottom line is *when we don't forgive, we don't change.*

Some Things Will Never Change: Mourning the Past

The discipline of mourning encompasses just about all we've been talking about. It involves facing reality, changing our way of thinking, relating differently, taking on a different attitude, and certainly relying on God to transform what we cannot.

To the Hebrew mindset, mourning was and is considered sacred. When a tragedy occurred, time was set aside to weep and mourn. People came alongside their loved ones and helped them enter into the pain they would rather resist. It is, after all, natural for us to avoid pain. It requires a disciplined mindset to face it. These people were purposeful mourners who had practiced the spiritual discipline of mourning and readily offered themselves to grieve with another who is grieving. These were people who had, as Oswald Chambers writes, "received themselves in the fire of sorrow." He states in *My Utmost for His Highest*:

> We say that there ought to be no sorrow, but there is sorrow, and we have to accept and receive ourselves in its fires. If we try to evade sorrow, refusing to deal with it, we are foolish. Sorrow is one of the biggest facts in life, and there is no use in saying it should not be. Sin, sorrow, and suffering are, and it is not for us to say that God has made a mistake in allowing them.

> Sorrow removes a great deal of a person's shallowness, but it does not always make that person better. Suffering either gives me to myself or it destroys me. You cannot find or receive yourself through success, because you lose your head over pride. And you cannot receive

yourself through the monotony of daily life, because you give into complaining. The only way to find yourself is in the fires of sorrow. Why it should be this way is immaterial. The fact is that it is true in the scriptures and in human experience. You can always recognize who has been through the fires of sorrow and received himself, and you know you can go to him in your moment of trouble and find that he has plenty of time for you. But if a person has not been through the fires of sorrow, he is apt to be contemptuous, having no respect or time for you, only turning you away. If you will receive yourself in the fires of sorrow, God will make you nourishment for other people. [88]

It's been said that nothing motivates change as effectively as the experience of pain. A child doesn't have to be told twice not to touch the fire once he burns his fingers. We learn very quickly when we are hurt by something.

C.S. Lewis says "God whispers in our pleasures and shouts in our pain." When a person truly enters and experiences pain, they learn a lesson not soon, if ever, forgotten. Interestingly, the very behaviors and ways of relating we most want to change are ones set in place to avoid pain!

People who walk through the fires looking for what God has in it for them not only learn a lesson, they also are changed. They "receive themselves" and find that a new capacity for loving is opened up in them as they mourn what they cannot change. It is a powerful dynamic because, as Oswald Chambers says, "People are not always made better by sorrow; some are made more bitter and resentful and hard." We are changed only when we are willing to trust God enough to fully feel the pain, to be willing to let go of our need to understand why we are in pain, and to accept that God will work all things for good (Romans 8:28). Many people use that Scripture to avoid the sorrow. It is quite a different matter to believe it enough to *find yourself* in "the fire of sorrow."

Those who learn to mourn their pain are truly released from the grip of the tragedy in a way that people who try to forget or avoid the pain never are. It's another paradox: "Blessed are they who mourn for they shall be comforted."

It is not an accident that the Holy Spirit is called the Comforter. The Greek word is *paracletos,* meaning one who "comes along side."[89]

As we mourn, God comes alongside us, comforts us, and draws us near (makes us intimate with Him), which definitely continues to transform us. We cannot be in the presence of Almighty Creator God and remain unchanged! Moses' face glowed after being in His presence.

In my work I encounter hundreds of people who are stuck in patterns or ruts of behavior, stuck there because they continue to relate to others in the same self-protective ways. Most often there is an element of refusing to mourn past hurts and forgive those who hurt them.

There is a God... and I'm not Him

Life doesn't usually work out the way we plan, and people don't behave the way we want, hope, and trust they will. Since things don't pan out the way I desire, I tend to question whether God is really working all things out for good. How can some of the senseless tragedies and betrayals that happen ever be turned into good?

This has, for me, been an ongoing consideration as I have been walking out my cancer diagnosis and treatment. I have fluctuated between trusting that God will work something good to cynically viewing my condition as an unnecessary, unfair trail.

I have eagerly assimilated the prosperity message so often put forward which basically says that by following God my life will be "blessed" in the sense of things going pretty much the way I would prefer. Sure, there will be some testing; I accept that, that's reasonable. But this?!

There it is: what I'm essentially saying is I don't trust God. I must have assessed He's unreasonable, random, dangerous. And I have evidence: Carlo's death, various betrayals, many disappointments... the observation that many things in my life are not in alignment with how I thought they would be by now (and perhaps made up that God should have had it be that way by now). In other words, *I know what is good for me* and the One who has the power to make it so hasn't delivered. He hasn't gotten into line with how I think my life should be. In my arrogance I may even conclude if I were God, life would probably work a lot better—it would turn out good.

What is *"good"* Anyway?

One reason we have trouble seeing God's good in tragedies is our limited definition of good. The question we must answer is, what does the Bible mean when it says God is working all things for good (Romans 8:28)? What if the good He is working out is the transformation of our character? When it's all said and done, isn't that what God is after: to transform us into the image of Jesus? Jesus is also referred to as the Suffering Servant and the Wounded Healer who has called us into the fellowship of His sufferings.

It is difficult for us to understand how suffering can be good and used by God to transform us. C.S. Lewis, who wrote often about pain, says, "What do people mean when they say 'I am not afraid of God because I know He is good?' Have they never been to a dentist?"[90]

In so many ways, Christianity has become flimsy and lacey, as opposed to the rugged, life-challenging, world-changing Christianity of our forebears. We need to examine both how we think and how we relate when it comes to life, suffering, and how life should be. Consider what Soren Kierkegaard says in his book *For Self Examination*.

> I have seen a person almost ready to drop in despair, I have also heard him cry out, "Give me life! life!" This is worse than death that puts an end to life, but I am as if dead and yet I am not dead. I am not a severe man, if I knew any mitigation, I would be quite willing to comfort and encourage, yet it is quite possible that the sufferer really lacked something else, that he truly needed harder sufferings. Harder sufferings? Who is so cruel as to dare say something like that? My friend, it is Christianity. The doctrine that is sold under the name of gentle comfort, whereas it is eternities' comfort... Christianity is not what we human beings, both you and I are all too eager to make it. It is not a quack doctor. A quack doctor is promptly at your service and immediately applies a remedy and bungles everything. Christianity waits before it applies its remedy... therefore Christianity's severity... the correctness of this you have no doubt already experienced on a smaller scale. Have not yourself experienced, as I have, that when you perhaps began to moan, that when you say, 'I can't take it anymore!' and then the next day you were treated more severely, what then? You could, you made it, you were treated more severely and you made it! When horses groan and pant, feel exhausted, when they feel that a hand full of oats is what was needed, but on the other hand, when with only a momentary halt the heavily loaded wagon would begin to roll back down the hill

and perhaps plunge the horses and the driver and everything down into the abyss, is it cruel of the driver that the lashes fall dreadfully, as dreadfully as he never before he had the heart to lash, especially this team of horses who are as dear to him as the apple of his eye? Is this cruel or is this kind?

Christ has a perspective on life and suffering that is quite different from ours. He, as God, sees how He will work all for good *in eternity* while we can see it only by faith. Therefore, what may seem cruel to us can indeed be eternity's comfort. Certainly the cross of Christ falls into this category!

Suffering, as we know, is a fact of life. And while it is one of God's instruments used to refine and transform us, we still refuse to fully embrace suffering and mourn what we cannot change.

Mourning can be exercised regarding so many aspects of life. We can mourn the years that have been lost as a result of foolish decisions. We can mourn each realization that we haven't changed, when in fact we "see with horror that despite all your efforts, you not only have not come nearer your goal but seem to have gotten farther from it."[91]

I have also encountered aspects of mourning when I realize how many ways I have missed it with the people I love the most. When I consider how I could have been different with my wife, son, daughter, and other loved ones, I truly feel a sense of mourning toward words and actions I can't go back and redo.

Somehow the pain of this kind of mourning awakens me. It drives me to seek out people I have been missing and address those aspects of our relationship that have suffered as a result of my actions.

Mourning is another paradox in that through it God, as we look to Him in it, takes the things we cannot change and somehow transforms our suffering, exchanging beauty for ashes and pulling the precious from the vile. Here again both God and we have roles, and ours is definitely a secondary one. We don't have a say in how much suffering we encounter, and can't dictate when it's over. Yet as we trust God enough to lean into Him in authentic anguish over what we can't change, He changes us.

Mourning also allows me to bury painful memories in a way that doesn't deny them but instead have them change me. I don't bury them by forgetting.

John, the man mentioned earlier, discovered the contribution mourning made to changing many things. An avoided sore spot between John and his wife was the fact that they didn't have the wedding she always wanted. Before they married, John made some decisions that led to a breakup. After a time they realized they still loved each other, so they made amends and decided to marry hastily. But it had always bothered his wife that she never experienced the traditional wedding and never wore the wedding dress she always imagined she would wear.

Their marriage was mostly harmonious and happy, and yet there was the sense of loss between them. Even though they had talked about it, the wedding they never had was always a lingering sad memory. It would especially be stirred whenever they attended a wedding or saw one on TV or in a movie. They were both aware that it still hurt. At weddings, he felt a little guilty, she tried to push the loss out of her mind, and both of them attempted to be fully present in the festivities. Sometimes they passed on even attending them.

One of the reasons their sense of loss was never fully explored was the mutual, unspoken question, "What good would it do to really go there?" After all, neither of them desired to make the other "pay" for what had happened, and they were genuinely thankful for their marriage.

When this couple attended our Art of Marriage Workshop, my wife and I introduced the concept of husband and wife mourning together over ways they hurt each other, whether the hurt was inadvertent or deliberate, forgiven or not. We made it clear that even two loving humans will at times hurt each other. These hurts can and should be forgiven, but just because an offense is forgiven does not mean you stop hurting. When you hurt, you grieve; it's just the way we're made. Dawn and I suggested to this couple that hurting together over their loss could actually be an avenue to greater intimacy. The Scripture says, "Blessed are they who mourn, for they will be comforted" (Matthew 5:4). The word comforted roughly means that someone draws near.[92] We become close as we mourn together.

They had never considered this possibility in regard to their lost expectation. It had nothing to do with being angry or vindictive; it had only to do with being honest about a deep hurt. As they mourned their loss, without either one attacking or being defensive, the tears and sorrow they allowed to surface brought great closure to this eighteen-year-old wound.

As John and his wife traveled all the avenues their mourning led them, they found many areas where forgiveness was needed anew. At the other end of their mourning process, they suddenly realized it was now possible to redeem, in a sense, what was lost. For their nineteenth anniversary, this couple participated in a renewal ceremony complete with bridesmaids, ushers, reception, and yes, a wedding dress.

God used the ceremony to bring healing to many among their family, friends, and church as John and his wife gave testimony about how the event came to be, authentically sharing their hurt and redemption. There wasn't a dry eye in the house, and the party that followed was happy and festive. Strangely, joy always seems to follow close on the heels of mourning.

Some people have asked me how to go about mourning a hurt or loss. I believe mourning is not so much a *how to* conversation as it is a *willing to* conversation. You see, mourning opens us up to hurting. And as we know, people resist pain. We are all born with the ability to feel emotional pain. Initially, this ability came as naturally to us as breathing. Somewhere along the way, however, we decided that we didn't like it, or that it wasn't supposed to be this way—that emotional pain was bad, not good. And so many people choose to stop hurting emotionally. Of course, some part of us does die when we choose this.

People are always looking for practical suggestions, steps, and processes for fixing things that aren't working. I assert the reason they want these elements is in order to control the process. The problem is that mourning our hurts and losses can't be easily packaged as something that can be fixed in three easy steps. Mourning is not tidy or packaged; it's messy and tends to undo us. It feels like we can never be put back together again if we allow ourselves to feel the depth of the pain of our losses for as long as they naturally last, and we don't really have control over how long that is.

You see, I think the problem is we want to be able not only to control these experiences that hurt but also bring them to closure. But we don't get over a significant loss because we decide to. I believe that's something God decides. Perhaps that is why we are told God will wipe our tears away in heaven.

Prayer and Prayer with Fasting

Prayer changes things. Either what we're praying about changes or we do. Either way, things do change. Transformation is what God is about, and as we invite Him to work in our lives and the lives of those we pray for, He uses the invitation to change us as well.

Prayer must be a central component in the life of anyone who is committed to transformation. Prayer is a discipline. As we all know, Christ Himself spent much time in prayer and combined prayer with fasting. Fasting is another discipline that directly confronts our desires. It is a decision to willingly suspend or deny what we think we need in order to gain something greater.

As I write about this I'm convicted about how I don't treat prayer as a discipline. I pray daily, but I don't often *labor* in prayer over things I would like changed. Too often my prayer comes out more like a well-intentioned heart wish.

As one prays regarding anything they earnestly want changed, there begins to come clarity regarding what is being sought. The hidden motivations of our hearts are revealed, and light is shed on the areas we pray about. You can't be in true communion with the Almighty and His Spirit while at the same time avoiding the revelation coming from Him.

The Bible makes it clear that God answers our prayers and that anything we ask in His will comes about. There is a caveat: "When you ask, you do not receive, because you ask with wrong motives" (James 4:3 NIV.) It is imperative to remember that God is ultimately after our transformation. It makes sense that He would use even the frustration of unanswered prayers to continue the refining process. When our prayers go unanswered we have opportunity to examine our motives. How we respond to unanswered prayer reveals what is in our hearts and how we relate to God when we don't understand His response—or apparent non-response—to our prayers. Seeing our hearts in this way, we usually find other things to repent of. Like I said, prayer changes things, or we change.

In the work I do with Reinvent Ministries, I know the results we see are so powerful because of the tremendous intercessory prayer covering each event. The penetrating, personal nature of our work encourages people to speak honestly, transparently, and frankly about their lives. This often results in situations that are free-flowing and dynamic, and sometimes it looks like things may really unravel. It is at these times I have seen intercessory prayer make the difference. As we invite God to work, we hold true to the principles we know to be from Him such as honesty, humility, love, asking forgiveness, etc. He makes an opening where there appears to be none.

I remember an example from a four-day training I was facilitating. The participants and I agreed that if a certain commitment was not kept (after promises were repeatedly broken during the first day and a half of the event), we would just call off the whole event and go home. Some people had come from faraway and took time off work and invested much to be there. These promises were completely possible to keep, on a level with the kinds of promises we expect our kids to keep. If we couldn't count on each other to keep these simple promises to each other, there was really no point in going through the motions. So we agreed I would leave if it didn't happen.

Well, it *didn't* happen. I kept my word and left the room, instructing the people to complete with each other by getting clear on what happened. They were to let me know when they were finished so we could close up the training.

I went into another room to wait for that process to work out. During that time, several team members and I began praying. It was an intense time, lasting almost two hours! We were literally on our face, groaning in our prayer. God revealed to me as I prayed how I had missed it with the participants. I had left the room confident that I had no part in the breakdown, but as I travailed a sorrow began to sweep over me. During that prayer time, specific participants came to my mind along with what was at stake for them in their lives. I began weeping profusely about what was happening and how I had contributed to it.

When I was finally asked to come back into the room and walked in, it was evident that a shift had taken place. They could tell I also had been laboring in soul-searching. I accounted for what I believed was my contribution. In a moment that still lingers sweetly in my memory, forgiveness was sought and given all around, and a new possibility for completing the training opened up from this authentic repentance. Prayer and the heart attitude of humility and repentance had made this possible.

There is an aspect of prayer that actually means *attitude* or *posture*. "Prayer, constituting as it does the most direct expression of religious feeling and consciousness, has been, from the beginning, the principal means by which men, created in the image of God, have given expression of their attitude toward Him."[93]

For centuries reflective prayer has been a primary avenue for God's transformative work to take place. Reflective prayer is simply a willingness to sit in God's presence and listen as our heart is revealed by His Spirit. At the end of this book I have included a sample reflective prayer called the "Prayer of Examen." The Examen is an ancient reflective exercise originally developed by St. Ignatius of Loyola, who is considered something of the godfather of discernment practices.

Another important and powerful aspect of prayer is when it is combined with fasting. In Matthew 17:21, Jesus lets us know there are some needs that require this kind of united approach. It's important to remember that prayer and fasting are not magic formulas that force God to do something He doesn't want to. Prayer, and prayer with fasting, are ways for us to partner with what God wants to do. He is sovereign and can do whatever He chooses whenever He chooses, and yet He restrains Himself and waits for our invitation.

Suffice it to say, without fervent prayer, the visitation God is waiting to bestow is hindered. Prayer must surround whatever it is we would like transformed. God is the one who ultimately transforms, and He responds to our invitation, not our demand in His timing.

Worship

Worship, in both the Old and New Testament, is always a function of sacrifice. In the Old Testament, a pivotal expression of worship was the sacrifice of unblemished animals to God—clearly a picture of the perfect Lamb of God who was to sacrifice Himself on our behalf. Because of His provision, we no longer have to make animal sacrifices to God to pay for our sin. However, we are called to live sacrificially, which is an expression of worship.

The pivotal New Testament Scripture regarding transformation is Romans 12:1-2: "Therefore, I urge you, brothers, in view of God's mercy, to offer your bodies as living sacrifices, holy and pleasing to God-this is your spiritual act of worship. Do not conform any longer to the pattern of this world, but be transformed by the renewing of your mind" (NIV).

Worship calls us to set ourselves aside, and it's clear that offering our bodies as "living sacrifices" involves dying to our prideful ways. Hebrews 13:15 refers to the "sacrifice of praise." Think about how difficult it is to enter into worship when things aren't going as we'd prefer. It's easier to worship when everything is going well, when God is meeting us the way we think He should. But when life is less than perfect, we tend to wallow in the mire instead of worshiping God and allowing Him to transform us, others, and circumstances in the midst of the difficulty. But this is exactly the time for a sacrifice of worship.

Too often we want to worship God on our terms instead of how God asks us to. We think it is our right to dictate when, where, how passionately, how reasonably, and how often we worship. Clearly, worship leads us headlong into a confrontation with our pride and self-centeredness and forces us to enter into humility and God-centeredness.

This transition leads us into the communal aspect of worship, for being God-centered means loving others. In fact, Paul's epistle to the Corinthians is written to a *community*, not an *individual*. How we are with each other matters greatly to God and is what God uses to transform individuals. While monastic lives of solitude can be godly, it is only in how well we love others that we can measure how well we love God (1 John 4:20). As you can see, our personal transformation is therefore tied to how we are with others.

This is very practical because living out our worship in community makes us open to the transformation of God in every aspect of our life, from sharing our gifts to sharing our material goods. Romans 12:3ff goes on to paint a clear picture of what it means to be "transformed by the renewing of our minds," and most of it has to do with how we give to others (cf. 2 Corinthians 8:1-2). Giving to others is part of the very essence of the Godhead, and God is out to make us more fully into His image. Loving and giving translates to life, and abundant life is what He wants for us.

This is why God calls us to worship, not because of a need He has, but rather because of what worship does for us. He knows that connecting to the Source of Life means life and fulfillment for us. Worship is also the entry point for His transformative grace in our lives. The entry of His grace confronts our fear of not having enough and causes us to engage in the fight against self-sufficiency.

The battle to change is fierce, and worship is a primary weapon in that fight. It is interesting to note that oftentimes the first wave of God's people to engage in battles were the worshipers. Consider this account in 2 Chronicles 20:21-23:

> After consulting the people, Jehoshaphat appointed men to sing to the LORD and to praise him for the splendor of his holiness as they went out at the head of the army, saying: "Give thanks to the LORD, for his love endures forever." As they began to sing and praise, the LORD set ambushes against the men of Ammon and Moab and Mount Seir who were invading Judah, and they were defeated (NIV).

Worship is more than the duty a derivative being offers the Creator. It is a life-giving and life-transforming encounter of love. We need to worship because worship invites God to touch and transform our very lives. Psalm 22:3 states that God is enthroned on the praises of his people. As with prayer, having an encounter with God through worship cannot leave us un-impacted and unchanged.

Not only does worship open the door to our transformation, it is also another entreaty for God to change our world. This can be seen in the Lord's Prayer. In it Jesus ties the worship of God (hallowed be Thy Name) to accomplishing His purpose in our lives and the world (Thy Kingdom come and Thy will be done on earth as it is in heaven). And heaven is what we lost with Adam's sin and what we have been chasing after our whole lives.

In Heaven we will find the fullness of what it means to revel and be fulfilled as we worship God and why worship speaks to the deepest level of who we were created to be. There, face to face with Reality Himself, we will be fully transformed.

TWENTY

The Final Awakening

Beloved, now we are children of God; and it has not yet been
revealed what we shall be, but we know that when He is revealed,
we shall be like Him, for we shall see Him as He is.

1 John 3:1-2 NKJV

"Have you not guessed? [said Aslan]... The dream is ended; this is
the morning." And as He spoke He no longer looked to them as a
lion; but the things that began to happen to them after that were
so great and beautiful that I cannot write them... All their life in
this world and all their adventures in Narnia had only been the
cover and the title page; now they were beginning
Chapter One of the Great Story...

C. S. Lewis, *The Last Battle*

The Wedding

We have explored many avenues that invite change. Since
transformation is central to Christianity, it is not surprising that so
many different topics are involved. In the end, God uses *everything* to
make us like Christ. Our transformation is His primary interest. We
will ultimately be made one with Him in Heaven at that great event
called the Wedding of the Lamb. In His great love, He longs for the
consummation of union with His Bride. "Let us rejoice and be glad and
give him glory! For the wedding of the Lamb has come, and his bride has
made herself ready" (Revelation 19:7 NIV).

I believe that the "bride has made herself ready" by all the means we
have been talking about in this book. First and foremost is the response
of our soul to the wooing of God through the Spirit. Our response

(our, "yes") invites Him to plant the seed of Christ in us. By this act we are regenerated and cleansed from the sin that initially separated us from God and brought us death. Here we are both passive and active (receiving and saying "yes").

As we begin to know Him, by prayer, Bible study, worship, and fellowship, we begin to grow in the knowledge of Him, begin to get a clearer glimpse of Who our Father is, and yearn to become more like Him. One of the disciplines we are to undertake here is taking thoughts captive and bringing them into alignment with the mind of Christ. Thus the transformation is continued. This aspect is more proactive. There is a diligence required of us.

Surrendering to life's trials and suffering opens the door to knowing a new dimension of the One into whose image we are being conformed. As Paul wrote, "That I may know Him and the power of His resurrection and the fellowship of His sufferings, being conformed to His death" (Philippians 3:10 NASU). In the mourning of our suffering we are comforted by God and drawn even nearer to Him. In the crucible of life's suffering and trials, the impurities are brought to the surface and we are continually refined. We "receive ourselves in the fires of sorrow."

C.S. Lewis, in his book *God in the Dock*, compares our transformation to that of a rabbit being transformed into a man. "We are to be re-made. All the rabbit in us is to disappear—the worried, conscientious, ethical rabbit as well as the cowardly and sensual rabbit. We shall bleed and squeal as the handfuls of fur come out; and then, surprisingly, we shall find underneath it all a thing we have never yet imagined: a real Man, an ageless god, a son of God, strong radiant, wise, beautiful, and drenched in joy."[94]

By participating in all of these dynamics we exhibit the attitude of "working out our salvation with fear and trembling" and take our appropriate responsibility to engage in new ways of thinking and relating. Again, in Matthew Henry's words: "*Let him be a new creature...* old things are passed away—*old thoughts, old principles, and old practices,* are passed away; and all these things must become new... The renewed man acts from new principles, by new rules, with new ends, and in new company"[95] (Emphasis mine).

Old ways are interrupted, and this new way of being leads us to change how we do life. As this happens, new territory is entered that leads us further into transformation. Employing the disciplines of confession, forgiveness, mourning, worship, and prayer all add to the process. Daily living the principles of paying attention to feedback and trusting God enough to enter the conflict of life will bring still further change. Embracing new attitudes and allowing God to increase our capacity to contain the paradox of our struggle, all the while pressing onward to glory, will work more character in us.

In short, all facets of what comprises life are brought to bear upon the fashioning of us into Christ's image. We already have Him in us and yet we have not arrived:

"Beloved, now we are children of God; and it has not yet been revealed what we shall be, but we know that when He is revealed, we shall be like Him, for we shall see Him as He is" (1 John 3:1-2 NKJV).

In reference to this verse, Matthew Henry states that we can see Him as He is only because of our likeness. "Their likeness shall enable them to see him as the blessed do in heaven. Or the sight of him shall be the cause of their likeness; it shall be a transformative sight: they shall be transformed into the same image by the beatific view that they shall have of him."[96]

In turn, seeing Him as He is brings a transfiguration not unlike the glow on Moses' face as he returned from Mount Sinai. We will have no need of a veil, however, as His glory will not fade from us. As His bride, He will remove our veil. We will bask in His presence and truly know Him. I believe there is a spiritual equivalent of the sexual knowing spoken about in the Scriptures. It is a knowing that is intimate and unifying and is an expression of love.

It should not be lost on us that the ones who will be allowed access to Heaven are the ones to whom the Lord of the universe can say, "I know you." This seems strange; doesn't the omniscient Deity know everyone? Apparently not—at least not in the way that is required. Matthew 7:21-23 says, "Not everyone who says to Me, 'Lord, Lord,' shall enter the kingdom of heaven... Many will say to Me in that day, 'Lord, Lord, have we not prophesied in Your name, cast out demons in Your name, and done many wonders in Your name?' And then I will declare to them, 'I never knew you; depart from Me'" (NKJV).

Being known by God is the ultimate joy.

Consumed and Consummated by God

Male and female both are an expression of God. In Scripture, we see both the Father-heart (many, many Scriptures) and Mother-heart of God (e.g., Isaiah 49:15; 66:13; Matthew 23:37). This is a mystery, and yet the evidence is incontrovertible. "So God created man in His own image, in the image of God He created them; male and female He created them" (Genesis 1:27 NIV). Our gender is more than our sex; it is something in our souls. God has no body; He is spirit (John 4:24). We are either male or female, yet ultimately, at some level, all human souls are relegated to being receptive to God's initiation: He initiates, woos, pursues, and, yes, romances both men and women. We love because He first loved us. We choose Him because He has chosen us. He calls Himself "The Bridegroom"[97] and calls us His Bride.

The beautiful hymn, *Jerusalem, Jerusalem*, provides another glimpse of what the Bridegroom has been working in His Bride and what He has waiting for her:

> I'll give you beauty for your ashes,
> The oil of joy for tears;
> A bridal gown shall clothe the sadness
> of many captive years.
> Every man shall see your glory,
> And kings behold your fame;
> Your righteousness will shine forever
> when God will change your name!

When we are wedded to the Lamb, we will get new names, as any bride does. One of them will be known to us alone (Revelation 2:17; 3:12); it will be between our Lord and us.

We will know Him and each other intimately. George MacDonald writes that in Heaven "I think we shall be able to pass into and through each others very souls as we please, knowing each others thought and being, along with our own, and so being like God."

Knowing others in this manner brings change as well. In Heaven I believe we will continue to grow in our understanding and appreciation for who our God made us, which will in turn spark new growth in us. Think about the times in your life when others have helped you just by exposing a struggle they were in or sharing a trial they had to endure. In their sharing you were able to get a new perspective on your own situation or know your own struggle in a new way. This in turn opened up a possibility for things to change. I wonder how knowing each other so intimately in heaven will continue to usher us from glory to glory.

Think of all the fascinating stories we will encounter from all the unique individuals throughout the centuries. Immediately the great characters of biblical history come to mind (what was Paul's thorn in the side anyway?). All the famous people who helped shape our earthly home will be intriguing as well. C.S. Lewis will be a personal favorite of mine. Without the constraints of time, these experiences will be a rich communion of the saints.

But I dare say that the most interesting nuggets of insight will probably come from seemingly inconsequential lives. The great depth of character that was produced in people who, day in and day out, diligently remained faithful to what God gave them to do. The incredible nuance that became developed in how they related to their circumstance and their God. Meeting a simple farmer or housewife who was able to cultivate incredible joy by persevering, not simply enduring, through situations others resisted because of the entitlement mindset of "I deserve better."

As we come to know these people, we will discover aspects of God revealed in their stories, uncovering subtleties of character in ourselves as we consider what they had to overcome.

Each and every story will contribute even more to our understanding and gratitude for who our God is. Each and every story becomes a mirror for us to look at ourselves even more deeply and identify other aspects in us where we can realize that more is possible. In this way, even in Heaven, I believe, we will continue to grow in our understanding, appreciation, and love for our God. We will see clearly how the Bridegroom has been passionately romancing us with everything at His disposal, using everything to invite us into knowing Him more clearly. We'll see how all good things in life are but a sign pointing us toward God and what awaits us in Heaven.

For instance, consider the aspect of God implied in earthly sexual union. Marc Gafni suggests that earthly sexual intimacy is the closest picture we have about how giving and receiving almost collapse into one. Surely, this is a faint glimpse of God; in His economy a giving act in turn becomes a receiving one. All of these intimate experiences cause us to hunger for more of Him and what He has for us. The taste we've had creates an ache for complete union with the Lover of our souls. As Peter Kreeft writes: "This spiritual intercourse with God is the ecstasy hinted at in all earthly intercourse, physical or spiritual. It is the ultimate reason why sexual passion is so strong, so different from other passions, so heavy with suggestions of profound meanings that just elude our grasp."[98]

The ultimate transformation He is after is making us like Himself, losing ourselves in Him (yet maintaining our uniqueness), thereby finding our true self, and becoming one with Him, just as Christ has been one with the Father from eternity (John 17:22-25). In this way too we come to participate in fellowship with the Godhead.

Before that happens, He must first make us fully into the individuals He created us to be—unique, special, and irreplaceable. It is this individuality that ultimately makes us able to lose ourselves. And strangely, it is the very fact that we feel so alone that propels us and allows us to ultimately connect. Another paradox to be sure! In his book, *Love is Stronger than Death,* Peter Kreeft writes:

> What is individuality *for*? In life, it is for union, for meeting, for relationships, for love... I become an individual self so that I may give myself to another and receive another's self. The paradox of *agape,* of self-giving love, is that it does the impossible... It shares the unshareable, gives the ungiveable, and receives from the other the gift that can no more be received than given: the gift of self, the gift of the giver, the *I. Agape,* as distinct from *eros* (desire) or *philia* (friendship) or *storge* (affection), is a gift not just of pleasure, or the body, or possessions, or time, or actions, or interests, or feelings, or thoughts, but of self.

There is a second paradox to *agape*: it performs the apparently contradictory feat of individuating by uniting, as well as uniting by individuating. The self, once given, is [truly] found. "He who loses his self shall find it" Matthew 10:39.

So it is true: Love is the purpose for everything. Even our primary purpose to worship and adore is an expression of love. We will in some way share in *agape* love, to participate in some manner in the love of the Father and the Son and the Holy Spirit, being swept up with the resulting joy emanating from the "laughter of the Trinity." We will truly get rapturously lost in this revelry and forget ourselves.

The amazing thing is that when we do this we discover who we really are. Instead of evaporating we become more substantial. We lose our sense of separateness, not our uniqueness. Again, by way of contrast, God's plan is made clearer. We get a glimpse of this contrast in *The Screwtape Letters* where a senior devil, through letters, is schooling a junior devil on how to have men lose themselves through sin.

> I know that the Enemy [God] also wants to detach men from themselves, but in a different way. He sets some absurd value on the distinctness of every one of them. When He talks of their losing their selves He means only abandoning the clamor of self-will. Once they have done that He really gives them back all their personality and boasts, I'm afraid sincerely, that when they are wholly His, they will be more themselves than ever.[99]

Having been created by God from the beginning to be unique, we find the full expression of that originality as we become joined to Him and, giving up our wills to Him, forgetting our self-centeredness.

In this ecstasy of self-forgetfulness (this is what ecstasy means: *ek- stasis*, "standing outside yourself"[100]), we then begin to truly enter into the joy of the Lord (Matthew 25:21. This kind of joy is bigger than anything inside us; it is something we actually enter. It envelops us, swallows us up, and sweeps away the limited self we've created. This is why, unlike the Buddhist mystic belief, we become more fully our self—the full expression of the eternal being God created. We have brief glimpses of this here on earth; those moments when we are so engrossed and lost in something that we lose sight of ourselves and identify with it more than with our own skin. Another way to think about this is that we find something that is so connected to a deep inner purpose of ours that it's as if we are one with it.

This unique experience can happen in a moment of contemplating the beauty of God's creation or being swept away in a moving piece of glorious music or relishing a conversation that is deep and satisfying or participating in sports when you are "in the zone" or enjoying an intimate sexual or non-sexual union with your spouse. These are times when you become so integrated—what you are doing with what you were truly created to be—that you are not aware of yourself doing it. It is such a natural and full expression that you truly enter a fulfillment unlike any other. All of these simply point us to, as Lewis says, "something other." He writes, in *Surprised by Joy*:

> I had smuggled in the assumption that what I wanted was a "thrill", a state of my own mind. And there lies the deadly error. Only when your whole attention and desire are fixed on something else... does the "thrill" arise. It is a byproduct. Its very existence presupposes that you desire not it but something other and outer...

> Images or sensations... were merely the mental track left by the passage... not the wave but the wave's imprint in the sand. The inherent dialectic of desire itself had in a way already shown me this, for all images and sensations, if idolatrously mistaken for Joy itself, soon confessed themselves inadequate. All said, in the last resort, "It is not I. I am only a reminder. Look! Look! What do I remind you of?"

> Inexorably Joy proclaimed, "You want—I myself am your want of—something other, outside, not you or any state of you.

Our true joy is God Himself. The only way to fully acquire joy is to set ourselves aside and be engrossed and lost in Him. It is in this way that a kind of death happens. Perhaps it is here that the Scripture about losing our lives to find them (Matthew 10:39; 16:25) finds its fullest meaning. Many saints through the years speak of such mysteries. Perhaps it is also in this way that we are "being conformed to His death" (Philippians 3:10 NASU). After all, our Lord set His life aside for us.

This kind of death however is the gateway to life.

Transformation

The prefix "trans" from the Latin, means "across, beyond, to go beyond," probably a preposition of a verb meaning "to cross."[101] As we cross over the river, passing from this life into the next, we will see Him as He is (1 John 3:2) and be changed (*trans*-formed). From that perspective, I expect our journey on earth will be very much viewed as a gestation period and birthing process. Upon being brought home we will, for the first time, awaken fully to what Paul wrote to the Corinthians: "Eye has not seen, nor ear heard, nor have entered into the heart of man the things which God has prepared for those who love Him" (1 Corinthians 2:9 NKJV). When our transformation is complete, and in the view of eternity, all of our temporal trials, suffering, and refining will finally be put into their proper perspective.

Then we will truly see what Romans 8:28-29 means: "All things work together for good to those who love God, to those who are the called according to His purpose. For whom He foreknew, He also predestined to be *conformed to the image of His Son*" (NKJV Emphasis mine).

All tales of transformation ultimately reveal the true creature waiting to emerge. Frederick Buechner, in *Telling the Truth*, gives a great perspective derived, of all places, from Fairy Tales:

> Maybe above all they are tales of transformation where all creatures are revealed in the end as what they truly are—the ugly duckling becomes a great white swan, the frog is revealed to be a prince, and the beautiful but wicked queen is unmasked in all her ugliness. They are tales of transformation where the ones who live happily ever after, as by no means everybody does in fairy tales, are transformed into what they have it in them at their best to be.

And of course, we must once again reflect on the magnificent picture of transformation presented by a crawling earthbound caterpillar undergoing a kind of "death" in it's sarcophagus like cocoon and emerging into a glorious creature which floats on the breezes and dances among the flowers bringing joy and beauty to those who view it. After this type of transformation of ourselves, all will be made right. Then, in light of who He has transformed us into, and what is before us, I believe we will exclaim with Paul that we "consider that the sufferings of this present time [on earth] are not worthy to be compared with the glory which shall be revealed in us" (Romans 8:18 NKJV).

I used to think that I will have so many questions to ask God when I finally see Him. All the questions that I still wrestle with: "Why did Carlo die? Why did I get cancer? Why didn't You intervene in _____ (insert innumerable references here) situation? But, I dare say, once in Heaven and joined with Him, I probably won't see it the same way anymore. It'll all fit in. Instead of discombobulated pieces of events that don't seem to have meaning, we will see what a glorious vision He has had from even before He first formed us in the womb. The mosaic of our life will be complete; all the pieces will be in place, and what a glorious fresco it will be! Like Job we will finally utter, after our awestruck silence, "My ears had heard of you but now my eyes have seen you" (Job 42:5 NIV).

We will finally look fully on the face of the Creator who, in love and for love, created us out of clay, breathed life into us, redeemed and refined us, and made us a magnificent work of art. Each piece of the mosaic has been obtained through the skillful blows of the events of our life, just as an artist uses the violence of a chisel to craft beauty. And He has lovingly set each piece in place.

Standing before Him as His masterpiece, we both offer our praise and inspire the praise of other masterpieces to the Artist. As we appreciate all His great works, transfixed by the unique signature and unmistakable mark of His hand on each, we will be moved to greater praise. The celebration will encompass all of creation, the angelic hosts and the redeemed exulting in the revelry and joining in the sacred dance.

As we worship Him we continue to move from glory to glory. Our eternal assignment is to joyously attempt to exhaust the Inexhaustible and plumb the depths of the Unfathomable and get swept away by the Mystery that is our God.

The End of The Beginning

APPENDIX A

"Prayer of Examen"

The Examen is an ancient reflective exercise originally developed by St. Ignatius of Loyola, who is considered something of the godfather of discernment practices. Set aside 10 minutes at the end of the day. Try and find a time that will work each day—just before or after dinner, or right at midnight as a study break, or whatever works best for you. You may want to avoid just before sleep to keep from falling asleep or to keep your mind from wandering.

1. Find an undisturbed location where you can sit and quiet yourself for a brief reflection.

2. Sit in a comfortable chair, upright, feet on the floor so you are relaxed but not falling asleep.

3. If you have not already determined what "filter" or "net" you're going to look at your day through, do that now (see Step 6 for an explanation of filter). Keep a list of the lenses (a Post-It note perhaps) and look it over a time or two allowing one of them to attract you. Once chosen, don't argue with it or rethink it.

4. Close your eyes and take a few deep breaths. Put your attention on your breath as a way of keeping your mind occupied, but slowing down. Use your breath as a way to bring your attention inward and be grateful for your life.

5. In the next step, you're going to recall your day, slowly looking at it through a question that is looking for a particular indicator of the presence of God. These include: Life and Light (II Corinthians 3:5-7; John 1:4; John 8:12; Romans 8:2), Freedom (II Corinthians 3:17; Galatians 5:1), Peace (Philippians 4:7; Colossians 3:15; Romans 8:6), Joy (Romans 14 17), Gratitude (Philippians 4:6), or the fruit of the Spirit (Galatians 5). Looking this way for the presence of God, Ignatius called looking for "consolation"

(moving toward God), while the opposite experience would be "desolation" (moving away from God). The most traditional filters have been to look for gratitude or light.

6. Now comes the actual examining of the day; this is the essence of the practice. Allow the video tape of your day, beginning from arising from bed in the morning, to play slowly before the movie screen in your head. As you review the day, ask "Where was I _____ (most alive, in the light, at peace, truly grateful, etc.) today?" Don't "think" about the question or try to go right to the particular moment when it occurred. Don't rush it and try not to leave anything out; it's all part of your day. As the movie plays, note where you most experienced what you are focusing on (light, peace, etc.).

7. If you want to do the full version (consolation and desolation), then run steps 6 and 7 again looking for the opposite (where was I least ____?) and note those moments in the same way.

8. Jot down what the moments of consolation and desolation were, and what your experience in them was. Don't attempt to interpret the experience, or draw lessons; just notice and note. Some journal reflection is appropriate, but less is more; don't overdo it.

9. You're done! The whole thing shouldn't take more than 7-10 minutes (Steps 1-5 = ~1 minute, Steps 7-8 = ~3-5 minutes, Step 9 = 3-5 minutes.).

After some time doing this (at least a week, preferably a month), read over your notes and reflect on them collectively looking for, "What do I notice here? What if any threads can I pick up? What if any current seems to be flowing underneath all of this that may be worth noting."

INDEX

F

G

H

I

END NOTES

Introduction
[1] Proverbs 22:6
[2] See 2 Corinthians 5:17.
[3] Paul David Tripp, *War of Words* (P&R Publishing, 2000).
[4] Werner Heisenberg (1901-1976) the German Physicist who developed the "uncertainty principle" and worked on the Atom Bomb.

Chapter One
[5] Thayer's Greek Lexicon, Electronic Database. Copyright (c) 2000 by Biblesoft.
[6] Marc Gafni,*The Mystery of Love* (Atria Books, 2003).
[7] John 10:10.
[8] Galatians 5:1.
[9] 1 Corinthians 13:12.
[10] Hebrews 12:2, the Greek word for "despise" is katafroneoo: "to contemn, despise, disdain, think little or nothing of" (from Thayer's Greek Lexicon, Electronic Database. Copyright © 2000, 2003 by Biblesoft, Inc. All rights reserved).

Chapter Two
[11] Michael Card, *The Poem of Your Life* from the CD *Poiema* Sparrow Records 1994
[12] C.S. Lewis, *The Weight of Glory* (HarperCollins 2001) pp. 18-19
[13] Genesis 1:26.
[14] 1 Peter 1:23.
[15] Matthew 8:19-22; 16:24; 19:21.

Chapter Three
[16] Amazing Grace John Newton 1772
[17] Blaise Pascal, *Pensee's* #427.

Chapter Five
[18] Noah Webster's 1828 Dictionary of the English Language.
[19] Blaise Pascal, *Pensee's* #978.
[20] Roger Fisher and William Ury, *Getting to Yes,* (Penguin Books, 1983) pg. 23.
[21] Henri Nouwen, *In The Name of Jesus, 1989.*

Chapter Six
[22] Matthew Henry, *Commentary on the Whole Bible,* (Hendrickson Publishers, 1991).
[23] W. H. Auden, *September 1939* (Vintage International).
[24] Matthew 6:34.

Chapter Seven
[25] Webster's 1828 Dictionary of the English Language.
[26] Isaiah 55:9, "As the heavens are higher than the earth, so are my ways higher than your ways and my thoughts than your thoughts." NIV.
[27] Taken from Peter Koestenbaum's *Weekly Leadership Thoughts.*

Chapter Nine
[28] Hebrews 13:8 Malachi 3:6.
[29] Webster's 1828 Dictionary of the English Language (Foundation for American Christian Education).
[30] www.dictionary.com.
[31] Webster's 1828 Dictionary of the English Language (Foundation for American Christian Education).
[32] Watson and Tocchini, *Killing the Victim before the Victim Kills You* (Mashiyach Press) pg. 237.

Chapter Ten
[33] Barnes' Notes, Electronic Database. Copyright (c) 1997 by Biblesoft.
[34] Matthew Henry, *Commentary on the Whole Bible: New Modern Edition* (Hendrickson Publishers, 1991).
[35] Jeff Bridges, *The Pursuit of Holiness* (Navpress), pp. 55.
[36] Barnes' Notes, Electronic Database. Copyright I 1997 by Biblesoft.
[37] William Harmon, *An Incomplete Guide to the Future* (Zondervan Publishing, 1983).

[38] Genesis 50:20.

[39] Rosamund Stone Zander and Benjamin Zander, *The Art of Possibility* (Penguin Books), pg.46

Chapter Eleven

[40] Exodus 20:5-6 and Deuteronomy. 5:10.

[41] Emily Pearl Kingsley, *Welcome To Holland.*

Chapter Twelve

[42] Marc Gafni, *Soul Prints* (Pocket Books).

[43] C.S. Lewis, *Mere Christianity* (Collier Books), pg.151

[44] Mark 12:31.

[45] This death to life is a recurring theme in Scripture: John 12:24, Romans 6:11 & 8:10; Hebrews 11:14 just to name a few.

[46] 2 Timothy 2:20 & 2 Corinthians 4:7.

[47] Adam Clarke's Commentary, Electronic Database. Copyright 1996 by Biblesoft (Emphasis Added).

[48] From Thayer's Greek Lexicon, Electronic Database. Copyright © 2000, 2003 by Biblesoft, Inc. All rights reserved.

[49] Ibid.

[50] Ibid.

[51] Richard Exley, *Perils of Power* (Tulsa: Honor Books, 1988), pp.80-81.

Chapter Thirteen

[52] In fact, I've also wondered if even what we remember is a function of our choice? What we remember, what we forget—what if these are disciplines? What would that say about the kind of life we are co-designing with God?

[53] C.S. Lewis, *The Voyage of the Dawn Treader* (Harper/Collins Publishers)

[54] I draw a distinction here between what I call a pop-psychology mindset, which is a mindset that many in the general public ascribe to psychology, and what most responsible psychologists actually advocate. I am not saying that these and other ideas have been promoted by the psychological community but rather that people often attribute false "pop psychology" ideas to this community.

[55] Exodus 20:3.

[56]Watson and Tocchini, *Killing the Victim before the Victim Kills You* (Mashiyach Press).

[57] John 16:33 NKJV (Emphasis mine).

Chapter Fourteen

[58] Strong, # 3340 "to think differently."

[59] Dr. Dan Allender and Dr. Tremper Longman III, *The Cry of the Soul* (Navpress Publishing Group, 1999) pp. 197-199.

[60] See Romans 2:14, 5:20 and 11:6.

Chapter Fifteen

[61] Webster's 1828 Dictionary (Foundation for American Christian Education)

[62] C .S. Lewis, *The Four Loves* (A Harvest/HBJ Book Publishers) pg. 13

[63] Ibid. pg. 33

[64] C .S. Lewis, *The Four Loves* (A Harvest/HBJ Book Publishers).

[65] C.S. Lewis, *The Four Loves*. (A Harvest/HBJ Book Publishers) pg. 33

[66] For a more philosophical and theological discussion on pain and suffering I recommend several brilliant works including C.S. Lewis's *The Problem of Pain* and *A Grief Observed*, Peter Kreeft's *Making Sense Out of Suffering*, and Sheldon Vanauken's *A Severe Mercy* (Harper Collins Publishers).

[67] C.S. Lewis, "As the Ruin Falls" *Poems by C.S. Lewis* (Harvest Books).

[68] C.S. Lewis, *The Problem of Pain* (A Touchstone Book/Simon and Schuster.) pg. 83

Chapter Sixteen

[69] *Websters 1828 Dictionary of the English Language*(Foundation for American Christian Education).

[70] Biblesoft's New Exhaustive Strong's Numbers and Concordance with Expanded Greek-Hebrew Dictionary. Copyright (c) 1994, Biblesoft and International Bible Translators, Inc.

[71] See Tracy Goss's book *The Last Word on Power* (Currency/Doubleday 1996).

[72] Romans 7:15-25.

[73] "I am the Vine, you are the branches" John 15:5.

[74] Jamieson, Fausset, and Brown Commentary, Electronic Database. Copyright (c) 1997 by Biblesoft.

Chapter Seventeen

[75] Wayne Grudem, *Systematic Theology* (Zondervan Publishers, 1995).

[76] Written by Derek Watson as originally posted on ACCD's website.

[77] Frederick Douglass, Letter to an abolitionist associate, 1849.

[78] Peter Koestenbaum's *Weekly Leadership Thought*.

[79] *The Confessions of St. Augustine,* The Eighth Book: 'I Hesitated To Buy The Goodly Pearl.' (Thomas Nelson Publishers)

[80] Strongs # 1468.

[81] *Devotional Classics* Richard J. Foster & James Bryan Smith Editors page 53.

[82] I believe we are made saints by believing in Christ- I am using the word "saint" in the traditional sense.

Chapter Eighteen

[83] Noah Websters *1828 Dictionary of the English Language* (Foundation for American Christian Education).

[84] Rosamond and Benjamin Zander, *The Art of Possibility* (Penguin Books 2000), pg.39

[85] Reinhold Neibuhr-1926 (Emphasis added).

Chapter Nineteen

[86] Vine's Expository Dictionary of Biblical Words, Copyright 1985, Thomas Nelson Publishers.

[87] Online Etymological Dictionary www.ctymonline.com.

[88] Oswald Chambers, *My Utmost for His Highest*.

[89] Strongs, Greek/Hebrew Definitions # 3875.

[90] C. S. Lewis *A Grief Observed* (Harper San Francisco) pp. 50-51

[91] *Bothers Karamazov* by Fyodor Dostoevsky (North Point Press 1990, translated by Richard Pevear and Larissa Volokhonsky).

[92] Greek: *parakaleoo* NT:3870 "as in Greek writings to call to one's side, call for, summon"
(from Thayer's Greek Lexicon, Electronic Database. Copyright © 2000, 2003 by Biblesoft, Inc. All rights reserved.)

[93] The New Unger's Bible Dictionary. Originally published by Moody Press of Chicago, Illinois.
Copyright 1988.

Chapter Twenty

[94] C.S. Lewis, *God in the Dock* (William B. Eerdmans Publishing Company), pg. 112

[95] Matthew Henry's Commentary on the Whole Bible: New Modern Edition, Electronic Database. Copyright 1991 by Hendrickson Publishers, Inc.

[96] Matthew Henry's Commentary on the Whole Bible: New Modern Edition, Electronic Database. Copyright 1991 by Hendrickson Publishers, Inc.

[97] Mathew 9:15.

[98] Peter Kreeft, *Everything You Wanted to Know About Heaven* (Ignatius Press).

[99] C.S. Lewis, *The Screwtape Letters,* (Harper Collins, Letter Thirteen.)

[100] Online Etymology Dictionary www.etymonline.com.

Made in the USA
Las Vegas, NV
12 June 2022